WHY READ THIS BOOK?

Whole Brain Power™ revolutionizes modern theories on brain training and reveals how each one of us can create within ourselves that elusive "fountain of youth," significantly rejuvenating our minds and bodies.

Ravaged by an undeniable physical decline, American society seeks refuge from increasing incidents of sleep disorders, obesity, Type 2 diabetes, ADD, ADHD, osteoporosis, Alzheimer's disease and dementia. While Americans get sick, pharmaceutical companies get rich. In 2007, Big Pharma took in a half a trillion dollars in gross revenues[1].

*In our attempt to take preventative measures to protect our health, Americans spent $225 million on brain training products in 2007, up from $50 million in 2005. According to **SharpBrains** co-founder Alvaro Fernandez, the 'brain training' market will surge to $2 billion by 2015.*

This explosive growth in products designed to improve the brain is a direct result of people recognizing that the human brain atrophies as we age through lack of use, just as do the muscles of the body. Compounding the decline in brainpower is society's pervasive addiction to excessive television viewing and violent video games, which studies prove lead to brain damage from the effects of chronic passive stress on the frontal lobes and the memory regions in the hippocampi, and the prolonged release of mind-numbing beta endorphins.

*Whole Brain Power™ presents training methodologies designed to help grow the brain at any age, and outlines a comprehensive approach that can lead the disciplined practitioner to a virtual "fountain of youth." The scientific **theories** that form the foundation of Whole Brain Power™ are the result of more than twenty years of applied neuroscience research by author Michael J. Lavery. His research into brain function, brain chemistry and brain development has led to a comprehensive understanding of brain dynamics. Conversely, his brain training methodologies developed for the average man or woman of any age are simple and straightforward. Even at forty-nine, when most men are easing into middle age, Lavery is accelerating his strength and athleticism, and is arguably the most ambidextrous athlete on earth.*

Whole Brain Power™ is a must read for anyone who desires to reverse the aging process, who aspires to athletic excellence, or who simply wants to develop the amazing untapped powers of the human brain.

---

[1] Source: http://money.cnn.com/magazines/fortune/global500/2008/industries/21/index.html
See Pharmaceutical Industry revenue/profit chart in the Appendix, page 293.

WHOLE BRAIN POWER
The Fountain of Youth for the Mind and Body

by
Michael J. Lavery

As told to
Gregory S. Walsh

First Edition

A Whole Brain Planet Book

Published through PRINT ON DEMAND
by LULU.com

A WHOLE BRAIN PLANET BOOK
P.O. Box 3888
Blaine, WA. 98231
Published through Print On Demand by LULU.com

Whole Brain Power ISBN: 978-0-557-00514-7

Visit our website at www.wholebrainpower.net

The Library of Congress has catalogued *Whole Brain Power* as follows:

Lavery, Michael J., Walsh, Gregory S.
Whole Brain Power: The Fountain of Youth for the Mind and Body/by
Michael J. Lavery as told to Gregory S. Walsh --
illustrations, Michael J. Lavery; photos, Michael J. Lavery, Gregory S. Walsh,

1st Edition, September 2008

Printed in the United States of America

DISCLAIMER

This publication contains the opinions and ideas of its author. The book does not set out to reinvent the wheel, simply to point to the wheel that has existed since the dawn of humankind and provide some ideas on how best to use the wheel as it was intended.

It is sold with the understanding that the author and contributors are not engaged in rendering medical, health, or any kind of professional services in the book. The reader should consult his or her medical, health or other competent professional before adopting any of the suggestions in this book or drawing inferences from it.

The book provides information about people who have practiced Whole Brain Power™ as a way of sharing their experiences with my training methodologies, but everyone who practices the training methodologies described here will have results unique to their efforts and application of the specific training regimens described. Again, it is strongly advise anyone desiring to follow these training guidelines (i.e. for penmanship, memorization, hammer drills) or nutritional guidelines, to consult his or her health care professional before doing so; and even under the guidance of a medical professional, one should always use moderation in learning new skills or changing one's diet, especially when attempting to improve one's brain and body.

The author and publisher specifically disclaim all responsibility for any liability, loss, risk, personal or otherwise, which is incurred as a consequence, directly or indirectly, of the use and application of any of the contents in this book.

Contents

Acknowledgements

I appreciate the support of my mom Beatrice, and my father Robert who passed away in 1988, without whose love and support I would not have been able to fulfill my quest. My sincere thanks are extended to my brothers Peter, Patrick, and James, and to my sister Mary, for being there through every step of the journey. I respect the wonderful mother that Diana has been to my four sons, Sean, Christopher, James and Steven.

My athletic achievements were enhanced by the great coaching that I received, including from my dad, all the way from Little League through my professional baseball career. As my pursuit of golf emerged as a major influence in my life, I am beholden to Jim Goss and the management from Aliso Viejo Golf Club for their generous support.

I want to thank Maria for her support in helping with this book. I extend my gratitude to all of my patrons throughout the years that have allowed me to pursue my creative endeavors and others who have helped financially to launch Whole Brain Planet. Along the way I have met some wonderful folks such as Rolly White, Claude Amesse, Pat and Jan Venditti, and the rest of the Whole Brain Power™ All Stars that I've worked with over the years. Mostly, I want to thank GW for the incredible effort that he has done in synthesizing my ideas into a coherent thesis, and then helping me write and design this first edition of *Whole Brain Power.*

FOREWORD

Dr. Craig McQueen
Orthopedic Surgeon, Salt Lake City, Utah

For the past forty years as a team physician I've been an active participant in high school, collegiate and professional athletics. During that time I've seen a marked evolution in sports medicine, sports science and the training of athletes. Today the main goals of sports science are to enhance performance in order to prevent injury, and to evolve the science of teaching athletic excellence.

In pursuit of these goals we must continually adapt our thinking and explore new ideas. Prior to Dick Fosbury, nobody thought jumping over the high jump bar backwards was a good idea. Then he won the 1968 Olympic gold medal in the high jump and set a new world record. Now every Olympic contender jumps backwards over the high jump bar. Known as the "Fosbury Flop", this unortho-dox, once mystifying approach to an athletic endeavor is now considered logical and the most effective method.

How will athletic performance be enhanced in the future? What is the next quantum jump in sporting excellence? As with auto racing, things learned on the track soon become applicable to the rest of us in our every day lives.

Training methods, nutritional guidelines, supplements, etc., that improve Olympic and professional athletes, will inevitably make their way into the health food store or the local fitness center. We have already witnessed one paradigm shift in athletic improvement with the Steroid Era (now being phased out in professional sports). This artificial enhancement of athletic performance has fueled unparalleled achievement on the field, but at what cost to the sanctity of the records books and to the athletes' bodies? Sadly, the taking of steroids has permeated the everyday world of young athletes in high school and college. Everyone wants that edge. At least for the moment professional sports are doing their best to condemn, outlaw and monitor this artificial enhancement that athletes seek.

A not-so-obvious paradigm shift in thinking about harnessing human potential in a natural and healthy way is the concept of ambidexterity, that is, developing equal skill with both hands or both feet. If it were not for my own experience into this realm, it would never have occurred to me to pursue it. Nonetheless, we are at a point in history where such a concept as ambidexterity is beginning to take hold. Neuroscience has advanced to a degree where we can now quantify changes in the brain that are occurring to an individual who practices ambidexterity.

Paradigm shifts in the athletic world are often born of necessity. For perspective we can take a look back to the 1950s when it was very common that high school and collegiate athletes were not allowed to have water on the field either during practice or during games. Since that time sports science has shown that athletic performance drops off significantly when the athlete becomes dehydrated. Cramping and muscle spasms become more prevalent if the athlete is dehydrated, and heat exhaustion, heat stroke and eventually even death can occur with those that are not allowed to have fluids.

During this period many coaches were against any off-field training, such as weight lifting, because they felt this would make the athletes muscle bound and that would affect their fluidity of motion on the field. Since then, strength training has become the backbone of almost all sports. Athletes now participate in some sort of off-field conditioning as a matter of course, including flexibility, strength, and agility training, weight lifting and hand-eye coordination.

In the 1970s, I participated with a sports science group on The Sports Medicine Committee of The United States Figure Skating Association. We had yearly camps at the U.S. Olympic Training Center where figure skaters were studied and placed on off-ice strength and flexibility training. This resulted in a marked *decrease* in the injury rate while improving the performance of the figure skaters.

Another evolution we saw in sports was in the 1950s and 1960s when most sports were seasonal. Football was played in the fall, basketball and hockey in the winter and then we had baseball, tennis, golf and track in the spring. Now athletes train year round and are required to train almost on a daily basis. This has led to a marked increase in the *overuse syndromes* seen in many athletes. These overuse syndromes include injuries to young baseball players in both the shoulder and elbow. Indeed, I have witnessed a marked increase in the need for surgery at the elbow in fourteen and fifteen year old baseball players. We have seen other athletes such as tennis players who play year round who have also experienced overuse injuries in their upper extremities, either in the shoulder, elbow or wrist.

How do athletes train properly and avoid overuse syndromes that can cause enough damage that they can no longer participate in their sport? I feel that younger athletes, pre-teen and teenagers, should participate in multiple sports rather than in just one sport. They can certainly specialize in one sport, but participation year-round in other sports could help mitigate injury from overuse syndromes and actually enhance their performance in their primary sport.

Speaking of sports-related injuries, it was just such a concern of my own that brought me into contact with *Whole Brain Power™* author Michael J. Lavery. Actually, I would describe my encounter with Michael as a life altering experience. In the summer of 2000, while my wife and I were attending an art exhibition in the famous art colony of Laguna Beach, California, I was attracted to one of Michael's landscape paintings on display at the art festival. As part of his presentation in his corner of the gallery Michael had an article about his ambidextrous tennis game hanging on the wall. It immediately appealed to my curiosity because I had recently undergone surgery for my right elbow. I was faced with the prospect that my tennis playing days were over and this was a discouraging thought for me.

Michael and I started up a conversation about this ambidextrous tennis concept and immediately I saw a ray of hope. I have always loved playing tennis and could be found on the court almost every day. I had been participating in regional and sectional tennis tournaments and now the depression of not being able to compete was affecting my life. Michael reassured me that with the proper approach that I could continue as an *ambidextrous* player. It was my right-handed serve that caused a lot of pain. The solution is simple he explained, "Just serve left-handed, doc."

He questioned me about my knowledge of the brain and any experience with ambidexterity. In all of my sports medicine experience I had not been familiar with an ambidextrous athlete or with any ambidextrous training. At this time the idea of being able to play tennis left-handed was quite foreign to me but the more I thought about it the more I realized this was the only way I would be able to participate in tennis in the future. He advised me to do a series of mental and physical training exercises unique to his theory and to contact him with any questions on his methodologies. We exchanged business cards and I went away from this art show with one of his paintings, and a whole new attitude about what was possible with my athletic interests.

The disciplines of the memory exercises and the cursive left-handed mirror image writing that Michael suggested were something that I could easily fit into my schedule. I immediately began to attempt to play left-handed, both with my ground strokes and with my serves. It took me only a few attempts on the court to get the ball into play. That initial success fueled my motivation to work through the awkwardness and strive to reach my goal to compete again -- *as a left-hander.* It took nearly three to four years of serving left-handed two to three times weekly with a bucket of balls to be able to reach the same level of tennis play that I was playing right-handed in previous years. Seven years have passed since meeting Michael, and I am playing at the same level at tournaments and with friends that I was playing right-handed in 2001. For a man in his late sixties to be able to accomplish this is amazing to me. I learned that developing ambidexterity is simply a matter of nurture, a matter of re-wiring the brain, and that in time many people will experience this new revolution through reading Michael's book and following his training regimens.

Now that I've had first-hand experience with developing my own ambidexterity through Whole Brain Power™ training methodologies, I support the effort to incorporate Michael's training for almost all athletes, especially those who seek performance enhancement and injury prevention without the aid of drugs or supplements. For example, on the *injury prevention* side, the overuse syndromes that we see in young baseball pitchers could be reduced if they threw half of the time right-handed and the other half left-handed.

On the sports *performance* side, a football quarterback would be much more effective rolling to his left side if he is right-handed but were able to pass the ball left-handed. According to Michael, training his left-handed passing will actually improve his right-handed passing.

We are already seeing examples of the emergence of ambidexterity in professional athletes.

For example, Pat Venditte Jr., a pitcher for the *Staten Island Yankees* (a New York Yankees class A team), has become the first *full-time switch pitcher* (ambidextrous) in modern professional baseball. And because he can use either arm, his coaches are able to rotate him into the pitching line up as a reliever more often then the other pitchers on staff.

Pau Gasol, a player for the Los Angeles Lakers, shoots hook shots right or left-handed and also does lay-ups right and left-handed. In the modern era most basketball guards have skill with either left or right-handed dribbling depending on where they are on the floor. In the tennis world, Rafael Nadal beat Roger Federer dramatically in the 2008 French Open. He was also victorious over Roger in the Wimbledon Championships the following month and more recently won the gold at the 2008 Beijing Olympics. Nadal is right-handed but plays tennis left-handed. He could use either hand when he plays, which is a great advantage and shows that athletes can reach a higher level by changing their dominant side. I know I did with my tennis game.

Ambidextrous training brings balance to the major muscle groups of the body and can help prevent injury to the *non-dominant* side as its strength and flexibility become more equal with the dominant side.

Ambidexterity for aging populations is no less beneficial as they practice the Whole Brain Power ™ training methods in order to develop both hemispheres of their brain, and muscle groups in both sides of their body. The ramifications of Michael's *theories, training and nutritional guidelines* related to possible prevention of the onset of Alzheimer's Disease, diabetes, obesity, osteoporosis and overall quality of life are significant, perhaps one of the most comprehensive approaches to mind and body health and fitness of the 21st century. It is my hope that clinical studies are soon taken up at major medical research institutions investigating the benefits to the brain and the body from practicing the full regimen of Whole Brain Power™ training methods.

I know that the anecdotal study of my own experience with Whole Brain Power™ leaves me with no doubt as to the fundamental benefits of Michael's program. In fact, meeting Michael Lavery changed my life, and inspired new thinking about brain development and athletic achievement. It has affected the way I treat patients, inspiring me to prescribe to those with upper extremity problems to begin training their opposite extremity, in essence, to become ambidextrous.

Michael is now entering new realms with golf, baseball, tennis and other sports, radically changing hand-eye coordination, functional strength and ambidexterity in athletes and non-athletes alike, people of all ages and walks of life. I feel this book will be a great value to those who are interested in increasing their athletic achievement and preventing injuries in their own and their family's athletic endeavors.

- Dr. Craig McQueen

Introduction

Americans want instant gratification and perpetual youth. We increasingly seek refuge from our decline through pharmaceuticals, cosmetic surgery, exercise machines and fad diets. We spent $225 million on brain training products in 2007, up from $50 million in 2005. Nothing works to our satisfaction. We continue to age, our brains shrink, our memory fades, our hormones diminish, our athletic prowess deteriorates, our bodies balloon in obesity or decay and wither away in frailty.

Then along comes Whole Brain Power™. Brains begin to grow, memory sharpens, steroids are produced endogenously, athletic prowess improves beyond youthful ability, fat melts away and bodies become strong and lithe. Yes, it sounds like a veritable *"fountain of youth."* Our case studies will support our thesis that Whole Brain Power™ may indeed be that modern day equivalent of Ponce de Leon's great quest.

Our case studies include:

- 15-year-old ambidextrous tennis players James Lavery
  and 17-year-old Chris Lavery
- 23-year old ambidextrous baseball pitcher Pat Venditte Jr.
- 27-year-old Whole Brain Power™ practitioner Dante Salazar
- 38-year-old ambidextrous baseball pitcher/switch hitter Chuck Mellick
- 43-year-old ambidextrous tennis player Suzanna McGee
- 52-year-old ambidextrous golfer and all-around athlete Les Taylor
- 60-year-old ambidextrous golfer, softball and tennis player, Rolly White
- 77-year-old Whole Brain Power™ practitioner Patricia Ford
- 91-year-old Whole Brain Power™ practitioner Harry White Sr.

Each of these individual practitioners of Whole Brain Power™ provide compelling anecdotal evidence that following Lavery's training methodologies leads to astonishing mental functioning, athletic improvement and -- we conclude -- endogenously produced steroids[1]. The ramifications are exciting for women and men of all ages, but especially for baby boomers and retirees. For all sports where hand-eye coordination and upper body, forearm and wrist strength are essential such as baseball, tennis and golf, the promises are endless.

Whole Brain Power™ is the result of more than twenty years of intense study and applied research into brain functioning, chemistry and development by author Michael J. Lavery. Lavery is the prime example of Whole Brain Power™ training methodologies in practice. But Lavery's theories and methodologies go far beyond his own astonishing ambidextrous skills in tennis, golf, baseball and hockey. Developing whole brainpower is about activating both hemispheres of the brain and harnessing the combined power in a way usually associated with great geniuses in history, like Leonardo Da Vinci, Michelangelo, Thomas Jefferson and Benjamin Franklin. Each of these key historic figures was ambidextrous, as were great athletes like Babe Ruth and Mickey Mantle. Now, Lavery takes whole brainpower beyond just the development of ambidexterity. His research has led to a comprehensive understanding of brain function, chemistry and growth. He has formed this understanding into cohesive *theories* that correlate brain development, endogenously produced hormones, improved memory, improved fine and gross motor skills, and increased energy with the daily practice of Whole Brain Power™ training methodologies.

A case in point is the story of baseball player Chuck Mellick. Mellick quit baseball for seventeen years after college, then in 2007 at age 37 he decided to take it up again. He also decided it would be fun to try pitching left-handed as well as right-handed. He is what is referred to as a mixed-handed person. He writes left-handed, but until age 37 he threw a baseball only right-handed.

---

[1] See the synthesis of cholesterol into the various steroidal hormones on pages 156-157.

Mellick posted videos of his ambidextrous pitching practice sessions on *You-Tube* where Lavery found them in January of 2008. Lavery soon made contact with the small town semi-pro player, and from that day forward Mellick began working with Lavery on all aspects of Whole Brain Power™. By the fall of 2008 as this book goes to publication, just seven months into intensive Whole Brain Power™ training, Mellick expects to be able to pitch more than 90 miles an hour with both his *right and left-hand pitches*, a feat no one in the history of baseball has ever achieved.

Mellick, emerging as a real life "Roy Hobbs," is poised for entry into Major League Baseball by the spring of 2009 as a free agent. Lavery is working with Mellick on his switch-hitting technique as well, so that just as fictional hero Roy Hobbs, Mellick will develop into a sensational switch-hit batter and switch-pitch pitcher, a rare "5 tool player." Mellick is anecdotal evidence that the more energy the brain produces, the more effective its functioning[2].

Lavery classifies his training regimens that create Whole Brain Power™ into the following three-step program:

> • *Penmanship drills*
> • *Memory drills*
> • *Ambidexterity drills*

He refers to his program as *"applied neuroscience."* The underlying premise of Lavery's brand of applied neuroscience is that the youthfulness, strength and performance of the brain, drives youthfulness, strength and performance in the body. Lavery offers a truly comprehensive theory and training methodology that can lead to whole brainpower through neuroplasticity: the brain's ability to reorganize itself by forming new connections and new neurons throughout life.

---

[2] Read more about Mellick's amazing story starting on page 210.

Whole Brain Power™ introduces readers to enough brain anatomy and chemistry to understand what is happening in their brain while they are practicing Lavery's training regimens. Of importance to his theory is what happens to *axons* in the central and peripheral nervous systems. Axons are the neural pathways that carry electrical impulses in the brain and body, and *myelin* is the *white matter* that surrounds and protects those pathways. Myelin thins with age, poor nutrition, passive stress from television and video game playing, and most importantly, lack of proper brain development and brain training techniques. The production of estrogen in women and testosterone in men declines as part of the normal aging process. But neither thinning myelin nor hormone decrease is inevitable. Lavery theorizes that the contrary is experienced through practice of Whole Brain Power™ training methodologies and nutritional practices.

Lavery's applied, anecdotal research has led him to his revolutionary theory that a direct connection exists between ambidextrous large and fine motor skill training of the forearms and hands, and *neurogenesis, steroidogenesis and synaptogenesis.* He concluded that bouncing golf balls on hammers and practicing the art of penmanship, are both highly correlated with the growth of new neurons in the brain and a thickening of the white matter (myelin) that protects the neural pathways (axons) throughout the brain and body. Lavery believes that thickening of myelin is correlated with steroidogenesis[3].

Studies done at the *University of Regensburg*[4] and *The University College of London study on Voxel-Based Morphometry*[5] support Lavery's theory through clinical research that found "environmental demands may be associated with changes in gray and white matter. For instance, it has been reported that the structure of the brain alters (the cerebral cortex grew on average 4% in the 90-day juggling trial) when human beings learn to navigate, read music, speak a second language and even perform a complex motor task such as juggling."

[3] http://www.ncbi.nlm.nih.gov/pubmed/9927319
[4] http://www.medicalnewstoday.com/articles/5615.php
[5] http://www.wholebrainpower.net/page25/files/page25_1.pdf

23

Lavery has created a complete and balanced regimen that includes not only widely recognized whole brain development activities such as playing a musical instrument, artistic endeavors, new language learning and juggling, but taps into much more powerful and efficient brain development through ambidextrous skill development including bouncing golf balls on hammers of all weights and sizes.

Michael "The Hammer Man" Lavery

Known as *"The Hammer Man"*, Lavery has unbelievable hand-eye coordination skills, including his ability to bounce a golf ball off of the round end of a *ball peen hammer* 300 times without dropping it. His official record set with a *standard claw hammer* through a Stanley Tool sponsorship is 3,192, and his unofficial record with the claw hammer is 7,148 hits without a miss. Those records might be considered an amazing parlor trick except that Lavery's hand-eye skills are completely and easily transferable as taught in the *Whole Brain Power™ training program* described in the pages of this book.

Lavery envisions that athletes, like our Suzanna McGee and Chuck Mellick, with their discipline and focus, and who practice all the training regimens and nutritional guidelines, will achieve astonishing improvements in their performance.

Baby Boomers who sense they are losing the battle with time should feel their

24

bodies rejuvenate and their memory ability sharpen, as has Les Taylor and Rolly White, two Baby Boom era practitioners who are outstanding athletes as well.

Senior citizens, like 69-year-old Dr. Craig McQueen, 77-year-old Patricia Ford and 91-year-old Harry White, can develop energy levels of someone twenty to thirty years younger, and their memory ability can sharpen, helping prevent or stave off the onset of dementia and Alzheimer's.

Even young people, like James and Chris Lavery, Ryan Walsh or Dante Salazar, will benefit from every aspect of Whole Brain Power™. Our holistic approach teaches them superior hand-eye coordination, functional strength, and the impact of nutrition on brainpower. It warns of the risk to their growing brains from violent video games and MTV-type television flash-editing imagery.

The 20th century was about training the body for optimum performance. The 21st century will be about training the brain for optimum *mind and body* performance. Lavery's research has led him to an understanding of brain functioning and performance that is cutting edge. His discovery that one of the keys to unlock whole brainpower is through the hands, through the development of ambidexterity, is unique and revolutionary. Conversely, his training methodologies for achieving whole brainpower are relatively simple and straightforward. Individuals in our Case Study chapter who have practiced Whole Brain Power™ for sixty days or longer see amazing results in their memory, hand-eye coordination, muscle density, functional strength and energy levels. Those Case Study participants who have practiced Whole Brain Power™ for six months or more have experienced a significant transformation of their brain power, memory, physical strength, athletic skill and energy.

The journey to developing that transformation begins with learning more about the man who developed the Whole Brain Power™ theories and training methodologies, Michael J. Lavery. Over the past twenty years he has transformed himself in phenomenal ways.

Chapter 1
The Michael J. Lavery Story

My journey into the world of Whole Brain Power™ started as an idea born out of necessity: I was determined to improve my tennis game. My forehand was a much superior shot than my backhand, which suffered from inconsistent topspin. Competitors attacked my backhand relentlessly until my game collapsed.

In September, 1988, the annual *Laguna Beach Labor Day Weekend Tennis Tournament* had come and gone and I was empty-handed at awards time once again. I had invested great effort in preparing for this event throughout the spring and summer and I took the loss hard.

During a casual match the day following the tournament my friend and practice partner, John Rushing, ran me from side to side on the court. He picked apart my backhand shot with his impressive topspin forehand. As I attempted to get to a ball far outside my reach, I unconsciously threw the racquet to my left hand and hit a forehand winner down the line. John stood in shock as he watched the ball sail out of his reach.

At that moment a thought came to me, "What if my back hand was as good as my forehand? What if I had a strong *lefty* forehand?" On the next rally I tried out the lefty forehand again; however, this time I missed, sending the ball over the back fence. Over John's objections I continued to try out the left-hand forehand during this match. He beat me effortlessly and made the following observation,

"It is a novel concept, Michael, but it could never work. Tennis is meant to be played only one way. It's a game with a forehand and a backhand." But the dye had been cast, I would develop a left-handed forehand.

I had never given much thought to being right-handed. As a matter of fact I was glad that I was born a right-hander. I had a successful athletic career as a baseball player, quarterback, and hockey player, all because of my coordination and strength of my right hand and arm. I was content with my athletic accomplishments, except for the game of tennis.

Once the idea of playing tennis ambidextrously took hold, I stayed with this new challenge. I practice relentlessly, hitting the left-handed forehand against the backboard. My regular playing partners eschewed my experiment.

"Come on and hit the regular way. You're slowing down our game with your missed shots."

Some were pretty adamant about it, "Unless you go back to the old style of play do not even call me. I'm not into suffering through your experiment in ambidexterity."

I searched out different courts where people did not know me and they found the novelty of what I was doing mildly interesting. Since they would generally win the match they just thought my ambidextrous approach was not an effective method.

My left-hand forehand was not *that* bad out of the gate. Some of the left-handed attempts would leave the court or be completely miscued, but occasionally I would hit a nice shot. These little victories were stashed away in my memory banks, and my intuition told me to stay the course.

At first this ambidextrous transformation resulted in my game going backwards in *tournament* play. This was my investment in loss, which became the foundation for the fantastic gains that I would experience at a later time and for the rest of my life.

The deeper I got into ambidexterity, the more I reflected on why our society is overwhelmingly right-hand dominant (86% of the population is right-hand dominant, 11% left-hand dominant and the remaining 3% are mixed-handed or ambidextrous) while we otherwise have such symmetry in our bodies and our brains. I became a library junkie, a voracious researcher on the topic of ambidexterity. I studied countless research papers on handedness and checked out or purchased books like the best-seller by Betty Edwards, _Drawing On the Right Side of the Brain._

I analyzed my personal history and thought about the skills I had developed with my left hand thus far in my life. As a shortstop in baseball I had a talented glove hand (left hand) as many players do. I had played the guitar from the age of fifteen, using my left hand on the fret board. Like everyone else, I remember how awkward it was at the beginning. Clearly, my left-handed skills were not something I was born with, they were talents nurtured and harnessed through tons of practice. More questions came to mind. Why did I play hockey as a left-hander and hit a baseball as a right-hander? I felt strongly that this quest to become an ambidextrous tennis player would have major ramifications in my life.

This is the point in my athletic career where I became a student and a teacher at the same time. My left-brain (which controlled by right hand) needed to teach my right brain (left hand) how to do the stroke mechanics in tennis. So my lefty forehand was the "protégé" and the right-handed forehand was the "coach". This forced the "coach" to focus and get a greater grasp on perfect stroke mechanics. This constant comparison of the skills of the left and right hand led to the conclusion that this experiment in ambidexterity had more to do with nurture than nature, specifically, with _re-wiring_ my brain.

When I was a few months into this ambidextrous tennis quest I realized I was never going back to my former self. I sensed something happening in my brain but I did not understand the mechanics of the changes that were taking place.

One day in the early 1990s, a man who had known me since moving to Laguna Beach in 1984 watched me play and he said, "Do you realize that you are re-wiring your motor cortex?" He knew me only as a right-handed player and now he saw my metamorphosis. This gentleman was involved in the medical field and his comment sparked my interest in learning about the brain, its features and its unlimited potential. Science had discovered that the brain's plasticity (its ability to grow new neurons) extended beyond our mid-to-late twenties. I became fascinated by the work being done by neuroscientists concerning this new theory on *neuroplasticity*.

A friend gave me a book titled, *The Fireside Book of Tennis*. To my surprise tennis history included ambidextrous players. A woman named Beverly Baker Flietz was a sensational dual-handed player in the 1950s. She was ranked number one in the USA at one point in her career. Australian tennis player John Bromwich was a tremendous athlete, a grand slam champion in doubles who served with his right hand and played as a left-handed ground stroker. When I saw Luke Jensen in the news serving tennis balls with each arm at speeds in excess of 120 mph, it was the inspiration to take my game to the next level. If Jensen could do it, so would I.

At this point my opponents in tennis had to accept my unusual double forehand game, but they complained about it nonetheless. The obvious awkwardness of the service motion left me open to ridicule. The more the players mocked me, the greater became my determination.

When I reached a plateau in my pursuit of ambidextrous tennis I wondered if I would ever progress further. Then the right hemisphere in my brain, my creative savant, popped out the answer -- I wasn't practicing ambidexterity across the board.

I decided it was necessary for me to eat, brush my teeth, comb my hair, shave and WRITE left-handed. That night I sat down at the kitchen table and began my first attempts at left-handed penmanship in mirror image -- backwards -- right to left across the page. I formed the letter $\underline{A}$ right-handed and then I mirror imaged it with my left hand. At first it felt strange. Then I formed the letter $\underline{B}$ and mirror imaged it on the paper, and so on all the way down to $\underline{Z}$. I then wrote my signature in mirror image cursive penmanship. I held the paper up to the mirror and there it was. I did not know that this was the way Da Vinci wrote in his journals. The first few nights I practiced simple sentences in left-handed mirror image writing, such as, *My tennis game will go to the Open Class level; I will serve left-handed aces against my opponents; I will hit winners with my left-hand forehand.*

I made a commitment to write every day in this new mirror image style. To my dismay, any attempt to share this skill with people often resulted in a strange look from them. Some would even ask, "Are you OK? Because this is kinda crazy." Their doubt was fuel for my commitment. Each day I wrote more and more, as much as an hour at a time. Sometimes my left hand would get cramps from the demanding sessions. Strangely, I sometimes felt tingling sensations on the scalp on the right side of my head. Were they right? Was I crazy? Or was I awakening dormant parts of my brain? The latter, I reasoned, for how else could one explain how I was able to write with my left hand in mirror image each day with more clarity, consistency and speed? I also became comfortable *reading* backwards, from right to left.

I bought an 8.5 x 11 inch hard cover journal book at the art supply store and began to document the experience. On one page I wrote right-handed in normal cursive format, and on the proceeding page I wrote left-handed mirror image. Each time that I went back to my dominant right hand I found a greater ease of writing. This ambidextrous theory started to have a foundation. One hand teaches the other; actually, one hemisphere of the brain teaches the other hemisphere.

30

As time passed I noticed that I needed to bring balance to my footwork on the tennis court as well. My right leg knew how to push off the ground with greater efficiency than my left leg. Now to learn how to serve effectively left-handed, my right leg needed to become a student of the left leg, my right hemisphere needed to teach the left hemisphere how to do something that did not feel natural.

This is when my brain started to become whole-brained.

For the first time I felt that I was having constant access to both hemispheres simultaneously. I visualized the electrical current passing across the bridge of the brain, the corpus callosum. As I switched the pen from hand to hand, or the tennis racquet, it was lefty, righty, lefty, righty, righty, lefty. I felt like a kid again. Why not practice the alphabet, only this time backwards? *Z-Y-X-W-V-U-T...*, I repeated it again and again. Soon I was saying the alphabet backwards as fast as I could say it forward. I was becoming an ambidextrous thinker, too.

This realization for me was a quantum jump in my journey. Could I develop the qualities of a left-brainer and a right-brainer? My imagination was ignited by the prospect of fully developing *whole-brain-power*.

For perspective, this adventure was also accompanied by my marriage and the subsequent birth of my four sons, Sean, Chris, James and Steven. As I started on this path, I was curious to see whether my children showed a propensity for hand and foot dominance at an early age.

My first son Sean showed a strong preference for right-handedness as early as the first 10 months. I would throw him a ball and try as best as I could to get him to throw it with his left hand. However, he kept on putting the ball into his right hand. Only when he was older and became aware of a financial incentive (money going into his piggy bank!) did he get coaxed to throw the ball with his left hand. He saw that there was a reward and he acted against his nature to throw left-handed.

31

From the time that my children became aware of their surroundings I shared with them my interest in ambidexterity. I used to tell them classic bedtime stories but then add a twist on the outcome. My tale of the three little pigs included the defeat of the big bad wolf after which the pigs would build a tennis court in the backyard and play the most radical game of ambidextrous tennis. Sometimes the story lead to a baseball diamond where the little pigs would strike out the hitters with an arsenal of switch-pitching. "You see guys; there were people in town who never gave a hoot about sports until they heard about the tales of the ambidextrous little pigs." I told my boys that the great baseball legend Mickey Mantle was taught to switch hit by his dad and his grandfather. When the young Mantle was a boy he asked his father, "Why did you name me Mickey?"

The dad's reply was, "Because you are a spitting image of the great Mickey Cochrane, the left-hitting wonder for the Philadelphia Athletics. He was one of my idols and a great all-around player, and so can you be, Son." Ask any dad or coach about the difficulty of rearing a switch-hitter and the sentiment is the same. It is not an easy task, for if it were, then switch-hitters would make up the majority of Major League line-ups. The Mantles had their way to bring out the best in this eventual *Hall of Famer*.

As the years passed people in Laguna Beach and surrounding communities saw my ambidextrous tennis game improve significantly. They saw ambidextrous athleticism in my sons as well, and comments changed from skepticism to amusement, "You know, Lavery, you might be on to something."

The first person that wanted to learn how to rewire his brain for his tennis game was orthopedic surgeon Dr. Craig McQueen, from Salt Lake City, Utah. I was at the Sawdust Festival art show during the summer of 2000. On the wall of my exhibit space was an article about my ambidextrous tennis game that was written up in the *Los Angeles Times* in December 1999. A sports reporter wrote a favorable story including the Da Vinci-style writing exercises. After Dr. Mc-

Queen read the article he turned to me. "That's impressive, but I presume you were already ambidextrous from birth. Don't you think it was latent in you and you finally unleashed this potential?" adding, " I seriously doubt I have any ambidextrous ability."

I replied, "If you had seen the beginning of my journey you would know that it took dedicated training to achieve these results. I don't think it came naturally to me. On the contrary, I believe I trained my brain to become ambidextrous, and I'm convinced you could train your brain to become ambidextrous, too." He shrugged his shoulders on that point.

I continued, "I'm sure in your career you've treated patients who severely broke their right forearm and now they were placed in a cast for two months. I assume you would encourage them that it was not going to be all that bad because they would still have the use of their left arm." McQueen nodded in agreement. "The question I have for you Doc is, do you really think they will develop any skill with their left arm while the right is in a cast, or is it a way of consoling them until they can recuperate their damaged arm and go back to using it full time again?" The latter, he responded. "I believe you should encourage them to develop as much skill as possible with their left arm for reasons far beyond necessity. Would you be willing to develop your left-handedness, with or without the necessity of a broken right arm?"

Little did I know that he had a problem with his right elbow, and that was one of the reasons he was intently listening to my argument concerning the nurture versus nature debate. He then opened up to me about an arthritic condition with his right elbow that two surgeries had failed to rectify. So he did have a necessity to develop his left-handedness after all. He professed his love for playing tennis, and now his game was being compromised by a painful condition. The stress of playing was aggravated by serving the ball, and by forehand and backhand ground strokes. He said it was the serve that caused most of the pain and that without this stroke he could not compete in tournaments that he enjoyed so much. "I have tried for some time, but the mechanics of the left-handed service motion is something that I can not seem to get. What should I do?" I suggested he buy one of my paintings so that I could give him my undivided attention for the next hour. He took my advice and purchased a painting for his daughter.

"Now Craig, I am a lay person with a passion for how the brain can be trained and you are a doctor of orthopedics. I would suspect that you had anatomy and physiology courses in Medical School; however your specific field of orthopedics made you focus more on the body than the brain, is that correct?"

"That is correct," he replied.

"Well if I asked you to name certain anatomical brain structures and neurotransmitters, you might find them somewhere in your memory banks."

He smiled and said, "I have not had that material to review in over 35 years. And even back then we did not have nearly the understanding that we have today." When I asked McQueen about his hand preference for all of the fine skill sets such as eating, brushing his teeth, shaving, writing and using the mouse on the computer, he agreed that he preferred the right hand to the left hand. I suggested he start to train the left hand and by extension the right hemisphere of his brain, that he start to write as Da Vinci did, left-handed and in mirror image, that he exercise the brain with mental gymnastics, and that he play the guitar more often, and memorize poetry. I recommended he do the alphabet forwards and backwards and from the middle out, and that he memorize the powers of 2 up to thirty. I started to throw every thing except the kitchen sink at the good doctor. He soaked it up. I knew that my sincerity and enthusiasm struck a chord with him. We exchanged contact information and bid each other adieu.

Two months later I received an email from Dr. McQueen in which he wrote that our meeting was a life-altering experience. He said that the changes in his life were nothing short of miraculous. "I am serving very well left-handed and doing a lot of mirror image writing. My guitar playing is better than ever and my tennis game is steadily becoming ambidextrous. My opponents cannot believe that I am learning these motor skills so quickly."

McQueen started this ambidextrous journey at age sixty-one and now eight years later people cannot tell he is the same player. A tennis pro who used to work at the tennis club where McQueen plays returned to visit after a number of years. Craig was out on the court playing left-handed and the tennis pro remarked to a member that the guy out there looked a lot like Dr. McQueen. But, he exclaimed, it could not be, because Craig is right-handed and this look-alike is playing smoothly as a lefty. McQueen loves to tell this story because it legitimizes all of the effort that he put into his game. He honestly claims that at age sixty-nine his best tennis playing days are a head of him.

That same year I was playing indoor tennis with a neurosurgeon doing his residency at Beth Israel hospital in Boston. He had heard about my ambidextrous abilities from my sister-in-law who worked at the hospital. He wanted to test out his right-handed tennis game against my dual-handed game. After seeing my right and left-handed ground strokes and ability to serve with ease with either arm and write fluidly with either hand, he delivered this opinion. "You are making me think that the brain is a muscle." He said, "You have theoretically thickened your white matter, and your **basal ganglia** is firing *bilaterally,* where mine is not." He gave me a crash course on the mechanics of action potentials and the speed that neuron bundles fire. He explained that the greater the **myelination** on the **axons** the faster you can think and move. He discussed the chemical **dopamine** and its uptake by the basal gangliam and the involvement with voluntary motor control. He was genuinely impressed that it was not until the age of 29 that I began this ambidextrous training. He suggested I study the properties of **pyramidal cells** and **Perkinji cells** and the **myelination** process that occurs in the **Central Nervous System**. Off to the library I went with renewed vigor for my research and a batch of new terms that I needed to come up to speed on.

One day in the fall of 2001, I was working out at a tennis club with my sons Chris and James. They were ten and eight years of age at this time. A gentleman named Rolly White stopped and watched our hitting session. He saw all three of us serving with either arm, hitting single-handed forehands from either side, and backhands from either side as well. He said to me, "Would you mind if I could join in on the fun?" He came on to the court and my boys and I put on an ambidextrous show. "This is wild stuff," he mused. "Do you think that it is teachable to a man that is in his fifties?"

I reassured him that it was and told him of the progress that Dr. McQueen was making in his late sixties. "You can learn to re-wire your brain when you are ninety," I told him.

We became instant friends and he called me the next day and asked about the application of my theories to the game of golf. "I enjoy tennis, but my true passion is golf. If you could help me lower my handicap I would be a very happy man." I explained to him that at this time golf was not my cup of tea. However, after seeing his eagerness to apply my theories to his game I accepted an invitation to hit a bucket of balls at the local driving range. I thought, "What better way to apply the concepts of learning a new skill than taking up the game of golf?" I had only played a few rounds in my life and was definitely in the hacker category. I was all over the place with my driver, and the irons shots were laughable. He had been playing for about thirty years and he had a nice swing. I was as eager to learn the basic fundamentals of the game as he was to lower his handicap, so we traded our skills. He would teach me how to swing the club and I'd teach him how to tap into the power of his brain to lower his handicap.

I was hooked on golf from that point forward. I signed up for the player development program at the course and a new chapter in my sporting life began. Immediately I understood why the game of golf is so difficult for so many. The golf club needs to be held with two hands and most people have a serious difference in skill levels with each arm and hand. So when a golfer aims straight, they often miss the fairway. When one actually thinks about how symmetry works for most sports, it becomes clear as day. 99.99% of people who throw a baseball or football, sink a basketball, serve a tennis ball, bowl, toss a Frisbee, play darts, shoot pool, fire a gun or rifle, do it with their dominant arm and hand.

In golf, however, if there is a slight error with the way that the club impacts the ball it will fly off the desired path. Where does this error come from? From a common sense perspective the hands do not work in harmony to strike the ball. If the hands are not in harmony then neither are the brain hemispheres working cooperatively. As a consequence, the many moving parts of the body have inherent errors and the club face either cuts across the ball, or the face of the club is too open or too closed upon impact. The ball cannot go straight as a result.

Just as I had experienced with my tennis quest, I knew I would apply my ambidextrous theory to this new challenge. From the beginning I committed to investing in right-handed and *left*-handed clubs. I became a regular at the driving range in the beginning of 2002. The feeling of really cracking the golf ball was a thrill, and I knew that I would eventually figure out how to hit it straight. Rolly took me out on the course and I would shoot scores around 110. One day I broke 100 and that day was a huge milestone for me.

Soon I was putting a few good holes together in every round and my "delusions of grandeur" came to the surface. I thought what a challenge it would be to break par on a good golf course. It was only four months into my golfing experiment that I said to Rolly during lunch, "I really think it is possible for me to become a scratch golfer."

He let out a load guffaw and responded, "Yeah, right! I've been playing for thirty years and my handicap is fifteen. You've been playing for four months and you think you have a shot at playing scratch golf?"

"Seriously Rolly, if I put my mind to it, I know it is within my potential."

He looked at me a bit funny as if to say, "Sure you will." I had gotten this look from others before with my tennis game so I was not offended. Then he said, "Okay, listen, set aside my skills on the course; professionals that have been out there for years have hit millions of practice balls in their journey to scratch golf. You could never catch up to just the sheer amount of practice the pros have done."

Huh, millions of practice balls, I thought to myself. I went home and got out my lob wedge and started to bounce the golf ball off the club face mimicking the *Nike* commercial where Tiger Woods does this ball trick. By the end of the night I could do it twenty-five times without a miss. Within a week I was bouncing it hundreds of times without a drop. Then I started to bounce the golf ball off the face of my putter. It was much more difficult, but eventually I broke 100 in a row. Then it was 200, then 500 and then I needed another challenge. That is when I took a hammer from my art supply box and started to tap the golf ball off the face of the hammerhead. It was a smaller surface and slightly convex. I was able to do ten in a row despite the curved surface. Then I did it 25 times. I had seen improvement with all of the other surfaces that I tried this ball bouncing skill with so I new it was only a matter of time before I would hit the magic 100 mark.

Just as I started to translate these talents into my golf swing, my golf teacher Rolly left for Europe on a two-year business assignment in England. I was on my own with my mission and revolutionary attempt to apply my ball-bouncing hand/eye coordination to my golf game.

I felt as though I was getting almost perfectly centered strikes every time. To test my theory I placed some carbon tape on the face of my driver and irons and got instant feedback. The tight groupings captured by the markings on the tape reinforced my determination to push for more hits on the hammers.

I was not content to stay with just a 16 oz. Stanley claw hammer. I went down to Home Depot and bought the biggest collection of hammers for a non-carpenter in the state of California. Within a week I was getting runs on various hammers up to 300 hits without a miss. Then it became 500. By this time it was clear to me that it was not luck any more; it was focused energy, improved eye muscles, grip strength and motor skill enhancement that was reaching into the subconscious strata of my cerebral cortex.

My goal with this coordination routine was to push up into the thousands of hits without a miss, and to do it ambidextrously. That meant I needed to get my left hand up to speed. Soon I could bounce a ball hundreds of times with the left hand without a miss and 2000 times in a row with the right hand. I felt a sense of motor skill balance that I had never known before in my life; meanwhile, my forearm and wrist strength were going off the charts. I would shake people's hands and not realize the power of my own grip. My wrist bones were getting thicker and the density of the muscle tissue was obviously greater than in my college sports playing days. At this time, in 2002, I did not fully understand the details of the brain changes and the chemistry changes in my body. But I continued my research at the library in search of an answer.

My golf bag was stuffed with a combination of left and right-handed clubs. I would hit fifty balls left-handed and then I would switch back over to right-handed. Many people tried to persuade me to stick to one side, saying, "Mike, you are bad enough right-handed, why be doubly mediocre from both sides?" They did not understand that my ambidextrous tennis experiment was now in-filtrating my golf game. The better I hit the ball left-handed, the easier it was to hit it right-handed. Soon I was driving even the lower compression range balls as much as 320 yards in the air. The course management banned me from using my driver for fear I'd hit the ball out into the traffic beyond the fence at the far end of the driving range.

Flush with the success of my ball striking ability, I pushed the ambidextrous fine and gross motor controls further in my training. I spent a great deal of time doing the hammer drills and the left-handed mirror image writing. I multi-tasked as I recited the power of two up to the 40th power while bouncing a golf ball on a hammer. There were days that I bounced the ball a total 10,000 hits on the different hammers in my tool kit. It was common for me in one week to bounce a golf ball 70,000 times. All of this was focused on my quest to be able to break par.

The funny thing about this whole experience was that I was not going out on the golf course testing my game. I had become a range rat. People would mock me and say this is no way to train at golf. They did not understand that my determination and my imagination had no limits, and that there was a method to my madness. Nonetheless, I realized people were talking about my eccentricities. People started to call me *The Hammer Man,* part out of ridicule, part out of amazement at my skill. It was OK with me to have this new nickname.

I had a machinist craft me a golf club out of the head of a hammer. He welded the housel from an old iron club, attached it to a 46-inch shaft, and now I had the perfect tool to train with to become a great ball striker. This club had only a ¾ square inch of surface area, thus I needed to focus in order to hit the ball on the center.

I sought even greater challenges for my hand-eye skill development and purchased a ball peen and a tack hammer. It wasn't long before I was bouncing a golf ball off the round end of the ball peen hammer. On the other end of the spectrum was the heavy hammer training I was doing with the short-handled eight, ten and twelve-pound sledge hammers. What I once would have considered impossible to achieve became commonplace. I tapped into something in my right hemisphere that made me savant-like in my ability to track a golf ball on the ball peen hammer over one hundred times without a miss. Soon I was able to run full-speed 50-yard dashes while bouncing a golf ball off of a conventional 16-ounce claw hammer.

One day my oldest son Sean and I went to a local park where we videotaped a sequence of *"The Hammer Man's Way to Better Golf"*. My boy has excellent video editing skills and we put together a five-minute presentation that went to the Stanley Tool Company in New Britain, Connecticut. This prompted them to fly me out to their headquarters where they filmed my ESPN world record of consecutive ball bounces off their *Number 1* claw hammer, 3,293 times. It made the *Top Ten Plays of The Day* on *ESPN* in October 2005. Next thing I knew I was back in New York for an appearance on *The Late Show with David Letterman* where I was called out of the audience during a segment called, *"Show and Tell."*

My two-minute demonstration of hammer skills on national television got the ball rolling on my golfing aspirations. Upon returning to California, the Aliso Viejo Golf Club (AVGC) manager Jim Goss, invited me into his office. He was intrigued by my ideas and skills and informed me that the Stanley Tool Company and his AVGC were going to sponsor my quest to play in tournaments. He understood my lack of knowledge of course management but he was willing to see if I could apply my unusual disciplines to play scratch golf on his course. He gave me a pass to play every day. I felt as if I died and went to heaven. I had no idea about how to navigate a golf course and my first two weeks were rounds with scores one would not write home about. This was three years ago, the year 2005.

That is when I got back to Whole Brain Power™ basics and began to write and post clippings in my journal about my golf game. What had worked for my tennis in the past was going to be applied to my quest to break par on this course. I clipped out pictures from golf magazines, wrote comments in my journal with either hand, drew sketches of golf holes and imagined how to play them. I watched other players and their ball striking techniques in the sand traps and the rough.

Slowly I was putting it all together and within two months of playing six days a week I broke par by one stroke. That was during a round in a skins game and for the first time I was on the receiving end of the small cash winning. From that day forward those guys no longer had me in their group when it came to playing for money.

In 2007, after two years abroad, Rolly returned to Southern California. He was blown away that I was getting complimentary golf from Aliso Viejo. We would go out in the morning and play a round and I did my best to put the pressure on him. He was in disbelief when I would post a sub par round. "If I were not there from the beginning of this journey, I would not believe it was possible," he said to me. "How on earth did you do this?"

I told him, "Just as you suggested, I hit millions of golf balls."

He blurted out, "You did what?"

I replied, "I hit millions of golf balls off the heads of different hammers. That does not count the 500 to 1000 balls that I would hit at the range per day.

"But what possessed you to do such a thing?" he asked.

"Well, you said the pros had hit millions of practice shots in their careers and so that set a baseline for me. When you said I wouldn't be able to play scratch golf, well, that inspired me." That was the day that Rolly got hooked on Whole Brain Power™. He signed up for the program and he committed to practicing all the training regimens, penmanship, memory and hammer drills. As I witnessed him make progress I became convinced that my theories had potential beyond my own skill development, that Whole Brain Power™ was transferable. All along I was doing tremendous amounts of research concerning *neurogenesis* and the theories on brain plasticity. The internet offered an opportunity to read papers from the top neuroscientists in the world. All the evidence was pointing

42

to the same conclusion: the human brain is the greatest mystery in the known universe. New discoveries were being presented on a daily basis. There were articles being published in *Time Magazine, Discover, Scientific American* and all of the top newspapers around the globe, and the consensus was all the same; neuroscientists were discovering that their previously held views on the brain were wrong. Terms like *synaptogenesis* and *steroidogenesis* further invigorated my investigation into this new paradigm.

The evidence pointed to the fact that the brain actually grows from nurturing it - from *training it*. UCLA's neurological department was involved with a study of identical twins and their conclusion was that left-handed men have a more flexible brain structure. When compared against their identical twin that happened to be right-handed, the left-hander in all those studied (70 pairs of twins, all men with the average age of 70) had more brain mass than their right-handed sibling. This discovery pushed me to become more left-handed on a daily basis. A new technology of looking at the brain used in a London College study based on a Voxel-Based Morphology scanner proved that learning the ambidextrous skill of juggling was growing the surface of the cerebral cortex by up to 4 percent.

It occurred to me that the thickening of the white matter (myelin) in the brain was correlated to the rewiring process of learning this ambidextrous skill (juggling), and that process was behind the increased mass of the cerebral cortex in the study participants. It was my first inkling that *the hands grow the brain.*

I researched many case studies that indicated the brain is much more plastic than science previously understood. There were stories of Hall of Fame baseball players that started out life as a right-hander and made it to the Hall as a lefty. And natural left-handed individuals who were "forced" or coerced into becoming a right-handed athlete, or vice versa, either because of parental pressure, coaches, superstition or lack of equipment. Among that list are such notables as Tiger Woods, Phil Mickelson, Venus Williams, and Rafael Nadal. If this were

43

not proof in itself of the ability of the brain to rewire itself, nothing else would be as persuasive. I saw a pattern emerging.

According to my research into *steroidogenesis*, experiments with castrated rats in which the adrenal glands and gonads were removed, researchers noticed that the rats did not lose muscle mass or bone density when put through certain exercises. How could this be since the obvious source of testosterone was missing? When they measured for testosterone levels they were at normal ranges. They did autopsies on the rats and when they removed the brains they were able to prove conclusively that indeed the *white matter cells or the glial cells* in the Central Nervous system called *oligodrendrocytes* were the source of the master steroid called *pregnenolone*. They were able to show the whole cascade of steroidogenesis (see pages 156-157), which eventually led to the production of the anabolic steroid -- testosterone -- in the rats. From my research I concluded that steroids could be endogenously produced throughout the body when the body and brain are trained in a certain manner - a manner in which myelination is accelerated. Could it be that the brain is the greatest pharmacy in the world?

Now my years of note taking and collecting articles and papers began to make sense, the puzzle was about to be solved. If the complexity of the brain and its ability to change itself was now a proven fact, then this Whole Brain Power™ theory might hold water. I knew what happened to me, and now others were telling me they were experiencing the same athletic development. After Rolly started the hammer program, the juggling, the writing and the memory drills, it was not more than one month before he started to hit his tee shot over the fairway traps that previously captured his drive. Within three months I watched him start to hit his drives at least 30 yards further than he ever had. There's Rolly, aged 60, jumping for joy in the middle of the fairway from a source of power and skill that he had never experienced before in his life. Here are our golf balls sitting side-by-side almost three hundred yards from the tee box.

44

In September of 2007, I had the good fortune to meet with my co-author of this book, Gregory S. Walsh ("GW"), a filmmaker from Seattle, Washington, who was producing a reality golf pilot show in the Laguna Beach area. My cameo on his pilot was just a few minutes, but the DVD that he sent me a month later of the final edited show inspired me to investigate GW's other film projects. There was a great selection of his diverse films available on his company's (Fivesun Entertainment) website, *www.fivesun.com*. Convinced that GW had the writing and filmmaking skills I needed to help share my discoveries with other people, I asked for his assistance. After our first serious discussions on the possibilities of creating a business model he joined forces with me. I brought him up to speed on my history and body of work concerning my ideas on the brain and my training methodologies.

GW, ever the director, influenced me to go in a new direction with my life's mission. He convinced me that my desire to play tournament golf should take a backseat to promoting Whole Brain Power™ training methodologies on a broad scale. The role he wanted me cast in was as "coach", not "player". I immediately grasped the wisdom of this new focus for my life and realized how much more interesting the role of coach or teacher would be as we both envisioned it.

As we got deeper into our discussions about my theories, GW coined the term *Whole Brain Power™* for the skills that we would teach, and *Whole Brain Planet™* for the name of the company we would form. He came back to Laguna a month later and filmed me demonstrating my training methodologies in a number of different venues here in Orange County. He returned to Seattle and built our web site at www.wholebrainpower.net, which became our initial effort to launch our company and to share Whole Brain Power™ with a broader audience. Over the next six months other practitioners, both men and women, joined the program confirming the skill transferability with people of all ages and physical abilities.

---

[1] You can read the article on our website: www.wholebrainpower.net

A front-page article in *The Orange County Register* (OCR) by staff writer Tom Berg appeared May 12th, 2008[1]. That article sent thousands of people to our web site to investigate this revolution in ambidexterity. People from all walks of life began to ask for training with me or a copy of this book (which was still only in proposal form at that time) so that they too could begin to harness Whole Brain Power™. At this point GW and I knew that our first priority was to publish this book. We were getting hundreds of emails requesting a copy or copies of the book as a result of Tom's article and we knew we had to find an agent and publisher for the book and get an advance so we could free ourselves up from our "day jobs" to start writing.

Soon after the OCR article circulated on the web in May, *ABC* contacted us. I remember the afternoon GW called from Seattle and asked if I was sitting down. "Michael, the cat's out of the bag. Peter Imber, a producer from ABC's *Nightline,* wants to interview you." Peter had visited our web site and looked at the people practicing Whole Brain Power™ such as Chuck Mellick, the 38-year-old ambidextrous baseball pitcher. Chuck is closing in on being the first pitcher in history to throw over 90 miles-an-hour with each hand. They saw Suzanna McGee working her ambidextrous tennis skills. Then they clicked on the page of my son Chris that shows him serving the tennis ball with either hand and slamming forehand shots from both sides.

Peter, and on-air correspondent Lisa Fletcher, brought their film crew down to Orange County a couple of days later and interviewed me and some of the practitioners of Whole Brain Power™, and filmed us doing ambidextrous drills. They seemed impressed by the skills of those involved and we went to several locations as they videotaped the four of us for more than 5 hours. Rolly White, tennis player Peter Larrieu age 52, and professional golfer Les Taylor also aged 52, all gave in-depth interviews.

The following day I received a call from Peter informing me that the story was now taking a different turn. He said that Lisa and he had decided to commit to a 30-day Whole Brain Power™ training program taking instruction on the different tenets from myself and WBP practitioner Rolly White. On top of that, Peter had contacted a neuroscientist from UCLA and would be including the scientific side of the equation, investigating the legitimacy of the theories being hypothesized by the Whole Brain Planet™ founders. I was thrilled to hear this as I want Whole Brain Power™ theories clinically tested.

The potential national exposure by ABC's Nightline offered a golden opportunity to share Whole Brain Power™ with the world. Figuring that the airing of the Nightline segment would occur sometime in late-summer or early fall of 2008, GW and I stopped our pursuit of an agent or publisher and moved forward in our "spare time" without an agent and without an advance and with the plan to self-publish the book through Lulu.com. By September 1st, 2008 we completed the manuscript for the First Edition of the book you hold in your hands:

Whole Brain Power: The Fountain of Youth for Mind and Body.

First Edition of Whole Brain Power™ published September 1st, 2008.

Chapter 2
The Blueprint for Your Brain

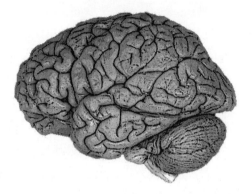

Throughout this book I will refer to scientific terms related to *brain anatomy, functioning and chemistry*. I believe that once you fully understand the impact that our penmanship, memorization and ambidexterity training have on *specific areas* of your brain and body development, you will be more compelled to hasten your development of Whole Brain Power™. New words will enter your vocabulary and have important meaning to you in your every day life; words like *hippocampus, amygdala, neuroplasticity, steroidogenesis, PH balance, neurogenesis, ATP, glucose, glucocortocoids and glutamate*.

Modern neuroscience is radically expanding our understanding of just how brain chemistry can be altered, in a positive way, without drugs. In fact in many ways, the brain is a natural pharmacy. You will learn that you can grow new neurons, produce steroids, more effectively metabolize cholesterol, and dramatically increase your energy, do all these amazing things *naturally* without supplements and without running to the drug store. Once you learn that real improvements in muscle and bone density, overall functional strength, superior hand-eye

48

coordination and a razor sharp memory come from *training the brain* first, you'll be well on your way to developing Whole Brain Power™.

The human brain is certainly the most complex organ in the known universe. The brain has been studied for centuries; however, we have learned more about how it functions in the last 15 years than in the previous 5000 years. Scientists have discovered and named the major and minor anatomical features, cells and chemical compositions. Most of the cell types have been isolated within the brain's 100,000,000,000 (100 billion) **neurons** and as many as ten times that number of **glial cells** or supporting cells. The identification of specific **neurotransmitters** has grown into the hundreds, and the proteins and polypeptides that are involved in brain functioning have also been categorized. We have a firm grasp as to how DNA is sequenced and how RNA works in regard to the brain producing its building blocks for maintaining its integrity. We have successfully mapped the human genome and have a better grasp of the number of genes that are associated with brain function. We have the equipment to measure in microns, the sizes of neurons, the thickness of axon sheaths, the dendrites, and the smallest gaps or synapses between communicating cells. As nanotechnology evolves, we can see and understand the mechanics of how neurons function and that the operations of the supporting role of the glial cells are comparable to that of precision micro machines.

Yet, neuroscience is still only scratching the surface in its understanding of the origin of consciousness within the brain and how to harness the brain's potential. *The Blueprint for Your Brain* will reacquaint you with some of the terms you learned in Biology class and some that will be new to you. Neuroscience is, in our view, only it its infancy and yet is still the most fascinating frontier of exploration imaginable. Whole Brain Power™ is all about that exploration; both from a neurological point of view, and from your own anecdotal study of how *you will train your brain and body* at any age.

The Autonomic Nervous System (ANS)

Within the brain, the **autonomic nervous system** regulates and adjusts base-line body functions and responds to external stimuli.

It consists of two subsystems:

• *The Sympathetic Nervous System*: nerves that activate our body's functioning or arousal. This system is "ergotropic", which means it *releases energy.*

• *The Parasympathetic Nervous System*: nerves that slow the body down for rest and repair. This system is "trophotropic," which means it *conserves energy.*

These subsystems of the Autonomic Nervous System are critical to our study of the brain and its application to Whole Brain Power™ as you will see in later chapters. They regulate two important functions of the brain: **growth or protection, releasing energy or conserving energy.** Because of the amount of energy both systems demand from the body, they must share the amount of energy between them depending on the needs presented. In high stress situations where the Sympathetic system takes over, there is an inhibition of *growth energy generation.* **The Hypothalamus-Pituitary-Adrenal Axis (H-P-A Axis)** mobilizes its defense in such situations against the *perceived* threat, real or imagined.

For example, in prehistoric times when faced with being mauled by a Saber Tooth Tiger, our *Sympathetic* system kicks in and uses the body's stores of energy to run and hide, or stand and fight and kill the tiger. After we've killed the tiger our *Parasympathetic* system kicks in using our body's energy to eat and digest the tiger, and to nourish our cells from the nutrients we take in. Substitute the acute stress in prehistoric times of fighting a Saber Tooth Tiger with the chronic stress of daily modern life (whether on the job, or in the home environment, etc.,) and the result is a prolonged energy-drain and debilitation that ultimately leads to depression, and suppression of the auto-immune system. Children who grow up in stressful homes are deprived of cellular nutrition and growth, in cellular energy-generation itself, and consequently suffer in their mental, emotional and social development. Energy in a stressed-out child (or adult for that matter) is diverted by the adrenal hormones which constrict blood flow to the frontal lobes and cortex, and divert energy and consciousness to the brain's limbic region survival faculties. Again, it is a matter of either *growth or protection,* and the necessary balance that the Autonomic Nervous System provides for the ultimate survival of the body.

The *Sympathetic Nervous System (SNS)* is the source of our fight or flight response, and is connected to the ***H-P-A Axis.*** This emergency response is controlled by the hypothalamus and amygdala. Under stress, the release of a chemical called *noradrenaline* stimulates heartbeat, raises blood pressure, dilates the pupils, dilates the trachea and bronchi, stimulates the conversion of liver glycogen into glucose, shunts blood away from the skin and viscera to the skeletal muscles, brain and heart, inhibits peristalsis in the gastrointestinal tract, inhibits contraction of the bladder and rectum and inhibits the immune system -- all to save energy.

All of this *SNS* response to protect the brain and body from danger was and is a necessary brain function for *real life* threatening events. However, you will learn later how viewing violent television shows, movies or playing violent video games are all perceived by the brain not as *fictional events* (as the producers of violent entertainment would like you to believe) but as *real events* by the primal regions of the brain in the *limbic system.* The result is the Sympathetic Nervous System realigns the energy to the amygdala in an attempt to deal with the perceived "real" violence it is experiencing.

51

The Homunculus Theory

The Homunculus Theory is taught in first year medical school where students learn about the Sensory Homunculus and the Motor Homunculus. The theory essentially states that there is a certain amount of real estate on the cerebral cortex reserved for the senses and the motor controls.

Cross-section of the cerebrum showing the Primary Motor Cortex

Figure 2.1

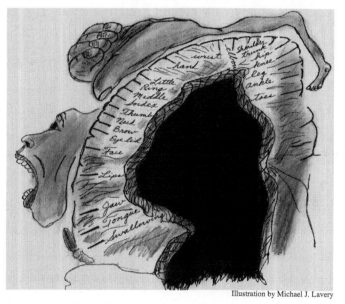

Illustration by Michael J. Lavery

Name: *Primary Motor Cortex*

Location: Dorsal part of the precentral gyrus

Function: The primary motor cortex works in association with pre-motor areas to plan and execute movements. The cortex contains large neurons known as Betz cells which send long axons down the spinal cord to connect onto alpha motor neurons which connect to the muscles. Pre-motor areas are involved in planning actions (in concert with the basal ganglia) and refining movements based upon sensory input from the cerebellum.

Sensory Homunculus

Figure 2.2

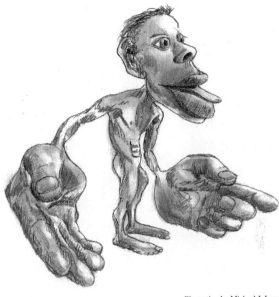

Illustration by Michael J. Lavery

This caricature illustrates what we would see if the human form had body parts drawn in proportion to the amount of area represented on the cerebral cortex. The *sensory* part of the brain is located in the ***Parietal Lobes*** and is referred to as the ***Somatosensory Cortex***. Notice that the figure has rather large hands, eyes, ears, nose and mouth. These areas represent our senses of touch, sight, hearing, smell, and taste. The hands in particular are drawn way out of proportion to the rest of the body because the hands have more nerve endings than any other region. For instance, there are hundreds of nerve endings in just the very tip of your index finger. The number of nerve endings on the upper arm or the thigh is considerably lower. We know from experience that there are certain parts of our body that are super sensitive to pain. When we burn the inside of our mouth from eating something hot or get a paper cut on one of our fingers, the pain can be intense.

53

Motor Homunculus

Figure 2.3

Illustration by Michael J. Lavery

The Motor Homunculus deals with the area of the frontal lobes called the motor strip. It is referred by science as M1. The drawing is done to illustrate the disproportionate amount of space that the lips, eyes, tongue and hands take up on the motor strip in relation to the other parts of the body. As with the Somatosensory Cortex, the hands are huge in proportion to everything else in the amount of landscape devoted by the motor strip to the hands. In fact, the hands take up approximately 25% of the motor strip. This is a major point in the hypothesis presented by Whole Brain Power™, that *the hands grow the brain.*

The hands actually have a major influence on the frontal lobes of the brain and therefore have much to do with the way the brain is sculpted. Research now shows that the hands actually help determine the size of many anatomical features of the brain, including the mass of the brain hemispheres.

We will be discussing in detail the concepts that underlie this theory in Chapter Five on Ambidexterity. Most of the training regimens of Whole Brain Power™ motivate the practitioner to train both motor strips through the exercise of fine and gross ambidextrous motor controls. The hands speak to the brain and the brain speaks to the hands, and this symbiotic relationship stimulates the activation of both hemispheres for whole-brain, motor strip potential.

Interesting Brain Facts:

• *The Human brain weighs on average about 3 pounds.*

• *The brain consists of over 1 trillion cells, 100 billion of which are neurons.*

• *Your brain is about 2% of your total body weight but uses 20% of your body's energy, including 20% of your sugar supply.*

• *The energy used by the brain is enough to light a 25 watt bulb.*

• *The brain can stay alive for 4 to 6 minutes without oxygen; after that brain cells begin to die.*

• *The composition of the brain is 77-78% water, 10-12% lipids (fats), 8% protein, 1% carbs, 2% soluble organics, 1% inorganic salt.*

• *36 ounces of blood flow through the brain every minute.*

• *1/5 of a cup of oxygen is consumed by the brain every minute. Of that oxygen consumed, 6% will be used by the brain's white matter and 94% by the grey matter.*

• *The slowest speed at which information travels between neurons in the brain is 260 mph, or about the record speed for the bullet train in Toyko.*

• *During early pregnancy the rate of neuron growth is 250,000 neurons a minute. While neuron growth slows significantly by age 30, scientists discovered in 1998 that new neurons can be formed at any age. This discovery has spawned an entire new study of the brain called* **neuroplasticity.**

• *Total surface area of the cerebral cortex (the outer surface of the brain) is 2,500 cm2 or 2.69 sq.ft. (The cerebral cortex is about 1/4 inch thick.)*

Brain Anatomy

As we blueprint the brain here is how we will organize the information in this section:

• **Name:** What is the anatomical name of the structure or chemical name of the substance found in the brain.
• **Location:** Where is it located within a region or system of the brain.
• **Function:** What role does it play within our brain or body.

We're not trying to turn you into a *neuroscientist* here, but if you read and comprehend this chapter you will have a very good foundation for understanding the *applied neuroscience* upon which Whole Brain Power™ theories and training methodologies are based.

The Central Nervous System (CNS)

Figure 2.4

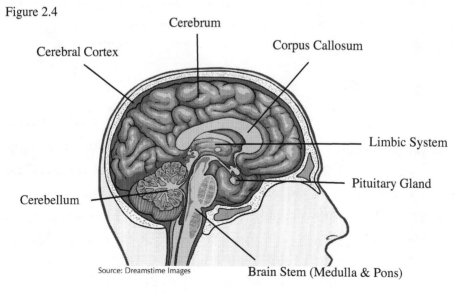

Source: Dreamstime Images

The CNS is comprised of the following large regions of the brain:

• **Brain Stem (medulla and pons)** • **Corpus Callosum** • **Limbic System**
• **Cerebellum** • **Cerebral Cortex (outer layer of the brain)** • **Cerebrum**

Name: *Brain Stem* or "reptilian brain", includes the *medulla* and *pons*.

Location: See Figure 2.4

Function: This is the most ancient and primitive part of our brain. It determines our general level of awareness and signals to the rest of the brain in a general way about incoming data, i.e., pain, heat, cold, shock, etc. It helps control basic bodily functions such as breathing, blood pressure and heart rate.

Name: *Corpus Callosum*

Location: See Figure 2.4

Function: This is the large bundle of axons which connect the two cerebral hemispheres and is used to communicate between the hemispheres through 200-250 million axons, or "wires". Of note is that the corpus callosum in left-hand dominant people is 11% larger than in right-handed people.

Name: The *Limbic System* or the "mammalian brain.

Location: See Figure 2.5

Function: This region plays a key role in primal emotional reactions such as hunger, sexual arousal and the 'fight or flight' reflex. It also helps to maintain hormonal secretions, body temperature, blood pressure, heart rate and blood sugar levels.

The areas of focus within the limbic system relevant to our theories and training include: *hippocampi, dentate gyrus, amygdalae, basal ganglia, thalamus, hypothalamus and pituitary gland.*

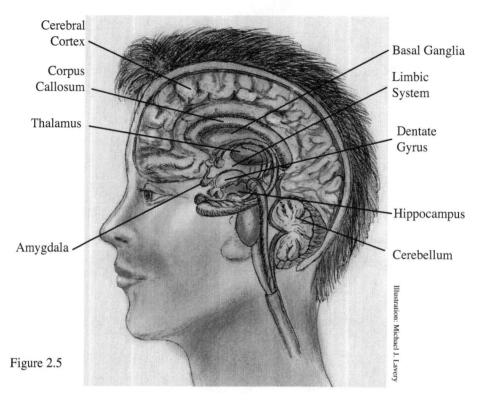

Cerebral Cortex

Corpus Callosum

Thalamus

Amygdala

Basal Ganglia

Limbic System

Dentate Gyrus

Hippocampus

Cerebellum

Illustration: Michael J. Lavery

Figure 2.5

Name: *Basal Ganglia*

Location: See Figure 2.5

Function: The basal ganglia (or basal nuclei) are a group of nuclei (bundle of neurons) in the brain interconnected with the cerebral cortex, thalamus and brainstem, and are associated with a variety of functions: motor control, cognition, emotions, and learning. This group of nuclei are essential elements in Whole Brain Power™ theories and training as they directly control outputting activities such as our spoken language, gesture preparation and our mastery of fine penmanship. The basal ganglia in essence "fires up" the cerebellum which in turn acts as a preamp to send commands to the rest of the brain through the *purkinje cells*.

Name: *Hippocampus*

Location: See Figures 2.5 and 2.6

Function: Buried deep in the forebrain, the hippocampi (plural for hippocampus, there is one located in each hemisphere) help regulate emotion and memory. The hippocampus is critical for the formation of new autobiographical and fact memories, and is a memory "gateway" through which new memories must pass before entering permanent storage in the brain. It is one of the first brain areas to show damage in Alzheimer's disease. The hippocampus is also part of the olfactory cortex, that part of the cerebral cortex essential to the sense of smell.

Figure 2.6: Detail of the hippocampus

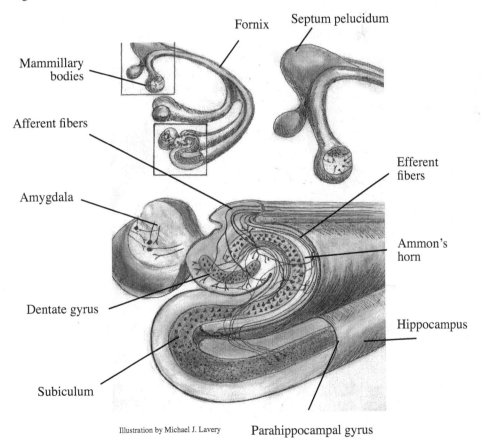

Fornix

Septum pelucidum

Mammillary bodies

Afferent fibers

Efferent fibers

Amygdala

Ammon's horn

Dentate gyrus

Hippocampus

Subiculum

Illustration by Michael J. Lavery

Parahippocampal gyrus

59

Detail of the Hippocampus (see figure 2.6)

The *fornix*, a thick bundle of nerve fibers which forms the outgoing pathway from the hippocampus. The *afferent fibers* bring impulses into the dentate gyrus and the area of Ammon's horn. The *dentate gyrus* which lies within the hippocampal sulcus and is thought to contribute to new memories and is one of the few areas of the brain responsible for *neurogenesis*. The *subiculum* is a region of cortex composed of up to six different cell layers and a multitude of nerve pathways. *Ammon's horn*, which merges with the subiculum and contains ovoid and pyramidal cells, the function of which are thought to be associated with memory. The *efferent fibers*, which carry information out from Ammon's horn to other regions of the brain. The *parahippocampal gyrus*, a highly specialized area of nerve cells concerned with memory pathways. The *mammillary bodies*, act as a relay station between the limbic system and the brain. The *septum pelucidum*, which links the amygdala with the hypothalamus and is believed to be concerned with pleasure reactions.

Name: *Thalamus*

Location: See Figure 2.5

Function: The thalamus processes and relays sensory information selectively to various parts of the cerebral cortex. The thalamus also plays an important role in regulating states of sleep and wakefulness as well as regulating arousal, the level of awareness, and activity of the brain.

Name: *Pituitary Gland*

Location: Limbic System

Function: The pituitary gland, or hypophysis, is an endocrine gland about the size of a pea located below the hypothalamus. The pituitary gland secretes hormones regulating homeostasis, e.g., growth hormone, oxytocin and endorphins.

Name: *Hypothalamus*

Location: Limbic System

Function: The hypothalamus links the nervous system to the endocrine system via the pituitary gland and controls body temperature, hunger, thirst, fatigue, anger, and circadian cycles. The hypothalamus protects the body from invading microorganisms by increasing body temperature, resetting the body's thermostat upward.

Name: *Amygdala*

Location: See figures 2.5 and 2.6

Function: The amygdalae (plural for amygdala) are groups of neurons located deep within the medial temporal lobes of the brain. They perform a primary role in the processing and memory of ***emotional reactions***. The amygdalae send impulses to the ***hypothalamus*** for important activation of the *sympathetic nervous system*, and to the ***thalamus*** for increased reflexes, as well as control activation of ***dopamine, norepinephrine and epinephrine***.

Name: *Cerebellum*

Location: See Figures 2.4, 2.5

Function: The cerebellum is responsible for maintaining and adjusting posture, coordinating muscle movement and storing 'memories' for correcting motor functions. The cerebellum has more than tripled in size in the last million years. It contains half of all the neurons in the brain but comprises only 10% of the brain. The cerebellum has been compared to a powerful computer, capable of making contributions to our motor dexterity and mental dexterity, both of which are required for the emergence of fluent human language.

61

Name: *Cerebral Cortex*

Location: See Figure 2.4, 2.7, 2.8

Function: The cerebral cortex is the outer layer of the brain and is about 1/4 inch thick. It plays a key role in memory, attention, perceptual awareness, thought, language, and consciousness. The illustration below shows the organization of the nerve cells responsible for information processing in the cerebral cortex, the vertical and horizontal position of the fibers, and the position of the blood vessels within the cortex.

Figure 2.7 - Detail of the Cerebral Cortex

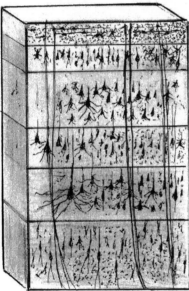

Molecular Layer

External Granular Layer

External Pyramidal Layer

Internal Granular Layer

Internal Pyramidal Layer
(See Figure C, page 63)

Multiform Layer

Illustration by Michael J. Lavery

Convolutions are the folds on the cortex (see Figure A, page 63). This convoluted covering gives the cerebral cortex a large surface area within the restricted confines of the skull. Each "hill" in the cortex is called a gyrus and each "valley" is a called sulcus. The hills and valleys give the brain its wrinkled appearance. Fusiform, basket and stellate cells are all types of neurons present in the cortex. They communicate with each other and sift and sort incoming information.

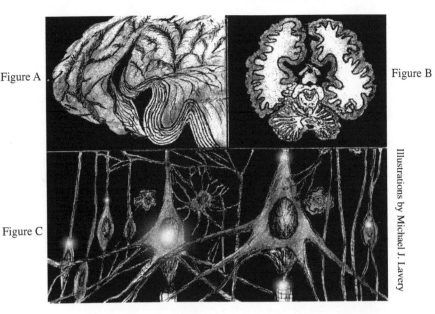

Figure A

Figure B

Figure C

Illustrations by Michael J. Lavery

Figure A: This illustration depicts the cerebral cortex and its convolutions or folds. It has been sliced to show the thickness of the cortex and the six layers that represent the different neural fields shown in Figure 2.7 on page 62.

Figure B: This detail is a cross section of the brain from above. Notice the outer edge of the brain in grey represents the cortex which approximates 1/4 inch in thickness. Within this area there are six levels (see figure 2.7 on page 62.) The lighter areas are considered to be the white matter tracks that send messages to and from different cortical regions.

Figure C: This is a close up of the super pyramidal cells normally found in layer five of the cerebral cortex, and they can have as many as 20,000 receptor sites. These are the largest neurons in the brain. These types of neurons are very important in the motor cortex, and output tremendous amount of information to the peripheral nervous system to aid in coordination.

63

Figure 2.8 Cerebrum

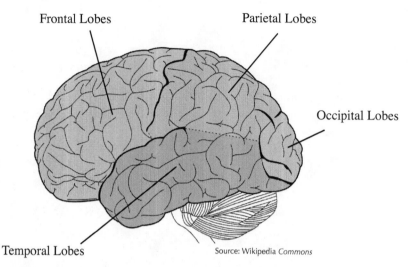

Frontal Lobes   Parietal Lobes

Occipital Lobes

Temporal Lobes   Source: Wikipedia *Commons*

Name: *Cerebrum*

Location: See Figure 2.4 and 2.8

Function: The cerebrum, which comprises about 85% of the brain's volume, directs the conscious motor functions of the body within the primary motor cortex and other frontal lobe motor areas where actions are planned. It is divided into four sections or lobes: the *frontal lobe*, the *parietal lobe*, the *temporal lobe* and the *occipital lobe.*

Name: *Frontal Lobes*

Location: See Figure 2.8

Function: The frontal lobes are in the front of the cerebral cortex and are involved in reasoning, planning, speaking, moving, emotions, and problem-solving. Maintaining brain wave activity in the frontal lobes is critical for impulse control and is related to prevention of Alzheimer's. As you will learn in "Chapter 6: System Killers," the frontal lobes are put at risk of degeneration from prolonged exposure to television viewing or playing violent video games.

Name: *Temporal Lobes*

Location: See Figure 2.8

Function: The temporal lobes are involved in: perception, recognition and pro-cessing of auditory stimuli and memory including semantics both in speech and vision. They play a role in memory formation (through the hippocampus) in-cluding comprehension, naming, verbal memory and other language functions. Temporal lobes also engage in a high-level visual processing of complex stimuli such as faces and scenes, and object perception and recognition. Finally, they are involved in episodic/declarative memory and transference from short to long-term memory and control of spatial memory and behavior.

Name: *Parietal Lobes*

Location: See Figure 2.8

Function: The *parietal lobes* are involved in perception of stimuli related to touch, pressure, temperature, and pain. The parietal lobe integrates sensory in-formation determining spatial locations of objects. For example, it is comprised of the *somatosensory cortex* and the *dorsal stream* of the visual system. This enables regions of the parietal cortex to map objects perceived visually into body coordinate positions.

Name: *Occipital Lobes*

Location: See Figure 2.8

Function: *The occipital lobes* are the posterior lobes of the brain. These lobes are involved with the visual processing center of the brain, containing most of the anatomical region of the visual cortex specialized for different visual tasks, such as visuospatial processing, color discrimination and motion perception.

BRAIN CELLS

Name: *Neurons*

Location: Cerebral cortex, cerebellum, basal ganglia

Function: Neurons are electrically excitable cells in the nervous system that process and transmit information. Fifty percent of the neurons in the brain are located in the **cerebral cortex**. The other neurons in the brain are located in the **cerebellum** which comprises only 10% of brain volume. The remaining neurons in the brain are found in the **basal ganglia**.

Figure 2.9

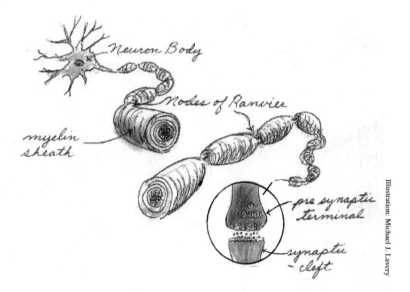

Name: *Myelin Sheath*

Location: See Figure 2.9

Function: The myelin sheath is the outer protective covering on axons and is one of the most important topics we'll discuss later in depth. Think of myelin as the insulation around copper wires in your home. The thicker the insulation, the more current (higher voltage) can run through the wire.

Name: *Glial cells*

Location: Throughout the central nervous system.

Function: Some glia function primarily as the physical support for neurons. Others regulate the internal environment of the brain, especially the fluid surrounding neurons and their synapses, and provide nutrition to nerve cells. Glia have important developmental roles, guiding migration of neurons in early development, and producing molecules that modify the growth of axons and dendrites. Glia are also active participants in synaptic transmission, regulating clearance of neurotransmitters from the synaptic cleft, releasing factors such as ATP which modulate presynaptic function, and even releasing neurotransmitters themselves. They are also crucial in the development of the nervous system and in processes such as *synaptic plasticity* and *synaptogenesis* and have a role in the repair of neurons after injury.

Figure 2.10

Oligodendrocyte

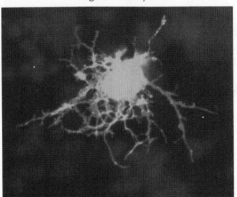

Source: Wikipedia *Commons*

Name: *Oligodendrocytes (type of glial cell)*

Location: Throughout the central nervous system.

Function: Oligodendrocytes are cells that coat axons in the central nervous system (CNS) with their cell membrane forming a specialized membrane differentiation called *myelin*, producing the so-called myelin sheath.

67

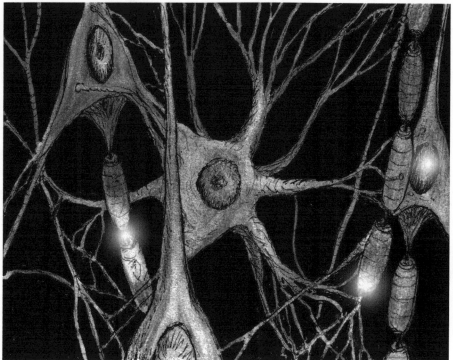

Illustration by Michael J. Lavery

Figure 2.11   An astrocyte (center) supports nearby neurons.

Name: *Astrocytes (type of glial cell)*

Location: Throughout the central nervous system.

Function: In the developing brain, a ***neuron*** depends on molecular signals from cells, such as ***astrocytes***, (protoplasmic or fibrous) to determine its shape and location, the kind of transmitter it produces, and to which other neurons it will connect. Astrocytes are the stars of the show. These glial cells have star like shapes and are very important to support the neurons physically by acting as scaffolding and holding the neurons in place. They also tap into the capillary system with their end feet and they take glucose and convert it into lactate to feed the neurons. They are responsible to aid in the repackaging of neurotransmitters at the synapses as well as maintaining the extra-cellular matrix around the neurons.

68

Name: *Schwann Cells*

Location: Throughout the *Peripheral Nervous System (PNS)*.

Function: Similar in function to oligodendrocytes, Schwann cells provide myelination to axons in the *peripheral nervous system*. They also have phago-cytotic activity and clear cellular debris that allows for regrowth of Peripheral Nervous System (PNS) neurons.

Name: *Pyramidal Cells*

Location: Hippocampus and cerebral cortex

Function: Pyramidal cells (or pyramidal neurons, or projection neurons) com-pose approximately 80% of the neurons of the cortex, and release glutamate as their neurotransmitter, making them the major excitatory component of the cortex.

Name: *Purkinje Cells*

Location: Cerebellum

Function: Purkinje cells (or Purkinje neurons) are some of the largest neurons in the human brain, characterized by a large number of dendritic spines. They are critical for language outputting and in some ways play the role of "general" for the brain, commanding many other areas of the brain into action. Purkinje cells send inhibitory projections to the deep cerebellar nuclei, and constitute the sole output of all motor coordina-tion in the cerebellar cortex.

Figure 2.12 Purkinje Cells

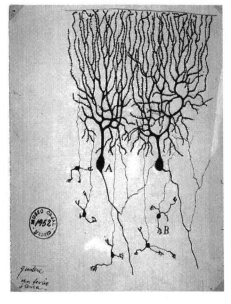

69

BRAIN CHEMISTRY

Name: *Neurotransmitters*

Location: Throughout the Central Nervous System

Function: Neurotransmitters are chemicals that are used to relay, amplify and modulate signals between a neuron and another cell. Examples of neurotransmitters include chemicals we will discuss in this section such as acetylcholine, dopamine, serotonin, epinephrine and GABA. Pharmaceutical drugs are designed to inhibit neurotransmitters in various regions of the brain, for example; *Prozac* is a selective serotonin re-uptake inhibitor, effecting the release of serotonin into the brain.

Name: *Glutamate*

Location: Throughout the Central Nervous System

Function: Glutamate is an amino acid neurotransmitter accounting for an estimated 40% of all *nerve signals* in the human brain, and is involved with neural development, learning, and memory formation. *In excess amounts it is an intense excitant of nerve cells and potentially toxic.* Neurotransmitters like glutamate act as excitatory signals, while GABA inhibits the firing of neurons.

Nerve impulses trigger release of glutamate from the *pre-synaptic cell.* In the opposing *post-synaptic cell,* glutamate receptors, such as the *NMDA receptor*, bind glutamate and are activated. Because of its role in synaptic plasticity, it is believed that *glutamic acid* is involved in cognitive functions like long-term learning and memory in the brain. All meats, poultry, fish, eggs, as well as dairy products are excellent sources of glutamic acid.

Name: *The N-methyl-D-Aspartate receptor (NmDa)*

Location: Throughout the Central Nervous System

Function: The N-methyl-D-Aspartate (NmDa) receptor is a subtype of gluta-mate-activated *ionotropic channels* which is implicated in synaptic mechanisms underlying learning, memory and the perception of pain. Because it is affected by anesthetic agents, the NmDa receptor is related to our state of conscious-ness.

Figure 2.13   Illustration of IGF-1

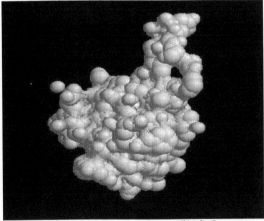

Source: Wikipedia *Commons*

Name: *Insulin-like Growth Factor (IGF-1)*

Location: Throughout the Central and Peripheral Nervous Systems

Function: IGF-1, which was once called somatomedin C, is a polypeptide pro-tein hormone similar in molecular structure to insulin. It plays an important role in childhood growth and continues to have anabolic effects in adults. We theorize that Whole Brain Power™ training methodologies help transport IGF-1 from the forearms up to and through the brain-blood barrier and thus provide this vital nutrient to the brain for maintaining mental functioning, neurogenesis, through conversion into *BDNF*.

71

Name: *Brain-derived Neurotrophic Factor (BDNF)*

Location: Primarily hippocampus, cerebral cortex and basal ganglia

Function: BDNF is one of the most active neurotrophins, and this protein helps to stimulate and control neurogenesis. It acts on certain neurons of the central nervous system and the peripheral nervous system, and helps to support the survival of existing neurons and encourage the growth and differentiation of new neurons and synapses. In the brain, it is active in the hippocampus, cortex, and basal forebrain—areas vital to learning, memory, and higher thinking.

Figure 2.14   Illustration of ATP

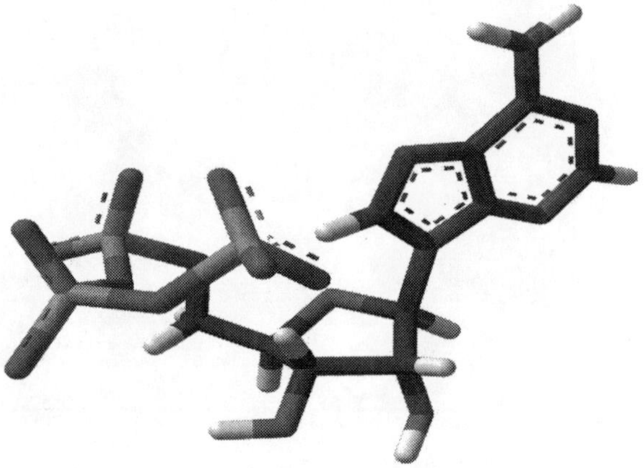

Source: Wikipedia *Commons*

Name: *Adenosine triphosphate (ATP)*

Location: Throughout the Central Nervous System.

Function: ATP is an important source of energy transfer within the brain and the body and we will discuss its role in more detail throughout this book. In scientific terms, ATP is a nucleotide that transports chemical energy within cells for metabolism. It is produced as an energy source during the process of cellular respiration, and is involved in cellular division, as well as in the process of DNA replication and transcription. It is very much involved in protein production.

Illustration: Dopamine molecule

Figure 2.15

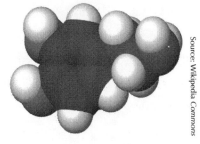

Source: Wikipedia Commons

Name: *Dopamine*

Location: Lower region of the basal ganglia.

Function: Dopamine is a hormone and neurotransmitter that activates the dopamine receptors in the brain. It is also a neurohormone released by the hypothalamus. Its main function as a hormone is to inhibit the release of prolactin from the pituitary.

Name: *Serotonin*

Location: Hypothalamus and midbrain. (also gastrointestinal tract)

Function: Serotonin is made from the amino acid *Tryptophan*. In the central nervous system, serotonin plays an important role as a neurotransmitter in the modulation of anger, aggression, body temperature, mood, sleep, sexuality, appetite, and metabolism. In addition, serotonin is found extensively in the human gastrointestinal tract as about 80-90% of the body's total serotonin is found in the enterochromaffin cells in the gut.

Name: *Nucleus Basilis of Meynart*

Location: Substantia innominata of the basal ganglia.

Function: The basal nucleus of Meynert (NBM) is a group of nerve cells that have wide projections to the neocortex and are rich in acetylcholine and choline acetyltransferase.

Name: *Calcium*

Location: Throughout the brain and body.

Function: Calcium is essential for living organisms, particularly in cell physiology, where movement of the calcium ion (Ca2+) into and out of the cytoplasm functions as a signal for many cellular processes. Calcium is also the primary mineral in our bones and teeth.

Figure 2.16   Illustration: Acetylcholine molecule

Source: Wikipedia Commons

Name: *Acetylcholine (ACh)*

Location: Throughout the Central and Peripheral Nervous System.

Function: Acetylcholine is the primary neurotransmitter involved with thought, learning, and memory. It sharpens our concentration and perception. For its manufacture, we need choline, a component of lecithin, known popularly as a "nerve food." A lack of choline can produce a decrease in memory. Some foods that contain choline are liver, egg yolk, as well as cheese, nuts, oatmeal, and soybeans. Drugs and medications can interfere with the manufacture and effectiveness of acetylcholine.

Name: *PH Balance*

Function: pH is the measure of the acidity or alkalinity of a solution. The pH scale ranges from 0 (the highest acidic) to 14 (the most alkaline). Perfect balanced human body pH is 7.4. Infections and disease proliferate when the body is too acidic as a result of acid forming foods.

Name: *Cholesterol*

Location: Throughout the body and brain.

Function: Cholesterol is a lipid found in the cell membranes and is transported in the blood plasma. It is also a sterol (a combination steroid and alcohol). Most of the cholesterol in the body is synthesized by the body and some has dietary origin. Cholesterol plays a central role in many biochemical processes, such as the composition of cell membranes and the *synthesis of steroid hormones*.

While acknowledging the correlation between abnormally high (LDL) cholesterol levels, "bad cholesterol," with cardiovascular disease we are most interested in discussing the more positive role of cholesterol related to the *natural* synthesis of steroid hormones, or *steroidogenesis*. Based on research done on primates, steroidogenesis can be activated throughout the Central and Peripheral Nervous Systems through the process of myelination and the subsequent cascade of biochemical processes that convert cholesterol into pregnenolone. I believe that research will soon prove that this process leads to the natural production throughout the body of testosterone in men and estrogen in women. (See pages 156-157 for synthesis of cholesterol into steroid hormones chart.)

Name: *Endorphins*

Location: Pituitary gland and hypothalamus

Function: The term "endor-phin" means "a morphine-like substance originating from within the body." Endorphins cause our breathing to slow, reduce blood pressure and decrease sensitivity to pain. Endorphins also reduce smooth muscle contraction, thus causing the smooth muscles in the arteries to dilate, increasing blood flow. Hypoxia or low oxygen creates acidosis stress which increases endorphins as part of the parasympathetic response to achieve balance.

Name: *Enkephalins*

Location: Throughout the Central Nervous System.

Function: Enkephalins are released as part of the fight or flight response. For example, in response to physical injury, terror, and severe emotional stress, the amygdala, hypothalamus, and related limbic system nuclei secrete enkephalins. The effect of opiates like enkephalins and beta endorphins is to inhibit the reaction of tissue to electrical stimulation. Without this inhibitory action to slow down neuron firing, the racing electric activity would result in convulsions and death.

Name: *Glucocortocoids*

Location: Adrenal cortex, throughout the PNS and CNS.

Function: Glucocorticoid hormones are important in the maintenance of many brain functions. Although their receptors are distributed abundantly throughout the brain, including the prefrontal cortex (PFC), it is not clear how glucocorticoid functions, particularly with regard to cognitive processing in the PFC. There is evidence of PFC cognitive deficits such as working memory impairment in several stress-related neuropsychiatric disorders, including depression, schizophrenia, and Parkinson's disease.

Name: *Gamma-aminobutyric acid (GABA)*

Location: Throughout the Central Nervous System.

Function: Gamma-aminobutyric acid (GABA) is the chief inhibitory neurotransmitter in the central nervous system. As such, GABA plays an important role in regulating neuronal excitability throughout the nervous system, and disrupted GABAergic signaling has been implicated in numerous and varied neurological and psychiatric pathologies, including movement and anxiety disorders, epilepsy, schizophrenia, and addiction.

Name: *Long-term potentiation (LTP)*

Location: Throughout the Central Nervous System.

Function: Long-term potentiation is the long-lasting strengthening of the connection between two nerve cells. Since neurons communicate via chemical synapses, and because memories are believed to be stored within these synapses, LTP and its opposing process, long-term depression, are widely considered the major cellular mechanisms that underlie learning and memory, including the more complex, higher-level cognition observed in humans. By enhancing synaptic transmission, LTP improves the ability of two neurons, one pre-synaptic and the other post-synaptic, to communicate with one another across a synapse. Enhanced communication is predominantly carried out by improving the post-synaptic cell's sensitivity to signals received from the pre-synaptic cell. These signals, in the form of neurotransmitter molecules, are received by neurotransmitter receptors present on the surface of the post-synaptic cell.

Figure 2.17 Illustration of Long-Term Potentiation synaptic process.

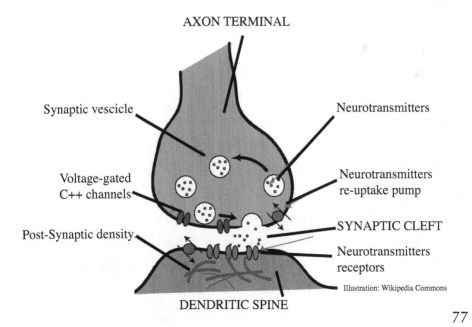

AXON TERMINAL

Synaptic vescicle

Neurotransmitters

Voltage-gated
C++ channels

Neurotransmitters
re-uptake pump

Post-Synaptic density

SYNAPTIC CLEFT

Neurotransmitters
receptors

Illustration: Wikipedia Commons

DENDRITIC SPINE

Name: *The Reticular Activating System (RAS)*

Location: Lower brain.

Function: The Reticular Activiting System (RAS) of the lower brain develops with the senses. The RAS is the focus and gateway of the different sense impressions, so that they are co-ordinated and can then be processed by the thought brain. The RAS enables us to give attention, to focus awareness, so that if the motor sensory pathways are poorly developed it may lead to children having short attentions spans and a poor ability to concentrate. Too much or too little simulation of the sense, together with underdeveloped fine and gross motor skills, can lead to poor attention. The action and feeling brains are 80% myelinated by the age of four. Brain development at ages six and seven moves on to the thought brain, the neocortex, with myelination starting first on the right hemisphere and then on the left. The right side helps process images, shapes and patterns, and it sees the big picture rather than detail. It is more intuitive, and is active in art, music, and color. As the right brain responds to color and novelty, it becomes dominate when watching TV.

Name: *Action Potentials*

Location: Throughout the Central and Peripheral Nervous Systems

Function: One of the most important elements of Whole Brain Power™ theory is the development of your action potentials through our training regimens. When we look at how neurons send messages electrochemically we see that *chemicals* cause an electrical signal. Chemicals in the body that are "electrically-charged" are called ions. We want to focus on the key ions: *sodium and potassium* (both have 1 positive charge, +), *calcium* (has 2 positive charges, ++) and *chloride* (has a negative charge, -). Nerve cells are surrounded by a membrane that allows some ions to pass through and blocks the passage of other ions. This type of membrane is called semi-permeable.

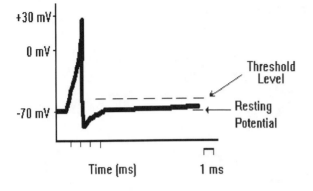

When a neuron is not sending a signal, it is "at rest." See the chart to the left, the resting membrane potential of a neuron is about -70 mV (mV=millivolt) - this means that the inside of the neuron is 70 mV less than the outside.

Propagation of an action potential: When an action potential depolarises the membrane, the leading edge activates other adjacent sodium channels. This leads to another spike of depolarisation the leading edge of which activates more adjacent sodium channels. Thus a wave of depolarisation spreads from the point of initiation. The sodium and potassium ion channels pump and all the action potential propagation is concentrated at sites between blocks of myelin called the Nodes of Ranvier. This myelin sheath allows the action potential to jump from one node to another, greatly increasing the rate of transmission.

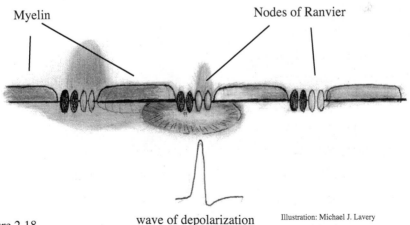

Figure 2.18   wave of depolarization   Illustration: Michael J. Lavery

Figure 2.19

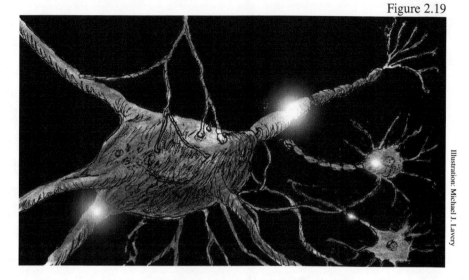

Illustration: Michael J. Lavery

An *action potential* occurs when a neuron sends information down an axon, away from the cell body. Neuroscientists use other words, such as a "spike" or an "impulse" for the action potential. The action potential is an explosion of electrical activity that is created by a depolarizing current (see the illustration above). This means that some event (a stimulus) causes the resting potential to move toward 0 mV. When the depolarization reaches about -55 mV a neuron will fire an action potential. This is the threshold. If the neuron does not reach this critical threshold level, then no action potential will fire. Also, when the threshold level is reached, an action potential of a fixed sized will always fire. Therefore, the neuron either does not reach the threshold or a full action potential is fired - this is the "ALL OR NONE" principle.

One of our goals with Whole Brain Power™ training is to build the myelin sheaths protecting axons so that neurons can effectively fire the action potentials. As we age, our myelin thins, which leads to ion leakage that prevents the firing of the action potentials at the node of Ranvier (see illustration on page 79). The result is fewer opportunities for the electrical signals to be communicated, and for signals to be carried to other parts of the brain or body.

This chapter, *The Blueprint for the Brain*, is meant to be a resource for you as you proceed through the remaining chapters of the book. Our goal is to convey to the reader the most basic information about brain anatomy, chemistry and function, that will be applicable to your Whole Brain Power™ practice. While you might not understand how your car's systems work, chances are you assume you can simply turn the key and it will start and run smoothly, and take you where you want to go. If your car gets old and starts falling apart, you can fix it, or replace it. We also assume that our brain will run smoothly upon command; but when we neglect or damage our brain, or it gets old and starts falling apart, we can't replace it. We can, however, repair it and replenish it with Whole Brain Power™ training and proper nutrition. If you want your brain to take you where you want to go in life, effortlessly, creatively and efficiently, you will want to know how its systems work, and how to not only maintain its systems, but actually improve their operation. Throughout this book we will explain in detail how your systems operate, and our discussions will be based on the basic facts outlined in this chapter.

Take a look at that image on the opposite page (page 80). In many ways, Whole Brain Power™ is about tending to the health of the neurons in our central and peripheral nervous systems. We want each neuron to fire properly and effortlessly. We want the myelin sheaths around the axons to be at their optimum thickness to help ensure the electrical signals (the action potentials) are strong. We want our astrocytes and oligodendrocytes to be healthy so that they can support the integrity of the neurons that they serve.

A healthy neuron system is the foundation of Whole Brain Power™. Each of the tenets of our training regimen, ambidextrous hammer drills, penmanship, and memory drills, are designed to work your body on a macro level, building muscle density and reflexes, as well as on a micro level, ensuring neuron health and neurogenesis is taking place. Let's get the training started with *Penmanship*.

CHAPTER 3: PENMANSHIP
SHARPEN THE PEN TO SHARPEN THE MIND

18th century "Penman": an expert in penmanship

With Whole Brain Power™ training I'm *not reinventing the wheel* but simply pointing to *the wheel that has existed for thousands of years.* I believe that **penmanship**, the art of communicating through symbols written with the human hand, is vital to brain health and brain development. I have discovered a fascinating correlation between major world cultures and their unique approach to handwriting that supports our theories underlying Whole Brain Power™. The significant attributes are these:

• **Chinese** calligraphy is written predominantly **right-handed** and from **right-to-left** and **vertical top-to-bottom on the page**. This indicates a left-brain dominance related to the use of the right hand, but the right-to-left direction and the vertical qualities imply more of a balanced involvement of the brain hemispheres and thus a more balanced emotional-analytical orientation in the Chinese culture.

• **Middle-eastern** cursive is written predominantly **right-handed** from **right-to-left on the page**. The use of the right hand indicates a dominant left-brain usage, but the right-to-left quality engages the right hemisphere and indicates more of an imaginative-emotional orientation in Middle-eastern cultures.

• **Western European** cursive is written predominantly **right-hand** from **left-to-right.** This style of writing focuses predominantly on the left hemisphere of the brain and indicates a process-analytical orientation to Western culture.

Figure 3.1: Sample of Chinese calligraphy (by Lin Zexu)

Top down
Right to left

Source: Wikipedia *Commons*

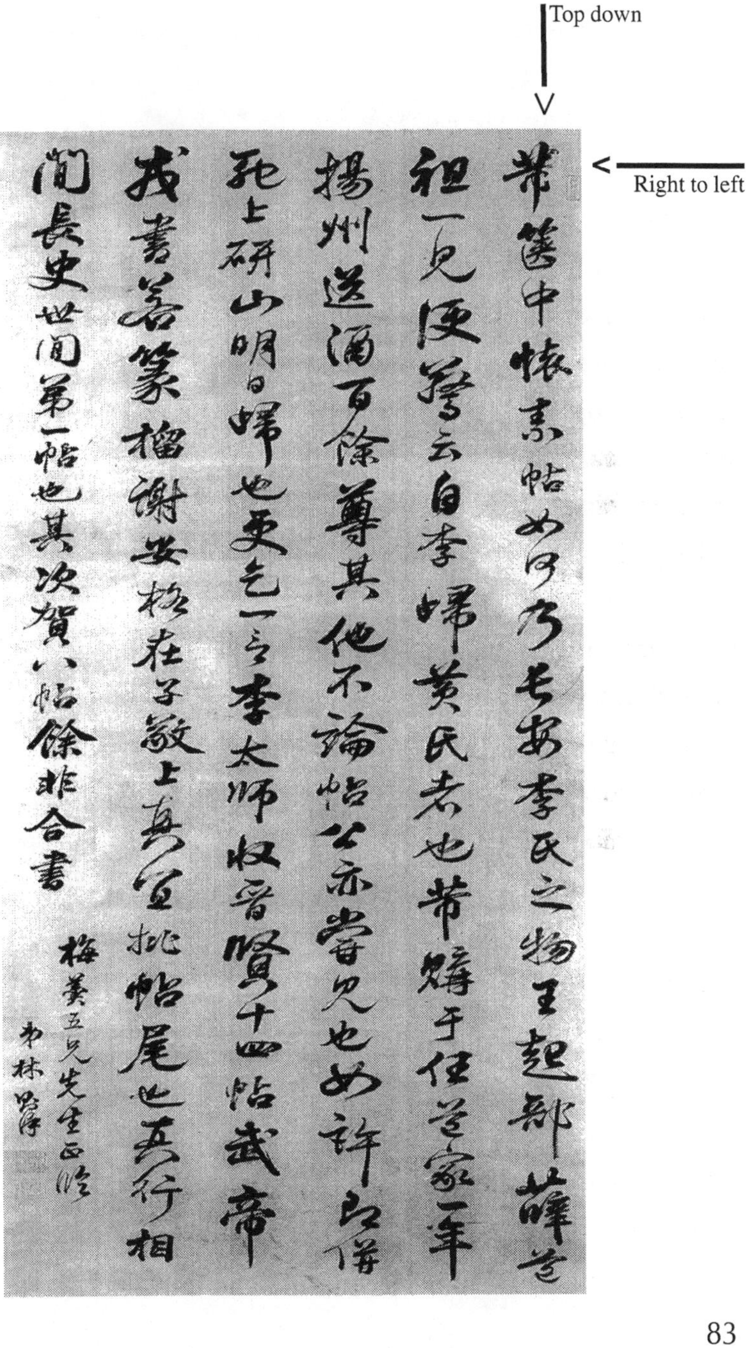

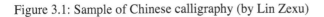

Figure 3.2: Sample of Arabic penmanship.

بيان صادر عن حركة التضامن الدولية وحركة نساء دوليات ومشروع تل الرميدة الدولي ومؤسسة الارض المقدسة (المنظمات المحلية
العاملة مع الدوليين وفرق السلام في فلسطين)

Right to left

نحن نستنكر بشدة الرسوم المهينه التي نشرت للنبي محمد التي تظهر عدم
الاحترام والتجاهل للقيم الاسلاميه وتغذي التحريض.
كما نعلن انزعاجنا من نشر هذه المواد واعادة نشرها في وسائل الاعلام في دول
تدعي التسامح مع كافة الاديان والثقافات والبشر.
وكدوليين من مختلف العقائد نعمل مع وبين المسلمين , ندعو الى اعتذار علني من وسائل الاعلام التي نشرت تلك الرسوم ومعارضة ورفض مواصلة حالة العداء هذه كما ندعو دولنا الى استنكار العداء للاسلام ومؤثراتها المختلفة .
ان العنصريه ضد الشعوب في الشرق الاوسط وضد المسلمين , لها تاريخ طويل في الثقافة الغربية,وتتغلغل في السياسات تجاه الشرق الاوسط وتجاه مواطنيها المسلمين.ان الصحافه الغربية تتجاهل هذه الحقائق عندما تناقش حرية الرأي وهذه التعبيرات تظهر المسلمين كرافضين للحرية
وتظهر العالم الاسلامي كمجتمع عنيف مع ان وخلال كتابة هذا البيان كانت ردود الفعل ضد تلك الرسوم غير عنيفه, فالستة اشخاص اللذين قتلوا هم جميعا من المتظاهرين المسلمين .نحن نؤمن بحق وقوة الشعوب في التصدي للعنصرية والظلم بطرق غير عنيفة
ونؤكد ان المقاطعة الاقتصادية والتظاهر ضد الرسوم كانت غير عنيفه .
مسؤولية ودور الصحافة وتقاريرها هي الاعتدال والموضوعية , والحكومات الواعيه هي التي لا تقبل غسل يديها من مسؤولية تنامي العنصرية في مجتمعاتها.
هذا البيان صادر عن المنظمات المحلية والدولية العاملة في فلسطين من اجل التضامن مع نضال الشعب الفلسطيني ضد الاحتلال الأسرائيلي, وسنواصل عملنا على امل ان يتحقق للفلسطينيين العدالة والعيش بحرية على ارضهم.

Source: Wikipedia *Commons*

Figure 3.3: Sample of English cursive penmanship.

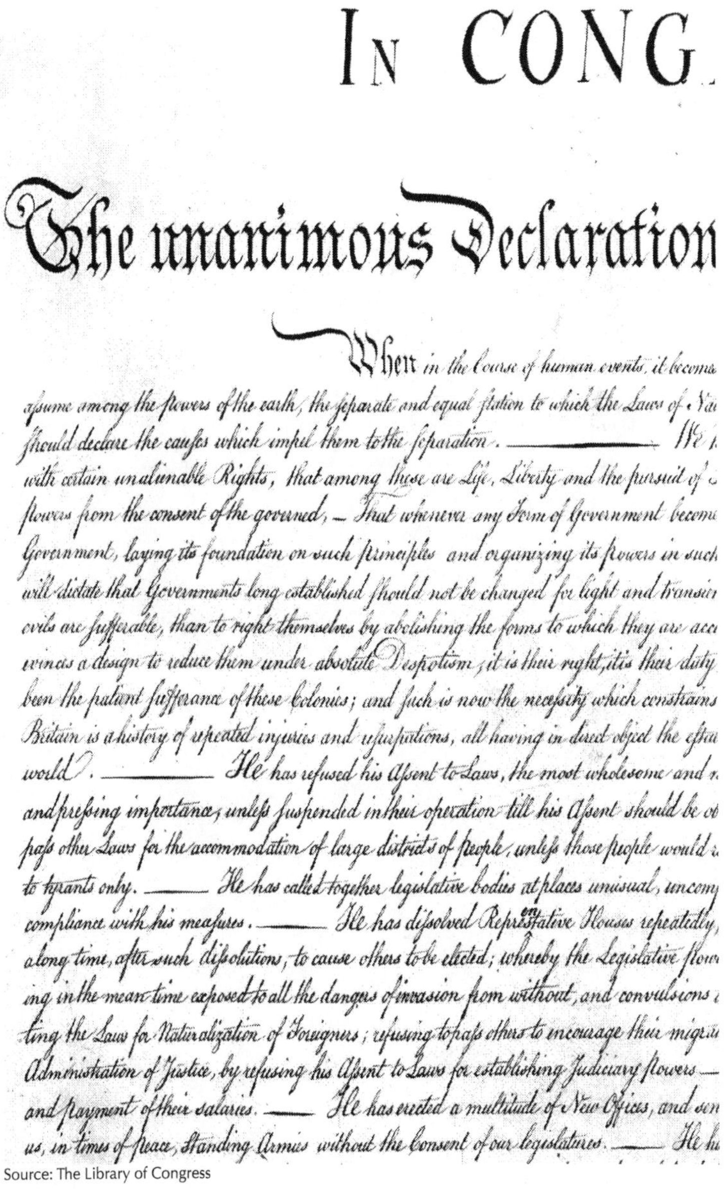

IN CONG

The unanimous Declaration

When in the Course of human events, it become
assume among the powers of the earth, the separate and equal station to which the Laws of Na
should declare the causes which impel them to the separation. —— We
with certain unalienable Rights, that among these are Life, Liberty and the pursuit of
powers from the consent of the governed, — That whenever any Form of Government become
Government, laying its foundation on such principles and organizing its powers in such
will dictate that Governments long established should not be changed for light and transien
evils are sufferable, than to right themselves by abolishing the forms to which they are acc
evinces a design to reduce them under absolute Despotism, it is their right, it is their duty
been the patient sufferance of these Colonies; and such is now the necessity which constrains
Britain is a history of repeated injuries and usurpations, all having in direct object the esta
world. —— He has refused his Assent to Laws, the most wholesome and n
and pressing importance, unless suspended in their operation till his Assent should be ob
pass other Laws for the accommodation of large districts of people, unless those people would
to tyrants only. —— He has called together legislative bodies at places unusual, uncom
compliance with his measures. —— He has dissolved Represtative Houses repeatedly,
a long time, after such dissolutions, to cause others to be elected; whereby the Legislative Pow
ing in the mean time exposed to all the dangers of invasion from without, and convulsions
ting the Laws for Naturalization of Foreigners; refusing to pass others to encourage their migra
Administration of Justice, by refusing his Assent to Laws for establishing Judiciary Powers —
and payment of their salaries. —— He has erected a multitude of New Offices, and sen
us, in times of peace, Standing Armies without the Consent of our legislatures. —— He h

—————> Left to right

Source: The Library of Congress

Until the last half of the 20th century, excellent penmanship was considered a natural by-product of a good education in western European cultures and the United States. U.S. Presidents were practitioners of quality penmanship. Here are an excerpt from George Washington's Revolutionary War diary, a detail of Thomas Jefferson's original draft of the Declaration of Independence, and an excerpt from Abraham Lincoln's draft of the Gettysburg Address.

Figure 3.4: George Washington's diary, 1781 (excerpt).

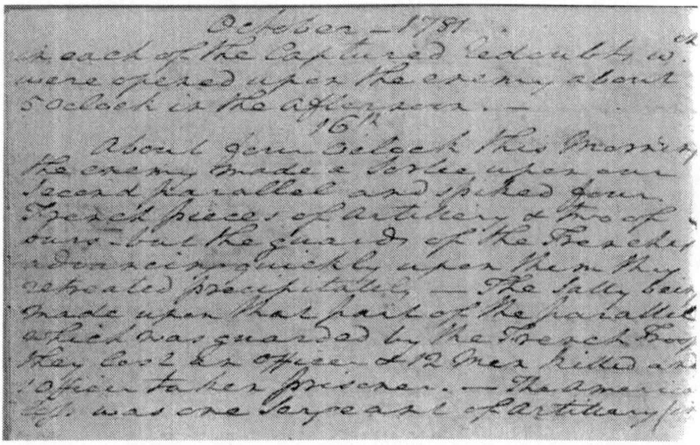
October — 1781
in each of the Captured Redoubts w
were opened upon the enemy about
5 Oclock in the Afternoon. —
16th
About four Oclock this Morning
the enemy made a Sortee upon our
Second Parallel and spiked four
French pieces of Artillery & two of
ours — but the guards of the French
advancing quickly upon them they
retreated precipitately. — The Sally being
made upon that part of the parallel
which was guarded by the French Troops
they lost an officer & 12 men killed and
1 Officer taken prisoner. — The Americ
loss was one Sergeant of Artillery

Source: The Library of Congress

Figure 3.5: Detail of Jefferson's original draft of the Declaration of Independence.

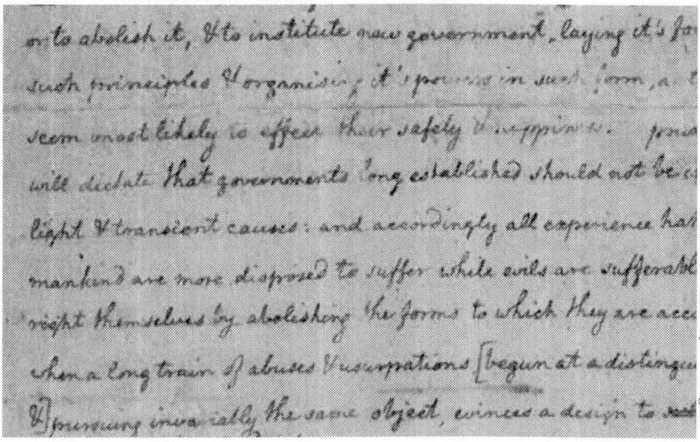
or to abolish it, & to institute new government, laying it's fo
such principles & organising it's powers in such form, a
seem most likely to effect their safety & happiness. pru
will dictate that governments long established should not be c
light & transient causes: and accordingly all experience hat
mankind are more disposed to suffer while evils are sufferabl
right themselves by abolishing the forms to which they are acc
when a long train of abuses & usurpations [begun at a distingu
&] pursuing invariably the same object, evinces a design to s

Source: The Library of Congress

Figure 3.6: Sample of President Lincoln's penmanship.

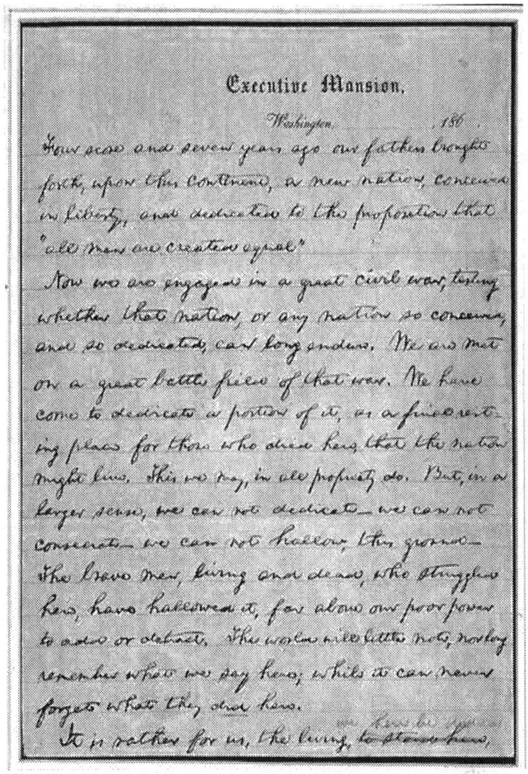

Executive Mansion,

Washington, , 186 .

Four score and seven years ago our fathers brought forth, upon this continent, a new nation, conceived in liberty, and dedicated to the proposition that "all men are created equal"

Now we are engaged in a great civil war, testing whether that nation, or any nation so conceived, and so dedicated, can long endure. We are met on a great battle field of that war. We have come to dedicate a portion of it, as a final resting place for those who died here, that the nation might live. This we may, in all propriety do. But, in a larger sense, we can not dedicate — we can not consecrate — we can not hallow, this ground — The brave men, living and dead, who struggled here, have hallowed it, far above our poor power to add or detract. The world will little note, nor long remember what we say here; while it can never forget what they did here.

It is rather for us, the living, ~~to stand here,~~

Source: The Library of Congress

Palmer Method

Many of us who learned cursive penmanship in grade school were taught what is known as the *Palmer Method* developed and promoted by Austin Palmer in the early 1900s. In 1912, sales of his book, *The Palmer Method for the Business World*, exceeded one million copies. It is interesting that the development of this style of writing by Palmer was conceived in order to help in speed and efficiency in penmanship over the more intricate Spenserian Method.

Prior to Palmer's style, *Spenserian Cursive* was the norm and was character-ized by a very stylized formation of the capitalized letters that included shading. This elaborate writing was too time consuming for the young Austin Palmer. He was employed to copy many documents and the necessity for speed led him to invent a faster way. He became so proficient at his own style of penmanship that a whole new form of writing evolved. However, the only educational system that truly embraced his style of penmanship was the Catholic school system. Palmer found great allies in the sisters of the convents who willingly became his first disciples of this penmanship revolution. He instructed many of the nuns over months of intensive training and they all became fluent in the standard way of writing in his penmanship format. Eventually more than twenty-five million people were practicing this type of writing. When one considers the discipline that was demanded of the children who grew up during this era it becomes read-ily apparent why the discipline of penmanship was related to overall civilized behavior. The impulse control that is necessary to produce the cursive writing carried over to other aspects of attention span and engagement of the frontal lobes of the brain -- the part of the brain that is responsible for impulse control.

Today, the public school system, and to a lesser degree Catholic schools, have reduced or almost completely eliminated cursive penmanship from its grade school curriculum. If teachers understood the *brain science* behind penman-ship, that knowledge may inspire a return to the power of the pen. While violent video games, television, poor nutrition, and a host of other factors can be associ-ated with lack of impulse control in today's youth, research shows a connection between the missing penmanship discipline and the failure to train the brain for impulse control. Studies also link lack of impulse control with the rise in ADD and ADHD. The brain of a young child is forming many new connections and developing insulation (myelination) of its axon sheaths. But the young brain will prune back underdeveloped myelinated fields not developed by such training as penmanship provides. Thus a chemical house cleaning often takes place at puberty and wipes out axons sheaths that are not fully myelinated. Use them or those them, as the saying goes.

Regrettably, instead of having children learn from tactile methods, such as penmanship, musicianship or art, the system (home and school) has turned over our children's brains to technology, increasingly to television programming and computer-based learning, keyboards and Big Bird. *Sesame Street* has for decades taught millions of preschoolers in what is undeniably a passive from of learning. The children's hands are idled and so are their brains. Once in school not only does computer-based learning increase with each passing year of study, but handwriting, if it is taught at all in the classroom setting, allows students to print in block letters. So, if they are given a choice of block printing versus the more difficult motor skill requirement of cursive writing, students naturally elect to print.

It was inevitable that penmanship would fall from grace. People embrace technology as a way to make their lives easier, more efficient, and convenient. The slide rule was a great invention but it went the way of the dinosaur when the electronic calculator was invented. No one uses or even knows how to use a slide ruler today, but when I was young my Dad's generation of engineers used them everyday. The proliferation of the typewriter in the 1920s helped lead to the demise of Palmer's great success, in favor of uniformity in written documents. Now, even typewriters have become archaic. Nothing it seems remains constant in society as far as technological progress is concerned. We are a product of our environment and our brains are affected accordingly. The price we pay as we move away from using our hands for fine and gross motor skills is an inevitable degeneration of our brain from lack of use. We have become a society of "inputers," technology consumers, instead of "outputers," producers of products with our hands, whether to share our ideas with a pen, or express our creativity with a musical instrument, paint brush, or make things with a textile loom, or welding tool. Increasingly, if technologists can design a machine that can do something that was once done exclusively by trained hands, then the hands lose every time.

Beautiful handwritten documents such as those shown at the beginning of this chapter by former Presidents, have given way to text messages in incomplete sentences. The failure to train the hands to follow the command of the frontal lobes of the brain is evident from the illegible writing of everyone I encounter with my consulting, from elementary school children, to Baby Boomers, to re-tirees.

The difficulty of writing in a penmanship format is much more demanding on the brain. It is analogous to training the voice to sing on key as opposed to simply speaking in a monotone voice. Everyone can speak in a monotone voice (and most do!) but few can sing pitch perfect melodies.

Penmanship practice is for the health of your brain, to help get the fine motor control exercise that it needs for impulse control, neurogenesis, and even steroidogenesis.

In an article in *Newsweek[1]* by Raina Kelley dated Nov. 12, 2007 titled: *The Writing On The Wall Good,* Kelley writes that penmanship is more than just a quaint skill.

'*...evidence is growing that handwriting fluency is a fundamental building block of learning. Emily Knapton, director of program development at Handwriting Without Tears, believes that "when kids struggle with handwriting, it filters into all their academics. Spelling becomes a problem; math becomes a problem because they reverse their numbers. All of these subjects would be much easier for these kids to learn if handwriting was an automatic process." That concern, in part, prompted the addition of a written essay to the SAT, which is graded for content, though not legibility. "If you put something like a writing*

[1] Link to article: http://www.newsweek.com/id/67956

90

test on the SAT, children's skill level will begin to be addressed," says Ed Hardin, a senior content specialist at the College Board. The trickle-down effect to middle schools should eventually reach third grade, where the trouble so often begins.'

I applaud the addition of the writing test on the SAT, but hope that a renaissance in penmanship leads to more than a "trickle-down" to 3rd grade. I envision a flood of interest on the part of teachers, administrators, curriculum developers and parents to bring focus back to cursive penmanship skill development in all grades.

While your own style of cursive penmanship is one way in which you *communicate and express your unique personality,* research by Dr. David Snowdon found another fascinating reason to practice cursive penmanship daily. His exhaustive study as reported in his book, *AGING WITH GRACE,* analyzed the brains (cognitive tests while living, anatomical tests after deceased) of more than 400 Catholic nuns. The results found that nuns who:

exhibited superlative language acuity (articulate, storytellers, facile memory)
+ *expressed* that language acuity through *penmanship skill*
= *maintained a healthy brain* into old age.

Snowdon's study revealed a marked absence of the symptoms of Alzheimer's disease in the nuns that lived well into their nineties, and as old as 105. Interestingly, the study of the deceased brains of the mentally healthy nuns showed some with, and *some without,* the neurofibrillary tangles most often associated with Alzheimer's. But while living, none had the cognitive symptoms of the debilitating and deadly disease.

91

The Brain Science of Penmanship

For more than a decade I have been researching the science behind the trans-formations in my brain and body as the result of my Whole Brain Power™ train-ing and practice. In my own personal journals, now hundreds of pages, I have written both right-hand cursive and left-hand mirror image as I took notes on my research. Here is what I have come to understand is happening in our brains -- *my theories based on years of canvassing scientific journals* -- when we put a pen to paper.

Through use of a PET Scan (**P**ositron **E**mmission **T**omography - which shows the uptake of oxygen and glucose by the brain) we can witness that much of the *cerebral cortex is engaged* by a person who is in the act of *cursive writing*. In other words, when you write cursive penmanship you're lighting up your brain, forcing it to maintain a high degree of focus, fine motor skill, and a host of other active responses. Just think, when you write something your tapping into your short and long-term memory banks, searching for words, spelling, sentence con-struction, grammar, mechanics, and much more. You're unleashing long-term potentiation in the hippocampus, firing neurons across the pre-frontal cortex. If you're writing mirror-image with your left hand then you're opening up your center of imagination and creative thought in your right hemisphere.

Remember, it was Da Vinci who was famous for writing left-handed mirror image in his journals, and he was arguably the most creative mind in the history of humanity.

Even when a person simply *thinks* about writing while holding a pen to write, the prefrontal lobes of the brain become engaged bilaterally. This is called an act of *Gesture Preparation*. This activity or *action potential* is firing billions of neurons simultaneously in anticipation of the act which is about to be initiated. The neurons deep in the *cerebral cortex* are called the *Pyramidal Cells* and they are highly excitable. The pyramidal cells begin to work in concert to send signals to the *cerebellum, the basal ganglia, the temporal lobes, the pre-motor strip, and the motor strip.* The eyes are also called into action so the *occipital lobes* are highly tasked to watch for the placement of the writing instrument and making sure that an even keel of writing is maintained. *Gesture preparation* puts the brain in a hyper-focused state. This is so different from what we are accustomed to doing when we tap the letters on a key board. The *Parietal lobes* are also engaged because of the sensation of holding the pen and the awareness of the body to be able to properly output the necessary penmanship. This seemingly simple act takes tremendous focus and energy. The uptake of glucose by the brain is elevated as you begin to burn calories.

As we move from the *Gesture Preparation Mode* to *the Gesture Production Mode, and the act of writing,* we fire neurons in the deeper strata of the cerebral cortex and the cerebellum; the basal ganglia and the motor strip also become engaged to execute the signals from the brain to the hand to perform the super fine movements of hand and fingers in *the act of penmanship* and the purposeful *expression of thoughts.* The chemical reactions taking place include the releasing of the neurotransmitter *dopamine* that is utilized by the basal ganglia for the fine motor controls. The dopamine is synthesized by the *Substantia Nigra Par Compacta.* It is important to note that the brain's production of dopamine is something it does normally under active stress. Dopamine levels are below normal when we engage in activities of passive stress such as watching television or playing video games. One result from low dopamine levels is an improper shift in normal beta (high energy) brain wave activity from the frontal lobes to the amygdala and lower regions of the brain.

Think about this whole process of cursive writing as a chain of events from a business model perspective. If the economy could be compared to a well-oiled machine and it is growing at a regular pace, then all aspects of the work force must be in place. There must be bosses who order things to get done and work-ers who comply with the orders. Factories must be running efficiently to handle the order of the goods that need to be brought to market so that consumer de-mand can be met with a surplus for any increased demand. This situation makes for homeostasis in the grand scheme of a country's welfare.

The brain also works on similar parameters. You are the boss or CEO of the brain. It takes positive volition to get this marvelous computer to do exactly what you want it to accomplish. It takes time to build up the skill and the en-durance to write in a fashion that is pleasing to you. The laser-like precision of directing a writing instrument requires stamina, and it is a skill that needs to be gradually built up as you train your brain to write perfectly formed letters and numbers.

Suppose that you write in your journal what *you just learned* about a brain that is engaged in penmanship; this information is at present still stored in your *dentate gyrus* of the *hippocampus*. Remember, it takes considerable time before these newly learned memories actually get moved out of the hippocampus and into our long-term memory storage banks. The act of *neurogenesis (birth of new neurons)* is happening with the newly learned terms about the brain. Your brain is also being stimulated by the expansion of your usable vocabulary. Just as London Cabby drivers grow their hippocampi by memorizing the names of 25,000 streets, so will you by learning and following the prescribed tenets of Whole Brain Power™.

Studies show that *astrocytes* are formed in the dentate gyrus of the hippo-campus from *granule stem cells*. These cells are necessary to be matured along with the *neural stem cells* that eventually become full grown neurons. Scientists have shown that in culture, an astrocyte expresses the chemistry that aids in the maturity of neural stems cells and that these newly formed *glial cells* also help form new capillary systems in the hippocampus. In layman's terms, when you learn difficult new terms and processes in the brain, you grow your brain, specifically your hippocampus. When you learn these new terms and then write down what you have learned in perfect cursive penmanship, right and left-handed, you stimulate growth of new neurons throughout the brain as the demands for outputting under active stress force the brain to adapt.

The NmDa (N-Methyl-D-Aspartate) receptor site activity is also strengthening as a result of the pen. The flow of blood is making its way to the hippocampus and the neurons in this area are firing aggressively. This is strengthening the *synapses*. This building of the synapses and the *dendritic spines* is called *synaptogenesis*. There is a building up of proteins at the presynaptic and post-synaptic terminals because of the pen. The more practice of an activity the brain gets the more efficient is the processing of the neurons. This is called *Long Term Potentiation (LTP)*. This means that the mature astrocytes are working extremely well at maintaining glucose delivery to the neurons. These helper cells not only act as a *scaffolding* (support) for the neurons, but also maintain the extra cellular matrix, regulating calcium concentrations, helping to form new capillary systems, regulating *ATP* levels, synthesizing *pregnenolone and DHEA*, and re-packaging neurotransmitters back into vesicles for the continuation of firing at the terminals.

In addition, the mechanics of the mammalian brain has all of the machinery for *steroidogenesis* (natural production of steroids) in place. As described above, astrocytes are also making the *precursors* that help the pyramidal cells of the CA-1 area of the hippocampus to produce testosterone and estradiol. Research[2] indicates that endogenously produced brain sex steroids such as testosterone and estradiol have an almost immediate impact on dendritic spines of pyramidal neurons. In laboratory conditions, expanding changes in the buds of dendrites appear within two hours. Also, writing is an *active stress* that raises the levels of the neurotransmitter *glutamate* for increased building of memory.

[2] Mellon, Synthia, N. *Neurosteroid regulation of CNS development*
link to article: http://www.pubmedcentral.nih.gov/articlerender.fcgi?artid=2386997

95

When glutamate is used for building memories it is a good thing for the brain. However, when glutamate's role becomes one where it is a neurotoxin, many negative ramifications result. Glutamate is necessary for calcium to get into the cell where it fulfills its role of maintaining cellular integrity. Conversely, when there is too much glutamate in the synapse the *calcium transition pore* stays open for too long a period and excess calcium floods in to the neuron and causes damage to the cell's *mitochondria*. There is a saying about oxygen. "You get too much you get too high, not enough and you are going to die." The same is applicable to the role of neurotransmitters. A balance needs to be maintained for the brain to work to peak efficiency, and this is especially true of glutamate.

The neurotransmitter called *acetylcholine* is also being synthesized by the *Nucleus Basilis of Meynart (NBM)*. The NBM is involved in neural plasticity in the hippocampus and is extremely important for the production of acetylcholine because of its role in the frontal lobes of the brain, the premotor strip and the motor strip, when they are all engaged in the act of penmanship. One of the problems identified with the Alzheimer's patient is the lack of acetylcholine in the brain. The deficiency of this neurotransmitter is one of the reasons that excess glutamate is found in the brains of people suffering from Alzheimer's. The brain is a very efficient organ and it will make substitutions (glutamate for acetylcholine) when the leading neurotransmitter for a certain purpose is not available.

As you practice your penmanship, you will increase your levels of *norepenephrine,* which is associated with alertness. Your improved relaxed nature will also help out with serotonin levels. Your improved speed of outputting penmanship will equate to greater fine motor controls which correlates with greater impulse controls. Theoretically, the myelination of your white matter tracks improves as the demand on the brain for increased focus and energy output increases. Studies indicate a by-product of the myelination process is greater expression of *pregnenolone* through the *oligodendrocytes.* Pregnenolone is known to be a mood-stabilizing chemical and a motivator of the stimulus that causes its manufacture in the first place. So the more you practice penmanship the more your brain inspires you to practice.

As you write, brain activity is *simultaneously* occurring across the *corpus callosum* as the right hemisphere fires up to output an original thought or idea. Drawing upon images, connections and memories in the *hippocampus, amygdala and cerebral cortex*, the right hemisphere's creative regions contribute the content while the left hemisphere diligently organizes the sentence structure and scans the *temporal lobes* for the proper spelling and for the rules of grammar.

The creative output process of penmanship is an unbroken chain of events as the brain:

-----> *produces electrical activity that is measured in beta waves,*
-----> *manufactures neurotransmitters that carry signals to compose and organize the content,*
-----> *fires action potentials,*
-----> *creates extensions on the dendritic spines,*
-----> *initiates neurogenesis in the dentate gyrus and improves synaptogenesis as a result of the demands placed on the brain to control the precise movements of the pen,*
-----> *expresses pregnenolone as a by-product of myelination,*
-----> *and creates long term potentiation, so that the act of writing becomes easier and more skillful with practice.*

All of this activity in the brain is further enhanced when one writes in mirror-image (backwards, right-to-left on the page) with one's left hand. Mirror-image penmanship not only engages all the regions of the brain associated with writing with the right hand, but it more directly engages the creative elements in the right hemisphere, since the left hand is controlled by the right hemisphere and vice versa.

Typing on a keyboard does not engage nearly this level of activity in the brain as the repetitive nature of writing with a word processor requires few demands on the brain once the typing skills (hitting keys with appropriate fingers) are accomplished. Plus, if you misspell a word or use poor grammar, you can go back and correct it, or the word processing software points out the misspelled word or poor grammar and offers to correct it for you. It is as though the error never existed. Not true with written penmanship where if you make a mistake you end up with words or sentences crossed out, smudged, or whited-out. Thus, a much higher order of focus and brain activity is required to produce a page of penmanship free of spelling, grammatical or content errors. As a result, it easy to understand why modern school systems and business environments have em-braced technology in pursuit of picture-perfect documents, but the price paid by the brain is a high one.

Proper Penmanship

To begin, the posture of the body, the head, the arms, wrists and hands is important. The placement of the paper and the arm angle helps focus the pen on paper and achieve a quality result. The non-writing hand is used to hold the paper to prevent it from slipping.

Downstroke

Upstroke

Upstroke

When the act of writing gets broken down to stroke mechanics, the pen goes up the slope of the letter and then back down at the consistent angle. The motion is simply broken down to an *upstroke - downstroke* output. It could be compared to the *back swing - down swing* of the golf stroke. This motion is in fact a simple contraction/release mechanism, a constant start and stop activity as well as flowing and graceful movements. The cerebellum is helping accelerate the pen upwards on the upstroke at a constant rate of speed. The counter action of the basal ganglia is ready to put on the brakes and stop the pen. Next, the down slope action is called upon and the cerebellum is firing once again sending signals through the Purkinje cells to the peripheral nervous system to the fingers to guide the pen in the downstroke. Most of the time the pen stays in contact with the paper until it is time to output the next word. The heightened sense of focus is a part of the mix in having to go back and cross the *t's* and dot the *i's*.

to life' as a common practice in American Society.

Sincerely,

Michael J. Lavery

Figure 3.8 Da Vinci's mirror image writing.

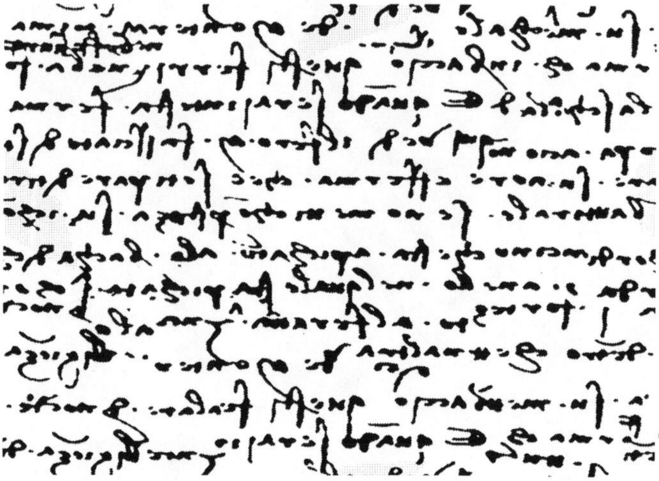

Source: Dreamstime Images

Now imagine being able to write smoothly with either hand and also in the mirror-image (backwards, right-to-left across the page). Mirror-image, left-hand writing is what Leonardo Da Vinci was doing during his lifetime.

When he wrote in his journals for personal reference, he wrote left-handed and in mirror image. If he was writing for others to appreciate his thoughts, Da Vinci wrote right-handed and in a normal left-to-right across the page.

Let's try mirror image writing. To begin, write your signature with your right hand in cursive on a piece of tracing paper with a felt tip pen. Then turn the piece of paper over and look at how it appears when it is in the mirror image format.

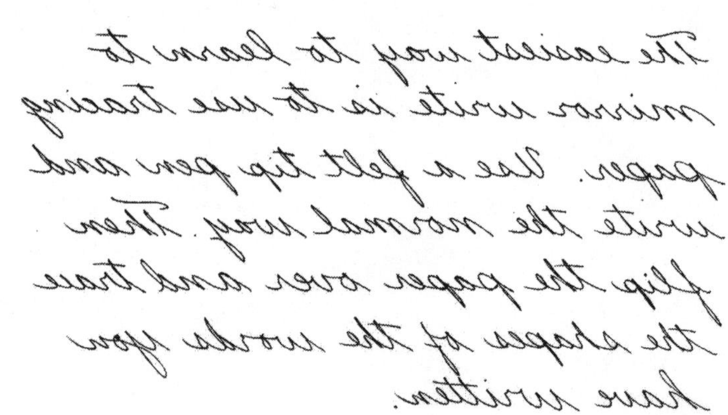

Now trace over the letters with the pen in your left hand. If you are left-handed, then reverse these instructions and do it with the right hand instead. Does your non-dominant mirror image handwriting flow smoothly or does it feel awkward? After a few weeks of practice my students tell me, "My dominant hand is working and writing better than ever, and my mirror image writing is slowly beginning to look exactly like my dominant hand writing." I tell them that part of the reason this is happening is that they are practicing more, but also because of the cross training that they are doing with their opposite hand. To handle this new demand on the brain, I theorize that *neurogenesis* is occurring as the brain adapts to the difficult skill of mirror image writing, as well as perfecting the skill of penmanship with the dominant hand.

I strongly encourage you keep a daily journal when you begin practicing Whole Brain Power™ training methodologies. The reason is simple: the journal has dated entries and the writing is concrete evidence of penmanship ability at day one. After thirty days it will be obvious to anyone that there is improvement, with both the dominant and non-dominant hand. If there is concerted effort on the part of the practitioner, then that progress will be documented in their journal. We recommend practicing five to fifteen minutes per day with your penmanship drills (about a half-a-page to a page-and-a-half total right-handed and left-handed mirror image writing).

As you begin the program, see your progress and feel the improvement in other areas of your life, the inclination to continue to train your brain's fine motor control is reaffirmed. Just imagine that your ability to communicate verbally was enhanced because of the penmanship training. What if your tennis game was getting better when it had hit a plateau for an extended period? How about the newfound confidence of making putts on the green when it is for making par? Many of my students call and say such things as, "Michael, you will not believe that my golf game is better than ever." They have never played a round of golf in the 70s and now they have just scored below 80 for the first time in their lives.

The ability to produce quality penmanship is such a rewarding experience, both for the brain's functioning at higher levels, and for the skill carrying over to other areas of our lives. Unfortunately, many people have been denied this training in today's public educational system, which began to abandon cursive penmanship twenty years ago. It is my conviction that you can learn or re-learn this important skill no matter what age you may be. Just as a person can learn to play the piano at age sixty-five, so can a person learn the basics of how to form the lower and upper case letters of the cursive alphabet. Literally, one has to return to the basics of letter formation as one did learn, or should have learned, in his or her youth.

On the following pages I will write in both the upper and lower case cursive format. Below, I demonstrate the method of writing each letter continuously across the page. The goal then is to be able to write the entire alphabet from a to z without taking the pen off the paper. Only when z is reached, does one go back and dot the i and j and cross the t and make the slash across the x.

abcdefghijklmnopqrstuvwxyz

The How-To's of Cursive Penmanship

Let's begin with your penmanship training. Commence by practicing each letter of the alphabet. On the line below my line of *a*'s, practice your own formation of the cursive small letter *a*. Find a comfortable way to hold the pen in your hand and try to slant your letters to the right as shown. Follow this format with each letter of the alphabet on the proceeding pages.

aaaaaaaaaaaaaaaaaaaaaaaaaaa

(a)_____

bbbbbbbbbbbbbbbbbbbbbbbb

(b) _____

ccccccccccccccccccccccccc

(c) _____

dddddddddddddddddd

(d)_____

eeeeeeeeeeeeeeeeeeeeeeeeeeeee

(e) _____

ffffffffffffffffffffffff

(f) _____

103

ggggggggggggggggggggg

(g) _____

hhhhhhhhhhhhhhh

(h) _____

iiiiiiiiiiiiiiiiiiiiiiiiii

(i) _____

jjjjjjjjjjjjjjjjjjjjjj

(j) _____

kkkkkkkkkkkkkkk

(k) _____

llllllllllllllllllllll

(l) _____

mmmmmmmmmm

(m) _____

nnnnnnnnnn

(n) _____

oooooooooooooooo

(o) _____

ppppppppppppppppp

(p) _____

qqqqqqqqqqqqqqqq

(q) _____

rrrrrrrrrrrrrrrrrrrr

(r) _____

ssssssssssssssssss

(s) _____

ttttttttttttttttttttt

(t) _____

uuuuuuuuuuuuuuuuuu

(u) _____

vvvvvvvvvvvvvvvvvvv

(v) _____

wwwwwwwwwwww

(w) _____

xxxxxxxxxxxxxxxxxxxxxxx

(x) _____

yyyyyyyyyyyyyyyyyy

(y) _____

zzzzzzzzzzzzzzz

(z) _____

Capital Letters

ABCDEFGHIJ

ABCDEFGHIJ _____

KLMNOPQR

KLMNOPQR _____

STUVWXYZ

STUVWXYZ _____

Now that we have the shapes of the letters down to a science, the goal each day is to produce quality penmanship. Remember, sometimes less is more. Write smoothly and hold the pen with very little tension in the hands. The picture of the hand position (shown on page 98) and the way in which the index finger, middle finger and thumb position looks should be emulated if at all possible. Relax the index finger and make sure that the first knuckle is not bowed inward. Penmanship skills help develop spatial awareness so make sure your journal entries are made on blank white paper, work as level of an outputting of sentences as possible. Work on the slope of the letters that you feel comfortable outputting. Ask yourself a question. "Would it be enjoyable to read the angle that I think is proper?" If your angle is too upright, it does not seem to flow as well. If your angle is too much forward, it is more difficult to read. We have put some angles on this page for you to see if your penmanship flows at or near an easily read slope.

abcdefghijklmnopqrstuvwxyz

If you were to output a half page of beautiful penmanship on a daily basis you would have almost 183 pages of writing in one year. This is about the length of most self-help books. Consider your daily journal to be your guide to self-improvement. My suggestion is for you to write in a narrative format. Enter your mission statements, or write the daily progress reports to yourself. For example, when I was playing golf on a daily basis in 2006, I wrote each day in my golf journal about what I wanted to accomplish. My goal was to break par and improve my overall game. I would record the experience of each round and focus on the areas of improvement I needed to address. I wrote down what I expected to do be doing in future outings. Constant affirmation of my expectations became a common thread that I would weave into my journal each day. Soon enough the ideas expressed through the pen were realized on the course.

I encourage you to use your daily journal writing as part of the holistic transformation of your brain and body. Focus on building your working vocabulary and avoid redundancy when writing. That is why I stress the less-is-more approach. If your writing entries can be very descriptive and your word density can have impact, then you are doing what the nuns in Dr. Snowdon's study have been doing for years. You are becoming a master with words, both in their usage and in their formation. It is as if you are becoming an artist with the beautiful images that your writing conveys. Let us remind the reader that the nuns with the least cognitive decline and the best brain tissue examined in autopsy were the best communicators through the spoken and written word.

The discipline of daily penmanship, both right-handed and left-handed mirror image, may not be easy at first. This is going to take some serious effort on your part and commitment to the time and focus involved. However, the benefits will astonish you as you mark your progress to flawless writing. You are going to be activating both brain hemispheres in order to be able to accomplish this aspect of Whole Brain Power™. Enjoy the awakening of your imagination and its integration with your organizational thinking. The increased activity across the corpus callosum will be greater than it has ever been. As the days and weeks slip by, you'll awake one morning and enter into your journal, "Day 90 of my penmanship practice." Compare that entry to Day 1, and that change is no less than an outward manifestation of your brain's journey to *Whole Brain Power™*.

PENMANSHIP PROGRESS JOURNAL

Day One and Day Thirty penmanship results.

On Day One

Right Handed, write: *Day One of my penmanship practice.*

Left-handed, mirror image, write: *Day One of my penmanship practice.*

On Day 30

Right Handed, write: *Day 30 of my penmanship practice.*

Left-handed, mirror image, write: *Day 30 of my penmanship practice.*

Day Sixty and Day Ninety penmanship results.

On Day 60

Right Handed, write: *Day 60 of my penmanship practice.*

Left-handed, mirror image, write: *ɘɔitɔɒɿq qiɦꙅnɒmnɘq ʏm ʇo 0ә ʏɒᗡ*

On Day 90

Right Handed, write: *Day 90 of my penmanship practice.*

Left-handed, mirror image, write: *ɘɔitɔɒɿq qiɦꙅnɒmnɘq ʏm ʇo 0ℓ ʏɒᗡ*

Dear Practitioner,

I trust that you have enjoyed the penmanship chapter. This skill is a rewarding one to develop and will pay dividends for years to come.

Let's review some of the techniques required to master this skill. The goal is to have consistency in slope production and letter formation, as well as levelness when outputting your penmanship. To refine your skill we encourage a dedication to writing daily in your journal.

As your penmanship confidence grows instead of jetting out an e-mail next time you want to send a thank you note, elect to write it by hand. Your family, friends and colleagues will appreciate this gesture. This will be received by them as something special and they will undoubtably enjoy seeing your fine motor control skills

When you make daily handwriting a habit it will do wonders for your brain. Penmanship training requires focus and alertness because of the need to avoid any mistakes and spelling errors. The first few letter attempts might frustrate you but with practice it will become second-nature.

From a historical perspective letter writing was once a very common practice. This is why millions of people had such exquisite handwriting in the 18th, 19th and early to mid 20th century. At one time popularity of the Palmer Method was widespread and fine penmanship used to be an integral part of the curriculum. Sadly, this is not true of today's educational system.

It is our intention through this book to inspire people once again to take up the pen and to harness the power of the brain by the method of fine penmanship. Nothing would make the authors of this book happier than to have Whole Brain Power practitioners bring penmanship back to life as a common practice in American Society.

Sincerely,

Michael G. Lavery

Chapter 4
Grow the Memory Grow the Brain

The ancient Greeks memorized Homer's Iliad and The Odyssey,
25,000 lines of poetry,
by visualizing a house filled with various rooms
and objects in those rooms were linked to lines in the poems.

From the dawn of civilization the world's cultures have, to varying degrees, tapped into the brain's powerful ability to remember what it has experienced. As a survival tool, a teaching tool and a storytelling tool, the *hippocampal* and *temporal* regions have performed an integral role in building and maintaining cohesive communities from China to Africa, from the ancient Greeks to native tribes of north and South America.

Starting with the ancient Chinese traditions, memory has shaped written traditions over the millennia. Confucianism promoted the memory and recitation of the stories of departed elders as well as memory-searches to answer the spiritual enigma of infant death. The Chinese also placed great value on personal memories for posterity, to supplement or correct imperial-sponsored histories.

Memory played a critical role in ancient Native American civilizations. Archaeologists have discovered that the Native American oral traditions dating back thousands of years are extremely accurate and reflect historical facts that can be verified with archaeological sites. According to Vine Deloria in his book, _Red Earth, White Lies_, Native Americans "have aggressively opposed the Bering Strait migration doctrine because it does not reflect any of the memories or traditions passed down by the ancestors over many generations." The lost city of _Troy_ and _Noah's Flood_ were both discovered based upon written evidence that was an exact copy of memorized ancient oral traditions. Homer's _Iliad_ and _Odyssey_, and the _Holy Bible_ are the written form of _oral traditions_ of the Greek and Hebrew people.

These historical examples of the power and importance of potent memory are astonishing, especially given modern society's reliance on technology that eliminates the use of our short-term memory banks. Today, if asked to remember a ten-digit phone number, we just tap it into our cell phone or _Blackberry_. If asked to remember a recipe, we request that the person pop it in an email. If we need directions, we plug the destination into _MAPQUEST_ and print them out, or even better, enter them into the _GPS_ on the dash board and let the gizmo tell us where to go. In fact, modern technology has made it all but unnecessary to remember much of anything. As a result, our memory regions are atrophying at a faster rate then any time in human history, and Alzheimer's and dementia are reaching epidemic proportions[1].

We want to reverse that trend by sharing with you training methodologies that will stimulate blood flow to the memory center of the brain, the **hippocampi and dentate gyrus**, and invigorate your short-term memory processing. Whole Brain Power™ memory drills can lead to improved short-term memory recall and may help prevent or delay of the onset of degenerative brain diseases. We have much more at stake than simply remembering ten digit phone numbers with ease.

[1] link to article: http://www.medscape.com/viewarticle/553921

Our research suggests that three things contribute to widespread memory loss:

• Too much *passive stress* from television and video game playing

(We'll cover this issue in depth in Chapter 6: System Killers)

• Not enough *active stress* from proper memory drills

• Not enough stimulation of blood flow to the hippocampi through proper exercise

There is evidence that the hippocampi can be trained and will grow in size even in adulthood based on the *London Cabby Drivers Study*[2]. If we can grow the memory regions of the brain while simultaneously reducing the degenerative chemical imbalances, we may have the ability to halt the epidemic of Alzheimer's, not to mention improve our memory performance in our everyday activities at work and at play.

Whole Brain Power™ takes an holistic approach to memory improvement and I want to help you understand:

• the basic brain chemistry and brain function of the hippocampus

• the importance of the three different types of memories -- working, declarative and procedural processing

• the damage that passive stress (i.e., video games, TV, movies) causes the hippocampal regions (covered in Chapter 6)

• the benefit of active stress memory drills on this region

• how long-term potentiation creates a greater expression of proteins and this improves plasticity as well as brings about a process called *synaptogenesis* in the hippocampus

• how *steroidogenesis* leads to improved testosterone (in men) and estrogen (in women) production and the direct link between normal or heightened levels of testosterone/estrogen with maintaining proper memory function

[2] Link to article: http://news.bbc.co.uk/2/hi/science/nature/677048.stm

The London Cabby Drivers Study

Source: Wikipedia Commons

Research done at the University College London, led by Dr. Eleanor Maguire, studied the hippocampal regions of the famous London black-cab "cabbie" drivers who must store a mental map of London, including up to 25,000 street names and the location of all the major tourist attractions. This research is the first to show that the brains of adults can grow in response to specialized use. The tests found the only area of the taxi drivers' brains that was different from the 50 other "control" subjects was the left and right hippocampus.

According to Malcolm Linskey, manager of London taxi school Knowledge Point, it can take three years of intensive memory training to pass the rigorous testing on 400 prescribed runs. Three-quarters of the candidates who begin this course for this lucrative cab assignment eventually drop out. Most of the cabbies learn by visualisation of the streets, but Linskey does teach aspiring cabbies some tricks for building the massive amount of data, for example '*L*ittle *A*pples *G*row *Q*uickly' gives you the order of the theatres on the north side of Shaftesbury Avenue: *L*yric, *A*pollo, *G*ielgud, *Q*ueen's."

The research discovered that the cab driver's grey matter enlarged and adapted to help them store a detailed mental map of the city, specifically, a larger hippocampus compared with other people. Interestingly, the longer the cabbies spent on the job, the larger their hippocampi.

The UCL researchers think evidence that the brain is able to change physically according to the way it is used could have important implications for people with brain damage or diseases such as Parkinson's.

According to Dr. Mcguire, "It has long been thought that if there's damage to the brain there's only a limited amount of plasticity in an adult that can help them recover. Now direct things in the environment, like [intense memorization of locations tied to] navigation, appear to show changes in the brain. So we could in the future see some rehabilitation programmes that use that kind of knowledge."

Enter Whole Brain Power™.

The London Cabby Driver's Study gives us insight into the power of memorization to enlarge the memory center of our brain. Indeed, the mechanics of memory are quite fascinating and are at the foundation of Whole Brain Power™. Why our memories are maintained or why they fade as we age has everything to do with how we currently live our lives.

When I do one-on-one consulting, one of the first things I do with a person is ask them a number of questions regarding where they feel they are having problems in their short-term or long-term memory. We discuss their interests and how they feel about such things as their progress in athletics, their confidence in their communication skills, their sharpness at work, if they are learning a foreign language, or playing a musical instrument. Sometimes the client will express his or her frustration at learning a new software program for their computer interests, etc. He or she is aware that memory processing skills are slowing down and that he/she has a "fogginess" to his/her thinking and memory.

Before outlining a training regimen for their memory banks, I explain that according to research, it takes 21 days for **neurogenesis** to occur after introducing some element of change in the environment; that is, 21 days for new **neural stem cells** to mature into full-blown **neurons** and **astrocytes** in the **dentate gyrus**. Not coincidentally, self-help books often remind readers that it takes 21 days to form the new habits being taught.

I underscore with my clients that their alertness, focus, and attention span will see improvements as well as a greater facility with their memory and energy levels increasing, usually within three to four weeks of consistent Whole Brain Power™ training. The first thirty days lay the foundation for the next sixty days; so that by day ninety into the training regimen my clients have experienced fundamental changes in their minds and bodies.

There are several forms of memory, but we want to focus on:

- *working memory* (short-term memory)
- *declarative memory* (long-term memory)
- *procedural memory* (long-term memory)

Working memory (short-term memory)

Working memory refers to the regions of the brain and the processes involved for temporarily storing and manipulating information. This immediate-memory functioning takes place in the frontal cortex, hippocampus, parietal cortex, and parts of the basal ganglia. There is a subtle but meaningful distinction between *working* memory and *short-term* memory in that working memory is (theoretically) associated with instant access and use of information, whereas short-term memory is associated with the temporary storage of information for later transfer to long-term memory.

119

Declarative memory

Declarative memory is our brain's capacity to store facts and memories that can be consciously discussed, or declared. The learning you did in school, text-book learning and knowledge acquired in lectures, as well as those memories that can be recalled by our "mind's eye" are in the declarative memory category. Our declarative memories are subject to being forgotten, but if we access those memories frequently they can last indefinitely. Declarative memories are best established by using active recall combined with mnemonic techniques (associating the memory with a visual object or phrase) and spaced repetition.

There are two types of declarative memory:

Semantic memory
Factual knowledge independent of time and place (e.g. knowing that ice is frozen water), common sense facts.

Episodic memory
Theoretical knowledge of a specific moment in time and place, personal experiences, such as your high school graduation ceremony or your first kiss.

Procedural Memory

Procedural memory is a form of implicit memory used everyday. Procedural memory gives us the ability to perform some actions (such as writing in cursive penmanship or playing guitar) even if we are not consciously thinking about it. It is the long-term memory of skills or procedures, our "how to" knowledge about accomplishing a task.

Trained or Untrained Memory

I often ask new clients, "What category do you believe yourself to be in, 'trained' or 'untrained' memory?" While most admit to being part of the "untrained" memory group, some feel confident about their working, declarative and/or procedural memories. However, when the confident group are taught new techniques to improve their golf swing or baseball pitch, they seem to have a hard time erasing their current poor techniques and replacing them with the proper ones. Even if I give them just three things to learn and practice, they will forget two of them. This indicates that their working and procedural memory powers are not up to snuff.

I explain that it is entirely possible to strengthen one's memory through training the areas of the brain responsible for procedural memory tasks or working memory ability, i.e., the hippocampus, dentate gyrus and frontal lobes.

Training the brain through the memory drills described later in this chapter helps trigger *neurogenesis (production of new neurons in the Central Nervous System (CNS)* and *synaptogenesis* in the memory regions *(production or strengthening of new synapses through activation of the NMDA receptors in the hippocampus)*. This revitalization of the critical areas of the brain for creating and accessing memories is important for more than day-to-day functioning. New research indicates that growing our memory regions can contribute to *steroidogenesis (endogenously produced hormones)* within the CNS. Thus, the brain may be capable of endogenously producing steroids as a practical matter for survival because studies indicate the importance of hormones, especially estrogen (present in both men and women) in contributing to memory functioning and prevention of Alzheimer's. So the benefits of a *trained memory* are much more far reaching than simply remembering to keep your right elbow tucked on your golf swing or keeping it off the table while you're eating dinner.

The Buzz Game

One of the first *working* memory tests that I share with clients is *The Buzz Game*. It is a rather simple, fun game, and it can easily have its rules altered once you get the hang of how it is played. It is an alternate counting game and it has three rules.

1) *The first rule* is that you insert the word *buzz* on any number that contains a 7, such as 7 or 17 or 27, 37, 47, 72 etc. For instance, as we are doing the alternating counting and I say the number 6, you should then say *buzz* instead of the number 7, and then I should say 8, and then you would say 9 and we keep alternating the counting until the number 17, which is another *buzz* number.

2) *The second rule* of the game is that you always insert the word *buzz* on any double number such as 11, 22, 33, 44, 55, 66 etc. For example, if you say the number 10 then I should say *buzz* and then you should say 12 and I would then say 13.

3) *The third rule* of the game is that the word *buzz* is inserted whenever you come to a number that is divisible by 7. Those numbers are 14, 21, 28, 35, 42, 49, etc. So for example, if I count 13 then you would say *buzz* instead of saying 14.

If someone goofs up and doesn't say *buzz* on a number they are suppose to, then you have to start the game over at 1.

You can always amend the rules, make them easier if you're just learning the game by only having two rules instead of three, or make them tougher if you want to add more rules.

If more than two people are present, then alternate around so that everyone gets a turn. This game may seem simple on the surface but you would be amazed at how poorly people do when they play it for the first time. Even after a few attempts, participants step on the memory "land mines" and self-destruct because of their failure to remember the rules or what number they are on during the game.

Try it yourself and then play this game with others and you will see that most folks do not fare well at all. Tell them before you play Buzz that this is not an intelligence test but rather a *working memory* exercise and *focus* game. Explain the rules only one time so that they are "forced" to pay attention. Naturally, the more often you play the game, the higher you get before forgetting to say *buzz*. You can always challenge yourself and your friends by changing the rules so that you must focus on new sets of numbers to buzz on.

This game of Buzz makes people very much aware that something is not working well in their brains. The analogy I often make regarding working memory is about being able to catch a thrown football, hold on to it, and then be able to run with it. The ability to catch but not hold onto the ball while running up field would be called a fumble. How many times in life do we fumble through our memories and feel the frustration that we do not have access to information at our fingertips? I ask my clients, "How much is it worth to you to develop great working, declarative and/or procedural memories?" The answers I get range from, *it would help with my school work*, to *it'd be critical to keeping my job*.

So if developing a strong memory is important to you if for no other reason than to help prevent the onset of Alzheimer's, here are the Whole Brain Power™ recommendations for training your memory.

Working Memory Training - Alphabet Drills and Coding

Remember, *working memory* refers to processes involved for temporarily storing and manipulating information.

Although the alphabet contains only 26 letters, most people can not say immediately what the 18th letter would be. Or how about the 14th, the 22nd, the 9th? For the record those letters are R, N, V, and I, respectively.

Practice the entire alphabet by saying aloud,

A is 1, B is 2, C is 3, D is 4, E is 5, F is 6, G is 7, H is 8, I is 9, J is 10, K is 11, L is 12, M is 13, N is 14, O is 15, P is 16, Q is 17, R is 18, S is 19, T is 20, U is 21, V is 22, W is 23, X is 24, Y is 25, Z is 26.

This is part of the outputting exercises that we recommend. In this case the goal is to be able to go from A to Z without making a mistake. If you falter please start over again and it is OK if you take your time. Speak the whole exercise just as it is written out for you. As times goes on it will flow easier and faster. Then it will become part of your Random Access Memory (RAM). Your goal is to develop a facility for "coding" the alphabet.

Now let's have you spell or "code" the word "excellent" using numbers that you practiced above for each letter of the alphabet:

e ____ x ____ c ____ e ____ l ____ l ____ e ____ n ____ t ____

(Here's the code.)   e=5 x=24 c=3 e=5 l=12 l=12 e=5 n=14 t=20

So *excellent* translates to 5.24.3.5.12.12.5.14.20. This coding of words creates active stress on your memory regions and its that active stress that pumps up your hippocampus and dentate gyrus. The faster you can code words, the stronger your working memory will become. Practice sending short emails to friends or family members (who are also practicing Whole Brain Power™) in which you use this simple alphabet code. If you really want to have fun and take this drill to the next level, make up your own code with your email buddies and completely encrypt your emails!   Use a *forward slash* to separate words, and a *hyphen* to set off a new sentence. 4.5.1.18/18.5.1.4.5.18 - 7.15.15.4/12.21.3.11

Declarative Memory - 5 words, 5 syllables, 50 states

Remember, declarative memory is memorizing facts you might have learned in school, or on the job, or online. See how fast you can come up with *5 words* that begin with the *letter A* that have *five syllables.* Time yourself as you write them down here, and don't forget to write them in your best cursive penmanship. (If you have trouble kick-starting your list read the paragraph on the top of the next page for some examples, then come back here and fill in your own list.)

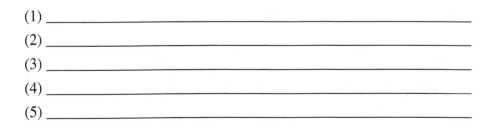

(1) _____

(2) _____

(3) _____

(4) _____

(5) _____

How well did you do? How long did it take?

Some examples include **ambidextrously, alleviation, abbreviation, anticipation, appreciation, anatomical**. Each day practice this at least once and continue with words beginning in all the letters of the alphabet. Time yourself to see how you improve the quickness with which you can access words stored in your temporal lobes. In your daily journal keep track of your words and the time it took to think of them. Track your progress for improved times at thirty days, sixty days and ninety days. To make it fun, challenge your friends or family members to this declarative memory builder. Not only will you sharpen your random access memory, but you'll also simultaneously build a phenomenal vocabulary.

One powerful drill for your memory is to recite the names of the United States in alphabetical order. Before looking them up, write down the states first from your learned experience. This will give you a baseline as to your long-term declarative memory. The second approach to memorizing the 50 states is to use *mnemonics. Mnemonics is a way of remembering using association -- associating easy to remember things with data.* This "visualization" of information assisted the ancient Greeks in learning the 25,000 words of Homer's famous poems, *Iliad* and *The Odyssey*. In fact, *Mnemosyne*, from which the modern word *mnemonics* is derived, was a goddess in Greek mythology. Here is the how Barry, an 80-year-old Whole Brain Power™ practitioner, used mnemonics to help him memorize the fifty states in alphabetical order.

"I first went to sweet home *Alabama*, and then took *Alaska* Airlines to see the icebergs. After freezing up there, I needed to get to some warm dry air in *Arizona*. Then it was off to see a replica of Noah's Ark in *Arkansas*. Then I went to meet Mickey Mouse in *California*. I stubbed my big toe in Boulder, *Colorado*, and got conned in to going to *Connecticut*. I took a ride down the Eastern Seaboard to see where George Washington crossed the *Delaware*. Then played some golf in the sunshine state of *Florida*, and still had the golf bug, so it was off to see the Masters in *Georgia*. By now the curiosity to see the volcanic activity in *Hawaii* was too much. Afterwards, I jetted back to get some *Idaho* potatoes, was a guest on the Oprah show in Chicago, *Illinois*, went to pick little green apples in Indianapolis, *Indiana*, and then volunteered for the *Iowa* Caucus. I thought to find Dorothy's home in *Kansas*, while taking time to see the *Kentucky* Derby. I had an itch to hear some jazz in *Louisiana*. I heard that there was a lobster bake happening in *Maine*. Then I went to see my old sweetheart Mary in *Maryland*. I learned that she moved to *Massachusetts* to watch the Boston Red Sox, so I went to get an electric car in motor city *Michigan*. Afterwards, I went swimming in *Minnesota*, the land of 10,000 lakes. Then I took a raft ride with Huck Finn down to *Mississippi*. Then I saw the arch in St Louis, *Missouri*. I did some cattle rusting in the mountains of *Montana*. After that, I went to get insured in Omaha, *Nebraska*. I had an urge to try my luck in Las Vegas, *Nevada*. I headed east to see the fall colors in *New Hampshire*. Then I tried my luck again at the casino in Atlantic City, *New Jersey*. Then I was off to the balloon Festival in Albuquerque, *New Mexico*. Then I partied in the city that never sleeps, New York, *New York*. I could not resist the accent of the girls from *North Carolina*, who migrated from *North Dakota*, where they say Hi if you're from *Ohio*. Then it was off to the see the Razorback football game in *Oklahoma*. I painted a seascape of the *Oregon* Coast and my curiosity led me to see the huge Pen sticking out of the ground in *Pennsylvania*. I took a short cut to *Rhode Island* and then it was over to see my sister Carol in *South Carolina*, who wished she was farming in *South Dakota*. I went to see a country music festival in Nashville, *Tennessee* and then was speculating for oil in *Texas*. Then I searched for another flame named *Virginia*, who loved the song Moonlight in *Vermont*. I always enjoyed the taste of Seattle Coffee from *Washington*. It made me excited about going east to see the historic monuments in *West Virginia* and then I satisfied my craving for some *Wisconsin* cheese."

127

Barry took only two days to memorize the 50 states by using this method, which included the time he spent creating his mnemonic storyline which he wrote out in cursive penmanship. This is an incredible feat for a man who is in his eighth decade. He can do the states fast now, forward or backwards, as well as all of the other assignments with the numbers and alphabet coding.

The interesting thing is that Barry claims he has never experienced the ability to memorize through visualizing. This is a major aspect of the whole brain way of thinking. The flexibility of a child's brain has so much to do with the right hemisphere's visual memory processing. Children can play *let's make pretend* until the cows come home, but as they get older there is less of a propensity to use the imagination as a conduit for memory enhancement. As we age, we get that imagination programmed out of us by the system. The original story that Barry learned has had an impact on his brain becoming flexible again. This is what **mnemonics** is all about. The more absurd the picture that you visualize in your mind the greater chance of linking up the association to the information that you want to remember.

Procedural Memory

Remember, procedural memory is the long-term memory of skills or procedures, our "how to" knowledge about accomplishing a task. Whole Brain Power™ strives to help initiate a new paradigm in thinking about how to engage the whole brain when it comes to helping cognitive functioning and speed of processing information.

Memory is more than reciting facts; it is about doing procedures as well. We believe that if all of the Whole Brain Power™ training regimens (penmanship, memory and ambidexterity) are followed, then the memory gets kick-started to a higher level than doing just memory drills alone. By engaging both hemispheres for the dual-handed skills of writing and doing the hammer drills, there is activity in the brain that is not normally harnessed. When the Whole Brain Power™ practitioner does the drills of reciting the powers of 2 to the 30th power and bouncing golf balls off of hammers *at the same time*, it is a form of multi-tasking that stimulates blood flow and brain activity not normally initiated from conventional brain-training modes.

Memory Drill: Memorizing 2^2 to 2^{30}

Another important drill for improving your procedural memory, and that has many other benefits to brain development, is the memorization of 2^2 to 2^{30}. Research shows that working with numbers, not only memorizing powers of 2 or powers of 3, but also forcing the brain to do the doubling without the aid of a calculator, is a very powerful active stress for the brain's frontal lobes as well as memory regions. And the pattern recognition of this kind of drill taps into the savant-like abilities of the right hemisphere of the brain.

Actively stressing the brain causes a cascade of changes in the brain including *myelination, neurogenesis, steroidogenesis* and *synaptogenesis*. All are processes that make the brain younger, stronger, and more resilient. Conversely, passively stressing the brain through such activities as playing violent video games or watching violent television programs or movies, leads to damage to the brain's memory regions, temporal and frontal lobes. Simply put: active stress is good; prolonged passive stress is bad.

Some practitioners of Whole Brain Power™ have found that this specific brain training technique, memorizing the powers of 2, not only enhanced their procedural memory, but because of the amount of energy needed by the brain to process and memorize long number sequences, they actually lost weight. We believe the reason for that is that the brain was using excess amounts of glucose (blood sugar) in its effort to compute the doubling of large numbers and lock those numbers into short and long-term memory.

129

In fact, if you only have time and energy each day to practice three of the Whole Brain Power™ training regimens you should focus on left-handed mirror image writing, bouncing golf balls off hammers with either hand and memorizing 2 to the powers of 30.

One fast way to learn the powers of 2, besides using mnemonics to create an imaginative visual story line, is to write them out in your daily journal, *without the aid of a calculator*, either right-handed or left-handed mirror image. (Your daily journal becomes the documentation of your journey to improve your brain and body, a record of your personal anecdotal study that will inspire you to improve.)

2 to the power of 30

$2^1 = 2$	$2^{16} = 65,536$
$2^2 = 4$	$2^{17} = 131,072$
$2^3 = 8$	$2^{18} = 262,144$
$2^4 = 16$	$2^{19} = 524,288$
$2^5 = 32$	$2^{20} = 1,048,576$
$2^6 = 64$	$2^{21} = 2,097,152$
$2^7 = 128$	$2^{22} = 4,194,304$
$2^8 = 256$	$2^{23} = 8,388,608$
$2^9 = 512$	$2^{24} = 16,777,216$
$2^{10} = 1,024$	$2^{25} = 33,554,432$
$2^{11} = 2,048$	$2^{26} = 67,108,864$
$2^{12} = 4,096$	$2^{27} = 134,217,728$
$2^{13} = 8,192$	$2^{28} = 268,435,456$
$2^{14} = 16,384$	$2^{29} = 536,870,912$
$2^{15} = 32,768$	$2^{30} = 1,073,741,824$

For those who found it too easy to learn 2 to the power of 30 here are ten more just for fun.

From 2^{31} to 2^{40}

2^{31} = 2,147,483,648

2^{32} = 4,294,967,296

2^{33} = 8,589,934,592

2^{34} = 17,179,869,184

2^{35} = 34,359,738,368

2^{36} = 68,719,476,736

2^{37} = 137,438,953,472

2^{38} = 274,877,906,944

2^{39} = 549,755,813,888

2^{40} = 1,099,511,627,776

2^{40} written out is:

One trillion, ninety-nine billion, five-hundred and eleven million, six-hundred and twenty-seven thousand, seven-hundred and seventy-six.

Whew, now *that's* actively stressing your memory banks! To paraphrase Jack LaLanne, "Pump those hippocampi!" Remember, the London cabbie drivers learn 25,000 street names, and the ancient Greeks memorized 25,000 lines of Homer's poems. Don't be intimidated next time somebody wants to give you his or her phone number with area code; it's only 10 numbers!

Why memorize numbers instead of Shakespeare or passages from Scripture instead? Actually, all three are excellent ways to actively stress your brain's memory regions, the hippocampus, dentate gyrus, and temporal lobes.

131

However, the numbers operate with patterns and there is a growing body of research that indicates that pattern recognition is a key component of brain functioning and memory development.

The *Kraepelin Test* of counting single digit numbers shows that indeed there is a tremendous amount of activity all across the frontal lobes of the brain on both hemispheres. There is also evidence that more than normal levels of right hemisphere processing is necessary to recall the phenomenal amounts of information that the powers of 2 demand.

Mnemonic Peg System

As mentioned earlier in the chapter, one way to help you learn large numbers like 2^{40} is something called the mnemonic peg system.

A peg system is a mnemonic technique for memorizing lists. It works by pre-memorizing a list of words that are easy to associate with the numbers they represent (1 to 10, 1-100, 1-1000, etc). Those objects form the "pegs" of the system. Then in the future, to rapidly memorize a list of arbitrary objects, each one is associated with the appropriate peg. Generally, a peg list only has to be memorized one time, and can then be used over and over every time a list of items needs to be memorized.

The peg lists are generated from words that are easy to associate with the numbers (or letters). Peg lists created from letters of the alphabet or from rhymes are very simple to learn, but are limited in the number of pegs they can produce. The Major System is often used to create pegs. While it is more complicated to learn than simple rhymes or alphabetic pegs, it is limitless in the number of pegs it can produce.

Peg Lists: *A rhyming example:*

1-gun: Visualize the first item being fired from a gun
2-zoo: Visualize an association between the second thing and a zoo
3-tree: Visualize the third item growing from a tree
4-door: Visualize the 4th item associated with a door
5-hive: Visualize the fifth item associated with a hive or with bees
6-bricks: Visualize the sixth item associated with bricks
7-heaven: Visualize the seventh item associated with heaven
8-plate: Visualize the 8th item on a plate as if it is food
9-wine: Visualize a glass containing the 9th item
10-hen: Visualize the 10th item associated with a chicken.

For example to remember the following grocery list of 10 items:

Apple: Picture an apple being fired from a gun
Butter: picture a gorilla stomping up and down on a stick of butter
Razor Blades: Picture a tree with razor blades for leaves
Soap: Picture a door made from soap
Bread: Picture bees flying from a loaf of bread as if it is a hive
Milk: Picture a brick house with milk jugs where the bricks should be
Cat food: Picture an open can of cat food with angel wings and a halo
Bacon: Picture bacon on a plate
Batteries: Picture a wine glass filled with batteries
Orange juice: Picture a hen being squeezed, and orange juice coming out

You can learn much more about the Peg System by going to the web sites of one of these well-known teachers of the mnemonic peg memory system: Harry Lorayne or Tony Buzan.

http://www.harrylorayne.com   http://www.buzantraining.com

Let me show you a technique that I use to memorize the Powers of 2. For example, let's take the group of numbers from 2 to the 21st Power to 2 to the 24th Power (please refer to the list on page 130.) These numbers have some interesting characteristics. I write them out and make special notes to myself to help in my original awareness processing of information. Let me demonstrate for you - in cursive penmanship.

Notice that I circled the numbers below. Each number starts and ends with the same number. When working on the Powers of 2, look for patterns and take notes to aid in your original awareness.

$2^{21} =$ (2),097,15(2) *This # is easy to memorize*

$2^{22} =$ (4),194,30(4) *This # has 3 fours in it*

$2^{23} =$ (8),388,60(8) *This # has 4 eights in it*

$2^{24} =$ (16),777,2(16) *This # has the # 777 in it*

While science has yet to fully understand the processing and storage of information in the brain such as is done by using the Peg System, it has been given a glimpse into one possibility. In a 2007 segment on *60 Minutes* about a savant known as the *"Brain Man,"* Daniel Tammet, a 27 year-old math and memory wizard, memorized PI out to 22,000 digits. As was suspected by scientists who have studied Tammet, at the age of four, he suffered a massive epileptic seizure. He believes that seizure contributed to his condition. Numbers were no longer simply numbers, and he had developed a rare crossing of the senses known as *synesthesia.*

"I see numbers in my head as colors and shapes and textures. So when I see a long sequence, the sequence forms landscapes in my mind," Tammet explains. "Every number up to 10,000, I can visualize in this way, has its own color, has its own shape, has its own texture."

For example, when Daniel says he sees Pi and he does those instant computations, he is not calculating, but says the answer simply appears to him as a landscape of colorful shapes. "The shapes aren't static, they're full of color. They're full of texture. In a sense, they're full of life," he says. Asked if they're beautiful, Tammet says, "Not all of them. Some of them are ugly. 289 is an ugly number. I don't like it very much. Whereas 333, for example, is beautiful to me."

This amazing story of Daniel Tammet underscores the potential of the brain to acquire vast amounts of information and to quickly access that information. Obviously, we don't want to suffer massive epileptic seizures or traumatic brain injury as did Tammet or "Rain Man," George Finn, in order to become fluid in our use of memory. But what we can do is tap into the right hemisphere of our brain and access the powerful resource of our imagination and visualization that resides there. Whole Brain Power™ training is designed to open up the savant-like powers in all of us, providing the foundation for exponential improvement in our working, declarative and procedural memories.

Chapter 5
Ambidexterity and Whole Brain Power

Ambidexterity is the Holy Grail of Whole Brain Power™.

T he one activity that will develop the human brain is the use of both hands equally well in almost everything we do. The development of whole brainpower through ambidexterity can lead to improved:

- *creativity, especially in concept development and fine arts skills*
- *athletic skills in all sports, but especially in golf, tennis and baseball*
- *muscle density and grip strength*
- *hand-eye coordination*
- *fine motor skills*
- *blood volume and circulation in the brain*
- *musical skills with almost every instrument and at every skill level*
- *memory improvement*
- *prevention or delay of the onset of Alzheimer's Disease*

Eighty-six percent of people in the United States are right-handed. In fact, every culture on earth re-trains their children that are born left-hand dominant, perpetuating dominant right-handedness throughout the world. I suspect that Tiger Woods was born a natural left-hander, but his dad re-trained him to play golf as a right-hander. As we know, the left hemisphere of the brain controls the right hand. If we use our right hand to carry out most of our daily activities, from brushing our teeth to handwriting, from swinging a tennis racquet to throwing a baseball, it stands to reason that we are predominantly generating neural activity on the *left side* of our brain. In that sense most of us here on planet earth are primarily half-brained in our daily life. More precisely, we're *left* half-brained, dominant in what is commonly thought of as the "logic-side" of our brain. The right hemisphere, or the "creative side," is largely an untapped resource.

I can't tell you how many times that I've been painting down on the sidewalk in Laguna Beach and people stand and watch, ultimately offering up their personal revelation, "I'm not creative like you." That's true to the extent that these folks are not tapping into the *creative savant* side of their brain, the right hemisphere. Keep in mind that some of the most creative minds in history, Leonardo da Vinci, Michelangelo, Raphael and Dante, were ambidextrous; all enjoyed a facility with either hand and were therefore constantly firing neurons in both hemispheres. It was noted that when Michelangelo was painting the Sistine Chapel and his right arm got tired he simply switched the brush to his left hand and continued painting.

The benefits of ambidexterity go beyond facility with either hand; there is an amplification effect in the brain from the use of both hands. One hand teaches the other and vice versa, leading to exponential growth in ambidextrous skills over time. And lastly, but not least of all, I theorize that ambidextrous training can lead to -- *neurogenesis, steroidogenesis and synaptogenesis.* For all the reasons listed above, I believe ambidexterity *is* the holy grail of Whole Brain Power™.

Why, if it's so important, is it that very few in the world are promoting ambi-dexterity with the same passion that I am? I can't answer that other than to say cultural mores are tough to break and for thousands of years, right-hand domi-nance has been the accepted norm for cultures on every continent.

Can anyone develop ambidexterity? I believe it is possible, absolutely, to nurture your brain's natural balance and complementary functions. I have wit-nessed the fact that every person who has followed Whole Brain Power™ train-ing for even a few weeks begins to develop some level of ambidexterity. The ten people we document in our case study chapter who are practicing the training regimens recommended in this book have experienced improvement in skills with their non-dominant hand. Some have practice *WBP* for just a few months, some for many years, but all have enjoyed measurable improvement in their am-bidexterity as well as the benefits to their brain health and/or athletic and artistic skills that result from tapping into Whole Brain Power™.

The reason they, and you, are able to develop ambidexterity is because of your brain's *natural ability* to re-wire itself, referred to in scientific terms as *neuro-plasticity*, and *neurogenesis*. In layman's terms, it is your brain's ability to grow new cells and sprout new connections as it learns new things.

We often learn new things when we have an intense desire to do so like learn-ing to drive a car or learning how to drive a golf ball 300 yards straight down the fairway. In rare occurrences, we develop some level of ambidexterity when forced to do so because we break our dominant hand or arm and must use our non-dominant hand while the dominant side heals. Famous early 20th century baseball player Tris Speaker broke his right arm when he was eleven-years-old and was forced to develop his left hand for throwing and for writing. After months of his right arm in a cast, he developed even more power throwing with his left arm. I conclude this had to do with the rewiring and new processing abilities of neural fields in the right hemisphere of his brain. He went on to become one of the best center fielders in history and one of the best hitters of all time with a .345 lifetime batting average.

Ambidextrous ability is a common thread that connects many great athletes, some who became legends from the opposite side of their natural inclination.

Ben Hogan was a natural left-handed golfer. As a young boy he mastered his left-handed five iron, and when he had saved enough money to finally buy a whole set of left-handed clubs, he was told that they did not have any. Faced with the choice of golf or no golf, he switched to being a right-handed player and he went on to master his non-dominant side. Ironically, some say his golf swing, *right*-handed, is the best the game has ever seen.

Earl Woods claimed to have changed the young Tiger from a left-handed grip to a right-handed one when Tiger was one-year-old. Tiger did display his ambidexterity in his youth as a switch hitter in baseball, and is left-eye dominant. There is strong speculation if left up to his natural inclination that Tiger would have swung a club left-handed and most likely would have written left-handed. Phil Michelson is known as "Lefty" to golf fans, but what makes Phil Mickelson a great player, I think, is the fact that he is a natural right-hander who plays golf left-handed, the reverse of Tiger Woods! Is it a coincidence that these are the top two players in the world today? I believe not; I think they have tapped into the brain's ability to rewire itself and therefore, into the essence of Whole Brain Power™.

Margaret Court and Ken Rosewall were both natural left-handed children, but were "taught" how to play tennis as right-handed players. Margaret is one of the best women tennis players of all time, and Ken is thought to have one the best backhands in the history of men's tennis. The brains of these two great athletes just learned how to play from their non-dominant side. Even to this day, many sports historians suggest that both players would have had even better service motions had they played from their left, their natural dominant hand.

A *Sports Illustrated* article[1] in June of 1991 discussed then 10-year-old future tennis star Venus Williams and her ability to hit from both sides with single-handed forehands. Venus later opted to play right-handed but her latent ambidexterity is there if she wants to develop it. Maria Sharapova also started out as an ambidextrous player until her coaches switched her to be a solely right-handed player. Football great Eldridge Dickey, an ambidextrous quarterback for Tennessee State University, was able to throw passes 60 yards with either his left or right arm.

Rafael Nadal won the French Open, Wimbledon and the Olympics in 2008. Rafael is a natural right-hander who, prompted by his uncle Tony, re-wired his brain and his tennis game to play left-handed. As of August 18th, 2008, Nadal has taken over the number one spot in men's tennis. The record shows that the sports of baseball, tennis, golf and football feature top stars who are ambidextrous, mixed-handed or players who changed their dominant hand to the other side by choice, or through demands made by parents or coaches.

In baseball, switch hitters have been around the game for decades, with Mickey Mantle as perhaps the most famous switch hitter of all time. But the baseball world has not seen switch pitchers. Not at least, until Pat Venditte Jr. strode onto the mound in a New York Staten Island Yankee uniform and into baseball history. As of the 2008 season, young Creighton University graduate Venditte is the only full-time ambidextrous pitcher in major league baseball today. In fact, Tony Mullane in the 19th century and Greg Harris in the 1990s were the only other "switch pitchers" of note in the MLB. Venditte was not born ambidextrous, but his father, Pat Sr., began to teach his son to throw and hit a baseball, and kick a football, with both arms and legs, from the age of three. Clearly, the Vendittes are pioneers in this ambidextrous revolution that is emerging in the 21st century. Today, the rookie Class A Yankee pitcher is setting team records and is swarmed by young autograph seekers, demanding he sign his name with both hands. He

[1] Link to article: http://sportsillustrated.cnn.com/tennis/features/williams/flashback/childs/

may single-handedly spawn a whole generation of switch pitchers in baseball.

In many ways what I encourage you to do is practice brain sculpting, that is, you decide how you want to grow your brain to achieve significant improvements in the areas of your life that interest you. Whole Brain Power™ training simply teaches you methods of achieving your goals quickly through ambidexterity.

With the benefits and the health issues associated with the development of ambidexterity in mind, let's drill down into the nuts and bolts of what is happening in your brain and body as you develop ambidexterity. We have found that the more practitioners of Whole Brain Power™ know about the impact of the training on their brain, the more inspired they are to overcome the initial awkwardness that accompanies the first few days or weeks of developing ambidexterity.

Our focus will be on three primary areas:

- *Ambidexterity and Creative Expression*
- *Ambidexterity and Athletic Performance*
- *The Brain Science and Brain Health of Ambidexterity*

Ambidexterity and Creative Expression

Opening up the right side of the brain through ambidextrous skill development will generate a significant increase in conceptual ability and original creative thought or imagination. Studies done by the *Centre for the Mind* proved that forcing neural activity in the right frontal lobe (creative side) stimulated the artistic savant latent in the average person. They achieved this by an artificial shut down of the left frontal lobe of the participants in the study. The result was a temporary state of savant-like creativity in which the participants in the study exhibit exceptional musical or artistic skills and abilities.

Typically, savants are rare individuals who, although severely brain impaired, display islands of astonishing excellence in specific areas including drawing, memory, music, calendar calculations, and arithmetic. They typically have no idea how they do it. We are all familiar with the savant character played by Dustin Hoffman in the film *RAIN MAN,* based on a real life story of a man named George Finn.

One view is that savants acquire their peculiar skills like any normal person, through repetitive practice. Another view is that savants have more highly developed brains in specific domains. These explanations do not fit well with reports that savant skills can emerge 'spontaneously', e.g. following an accident or at the onset of fronto-temporal dementia, and that these skills do not improve qualitatively with time, even though they may become better articulated. Furthermore, it would appear highly coincidental that a single savant can display several of these peculiar skills and that the same skills are so compelling to savants across cultures.

An alternative explanation, and one that I subscribe to, is that savant skills are largely innate. The Centre for the Mind attempted to simulate these innate savant skills in healthy people by directing low-frequency magnetic pulses into the left fronto-temporal lobe. Its conclusions were derived from eleven right-handed male university students, eight of whom underwent placebo stimulation. They examined performance before, during and after exposure to the stimulation.

Through repetitive *transcranial magnetic stimulation (rTMS)* of the left front temporal lobe, the Centre for the Mind's study temporarily facilitated savant-like skills in the test subjects. As predicted, this shutting down of the left front temporal lobe triggered activity in the right front temporal lobe.

To see evidence of the improved artistic skill by the test subjects receiving the rTMS, check out the Centre's web site at:

www.centreforthemind.com

While this rTMS test provided a temporary glimpse into the artistic savant by creating a lesion on the left frontal lobe, we believe you can tap into your savant qualities naturally and permanently. Specifically, three areas of the brain are influenced through ambidextrous training methodologies that unleash creative expression:

• Left-handed mirror image writing fires neurons in the right temporal lobe that aids in the development of spatial intelligence. For example, an artist will rely on spatial intelligence to accurately place drawings of items in a still life based on his or her observations of the actual set up of those objects. An orange is one inch from the sugar cup, two inches from the apple.

• The corpus callosum thickens through ambidextrous dual-hammer drills where you bounce the golf ball back and forth between hammers in your right and left hands. This assists in improved bilateral communication between the hemispheres, coordinating the right brain's interpretation of the object being rendered (an apple) with the left-brain's motor strip control of the hands that control the charcoal or paintbrush to accurately draw or paint the apple.

• The cerebral cortex, the motor strip and the hippocampus in the right hemisphere are all stimulated through the left-handed hammer drill, helping the mind to connect to the imagination, remember those details of what is imagined and then communicate that information to the executive function in the frontal lobe. For example, the artist may see an apple that she is painting sitting on a plate in front of her, but her creative imagination ties that reality with a memory of her childhood of an apple that had a small leaf on the protruding stem. That leaf conveyed to her mind that the apple was freshly picked, so instead of painting the apple as she sees it in present time, she adds a leaf to the painted apple, giving a new meaning to the expression of her still life.

The Creative Savant - A Case Study: C. Ryan Walsh

A young man named C. Ryan Walsh, who had no formal training or experience in drawing or painting, participated in a 45-day Whole Brain Power™ anecdotal study. The study was the focus of a documentary film titled, *"Brain Dead: The Resurrection of a Video Game Junkie"* in which Ryan's progress with WBP training regimens included hammer drills, penmanship, art and music. You can watch the documentary on the www.wholebrainpower.net website.

On Day One of his Whole Brain Power™ training he was given the assignment to draw an *apple on a plate* in pencil and charcoal. For this assignment he was given no art lesson so that the result would be from his natural ability and skill. Below is the final artwork he produced on Day One. While the final piece clearly showed the representation of an apple on a plate, the artwork showed minimal artistic skill or control.

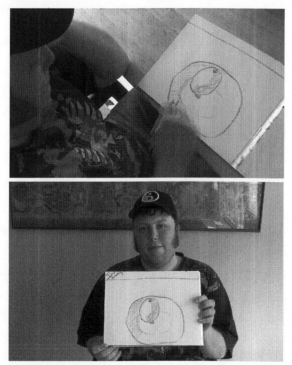

144

Day One Assignment - the resulting finished artwork.

On day five of his WBP practice Ryan began work on a pencil and charcoal sketch of the Cezanne still life "Pommes and Oranges" pictured below.

On day eleven Ryan continued his work on the initial pencil sketch of the Cezanne in his effort to complete a full charcoal sketch of the still life prior to moving on to an acrylic painting on canvas.

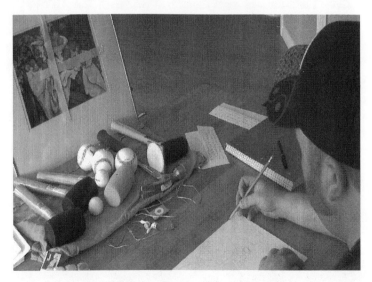

(Day 11: Note the various hammers, journal, penmanship samples and juggling balls on his work desk, all part of his Whole Brain Power™ practice.)

On day thirty of his WBP training Ryan completed the final charcoal sketch of the Cezanne still life. Note that this work is now quite sophisticated and shows clear spatial intelligence, shading quality and an accurate representation of the Cezanne still life.

Ryan puts the finishing touches on his charcoal sketch.

On Day 33 he moved on to the next step in the assignment, the acrylic painting on an 18"x 24" canvas. He finished the painting on Day 36.

Ryan signs his finished painting on day 36.

Below are the final results of opening up Ryan's right hemisphere and tapping into his creative savant. On the left, his day one "*Apple on a plate*", on the right is the final result of his day 36 attempt to replicate the Cezanne still life, "*Pommes and Oranges*." in acrylic paint. Ryan's actual time spent on this art project during the 36 days was less than 15 hours, during which he received a total of *less than 30 minutes* of artistic advice from GW on layout, charcoal shading and paint color.

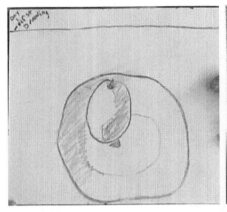 

Day One: Ryan's Apple on a Plate   Day 36: Ryan's Pommes and Oranges

Ambidexterity and Athletic Performance

Perhaps one of the most powerful aspects of improved performance through ambidexterity will be manifested in athletic abilities. While the hammer drill training methods recommended at the end of this chapter have mild cardio-vascular conditioning value, readers are encouraged to maintain whatever cardio-vascular training they are now engaged in to help maintain or increase heart-lung conditioning, and also increase blood flow to the brain. Studies have proven that increased blood flow to the brain helps maintain brain health and is vital to neurogenesis -- brain growth.

According to an article in the *New York Times*[2], a landmark study published by *Columbia University* and the *Salk Institute* shows that subjects had grown new brain cells after a three-month program of aerobic exercise. Until this study science did not know of a correlation between exercise and brain development. The study showed that every time a muscle contracts, it sends out the IGF-1 protein (insulin-like growth factor) that travels through the bloodstream, across the blood-brain barrier, and into the brain itself. In turn, IGF-1 issues an order to increase production of brain-derived neurotrophic factor (BDNF), which fuels almost all the activities that lead to higher thought and improved memory functioning. With regular exercise, the brain builds up levels of BDNF, and the Central Nervous System nerve cells start to branch out, join together, and communicate with each other in new ways. This is the process that underlies learning.

Additionally, research done by the *University of Regensburg* and *The University College of London,* proved the ambidextrous skill of juggling grew the participants cerebral cortex by an average of four percent in 90 days. I theorize that our hammer drills done with both the right and left hands, and simultaneously in *dual hammer drills* from right *to* left hand, have the same impact on brain growth as juggling. It is possible that our heavier hammer drills (4 pound sledgehammers) have an even more potent impact on brain development because of the possibility that more IGF-1 is pumped into the bloodstream and makes its way through the brain-blood barrier. Since my Whole Brain Power™ theory is tied into the premise that the hands grow the brain, my hammer drills, which put so much active stress on the hands and forearms, should be one of the most effective means by which you can provide muscle contraction that releases IGF-1 into the bloodstream. Again, hammer drills are not intended to replace your normal aerobic routine such as walking, swimming, treadmill, bicycling, etc., which target the heart and lungs as well as the brain. However, hammer drills should

[2] Link to article: http://www.nytimes.com/2007/08/19/sports/playmagazine/0819play-brain.html

provide a more effective method for specifically targeting the brain with IGF-1.

With that in mind, let's discuss the three essential areas that are influenced in Whole Brain Power™ training methodologies that take athletes to higher levels of performance:

• Improved upper body, forearm, wrist and grip-strength
• Improved hand-eye coordination
• Improved muscle density throughout the body

Other aspects of improved athletic performance such as *spatial intelligence* (Chapter 3, left-handed mirror image writing, and above in this chapter -- the C. Ryan Case Study) and *procedural memory* (Chapter 4, learning 2^2 to 2^{30}) were covered earlier. Let's drill down into the three areas improved for athletes through ambidextrous training.

Improved upper body, forearm, wrist and grip-strength

Whole Brain Power™ hammer drills are done with 16-ounce rubber mallets to start, but as you develop your hand-eye coordination you will want to move on to heavier hammers including sledgehammers when the lower weighted hammers no longer pose a challenge. Within 30 to 90 days practitioners often move on to two-pound sledgehammers for women and seniors, and four-pound sledgehammers for men and athletes of both genders. Within six months to a year, trained athletes may find the need for even heavier sledgehammers in the six, eight and ten pound weight range.

Performed with both the left and right hands, the heavier sledge hammers create amazing strength in the upper body, forearms, wrists and hand grip in a relatively short amount of time.

Some sports definitely benefit from the kind of strength developed through the hammer drills, including golf, tennis and baseball. The reason these sports derive so much benefit is that swinging a golf club, a tennis racquet, a baseball bat, or throwing a baseball, all use speed and strength as key components to ensure effectiveness.

One aspect of the golf swing, tennis serve, bat swing or baseball pitch is the centrifugal force produced in the swing, serve or pitch. Heavier, stronger forearms aid that centrifugal force as they act as counter weights in the arm motion, exerting power to the club, racquet, bat or ball. The added wrist and grip strength gives the golfer, tennis player or baseball player added control over the ball as it leaves the club, racquet, bat or hand. Once you've given the ball the increased velocity through improved centrifugal force, you also want to add more finesse into where the ball goes or how it goes there. For instance, in golf, your forearm strength will give the ball distance and your wrist and grip strength will give your ball flight dynamics. You may want more or less spin on the ball depending on whether you want it to roll down the fairway or stop sharply on the green. And since you're hitting the golf ball with both hands on the club, the ambidexterous nature of Whole Brain Power™ training helps ensure that both the right and left sides of your body have equally developed strength, coordination and reflexes so that you have improved accuracy when you connect with the ball.

In tennis, it is often desirable to reduce rotation of the ball after you hit your serve or ground stroke. You can add more "weight" (less spin) to the ball by hitting the ball flatter, thus reducing its rotation in flight. More speed = more air molecules traveling along with the sphere, the "heavier" the ball on impact with your competitor's racquet. That ability to hit a tennis ball with lower rotation is easier to master if your hand/eye coordination is improved and your wrist and grip strength are maximized. The ambidextrous training in tennis adds a completely new dimension to your competitive game. Imagine being able to serve 100 to 120 mile-an-hour with your left hand with no spin on the ball, then volley back right-handed cutting angles the competitor can't handle.

In baseball, if you're a pitcher, you can add the same "weight" to the ball as in tennis by having greater hand and finger strength. Thus, the ability for you to reduce rotation of the ball in flight. Batters will think they're hitting a lead ball if they can connect with it at all.

I want the reader to understand that while golf, tennis and baseball participants are obvious beneficiaries of hammer drill training, I believe that Whole Brain Power™ training is applicable to most sports, and anyone can profit from this training. I have a particular concern about heavy weight lifting done by athletes in sports where large, bulky muscles aren't required or even desired, such as swimming, basketball, volleyball, track, etc. All of these sports required flexibility and functional strength, not necessarily absolute strength gained by pumping iron. Take swimmers, for instance. The kind of strength they need to pull themselves through the water is ideally suited to the kind of functional strength conditioning achieved through the hammer drills. I talk to too many athletes in all types of sports who have suffered torn muscles in the shoulders, chest and back from pumping iron. The kind of upper body and arm strength gain from advanced hammer drills is going to provide that kind of strength support they are looking for with weights, perhaps better, but without the same high risk of torn muscles.

Improved Hand-Eye Coordination

We have developed a whole series of hammer drills with Whole Brain Power™ that are designed to *not only* increase your upper body, forearm, wrist and grip strength, but also to take your hand-eye coordination to a new level.

151

Whereas you can develop great functional strength by increasing the weight of the sledgehammers used in your drills, you can dramatically increase your hand-eye coordination by moving to smaller surfaced hammers. The development of the eye muscles is also enhanced from the intense tracking of the ball hundreds, even thousands, of times in a single hammer drill workout.

Bouncing a golf ball on a hammer 500 hundred times in a row without dropping it develops precision in ball tracking ability, but just as importantly, this skill requires absolute focus by the practitioner. It is this combination of forcing the brain to both track and focus that develops split second reaction responses, spatial intelligence, and when done with two hammers at once, development of the corpus callosum.

As you progress from the 2" diameter of the rubber mallets to the ¾" diameter of a 16 oz. claw hammer surface, and ultimately to a tack hammer and then the round end of a ball peen hammer, you will develop focus and hand-eye control you never thought possible. This focus and hand-eye control will then translate to your athletic endeavors, especially your golf, tennis or baseball swing, giving you unrivaled ability to connect with the ball with precision. Gone will be the days of constantly hooking or slicing the ball off the fairway, or numerous missed hits on the tennis courts or excessive baseballs hit into foul territory. But one of the exciting things about this skill is that you will develop it ambidextrously, so that your dominant and non-dominant hands are both highly trained for hand-eye control.

Mirror Imaging Methodology™

The added bonus of developing ambidexterity with your hand-eye coordination is that whether or not you hit a golf ball, tennis ball or baseball with your *non-dominant hand* in competition, the act of training to do so actually improves your dominant hand. We call this phenomenon *Mirror Imaging Methodology™*.

It basically refers to one hemisphere of the brain training the other hemisphere in a specific skill. For example, we're working with ambidextrous baseball pitchers who are natural right-handers, but who have developed their left-hand pitching to an almost equal or effective degree. Inside the left hemisphere is the stored memory of how to control the body to pitch a baseball right-handed.

As the player practices pitching with his left arm, the left hemisphere begins to transfer this stored skill to the right hemisphere. We have found as time goes by, and the right hemisphere gains the skill from the left hemisphere, that the player's left-handed pitch approaches the skill of the right-handed pitch. Simultaneously, an amazing thing happens: their right-handed pitch begins developing an even higher level of skill. It is as though the dominant hemisphere is challenged to exceed the newly developed skills of the non-dominant hemisphere. The result is that ambidextrous training feeds on itself, exponentially improving one side then the other and back again in a resonating echo of skill development.

Improved Muscle Density

There are three reasons that ambidextrous hammer drills are so important to muscle and bone density.

• Ambidexterity ensures *neurogenesis, myelination and blood flow* is maximized in both hemispheres of the brain. Strengthening both hemispheres is vital to stave off the potential for stroke, as the blood vessels and thinning of the white matter (myelin) protecting the neural pathways degenerate as we age.

• Ambidexterity facilitates *steroidogenesis*: the endogenous production of pregnenolone, DHEA, testosterone, estradial, estrogen, and progesterone throughout one's lifetime. The decline of these endogenously (naturally) produced steroids leads to premature aging of the brain and body. Moreover, studies indicate that estrogen and testosterone play key roles in protecting the cellular structures in the dentate gyrus, where new memory cells are formed inside the hippocampi,

153

and thus help prevent memory loss and progression of Alzheimer's and dementia.

• Ambidexterity nourishes the pre-frontal and frontal lobes through sustained beta brainwave activity creating a cascade of chemical reactions resulting in the production of adenosine triphosphate (ATP). Other than its role as the key contributor to fueling our metabolism, ATP is essential in the process for synthesizing cholesterol into steroids. Also, low ATP output significantly increases the risk of high levels of bad cholesterol and the associated health risks with atherosclerosis and stroke.

The hammer drills significantly challenge the brain as you evolve your training to successively smaller hammer surfaces or to heavier hammers. I believe that these drills generate the formation of myelin in the Central Nervous System (CNS) and Peripheral Nervous Systems (PNS) because of the intense demands that the drills place on the brain and body to successfully bounce the ball hundreds or thousands of times without dropping it. This kind of intense conditioning requires the signals from the brain to the hands be optimized. Thus, the nerves must carry increased levels of electrical current, and they can't do that if the myelin isn't thick enough to protect the axons and allow for proper **action potentials.**

The brain and body respond by producing the white matter that not only protects the axon connections between neurons, but helps reduce ion leakage. It is known that any increase in the thickness of the myelin sheath helps speed up the conduction of the action potential of any given signal from neuron to neuron or from neuron bundle to neuron bundle. Studies indicate a direct correlation between myelination and the cascade of chemical reactions (oligodendrocyte formation in the CNS as well as new Schwann cell proliferation in the PNS) that result in the production of pregnenolone and the other free steroids in the central and peripheral nervous systems. Pregnenolone is known as the master steroid, and thus extra pregnenolone is available to create the synthesis of endogenous steroids. (see Cholesterol Synthesis chart on pages 156-157.)

As mentioned earlier, the very idea that the brain actually enlarges with ambidextrous training methods has been proven by a research facility at Regensburg University, Germany. The study on juggling's effect on the cerebral cortex proved *neurogenesis* was taking place. They took people who did not know how to juggle, and each one had a scan done with a technology called Voxel-Based Morphology. This machine can detect increases in the surface size of the cerebral cortex. After three months of intense training, the participants became very proficient at juggling, and then a new scan was performed. Interestingly enough, all the participants showed a significant increase on the surface of the cerebral cortex averaging 4%.

Neurogenesis Process (birth of new neurons and glial cells)

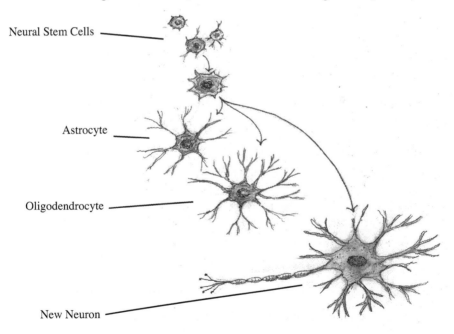

Neural Stem Cells

Astrocyte

Oligodendrocyte

New Neuron

Illustration by Michael J. Lavery

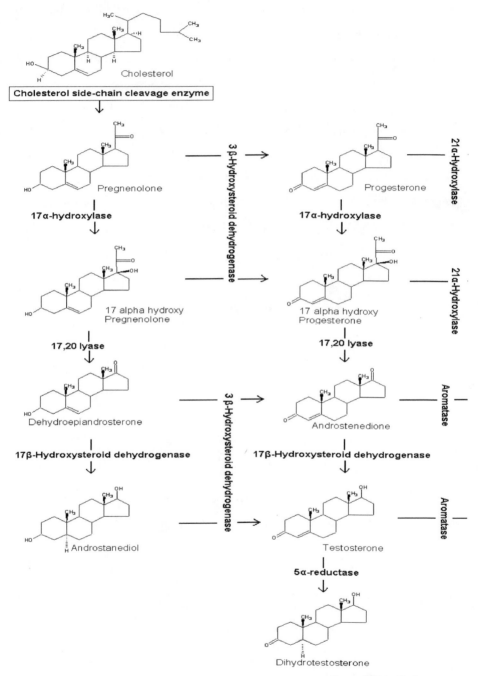

Source: Wikipedia Commons

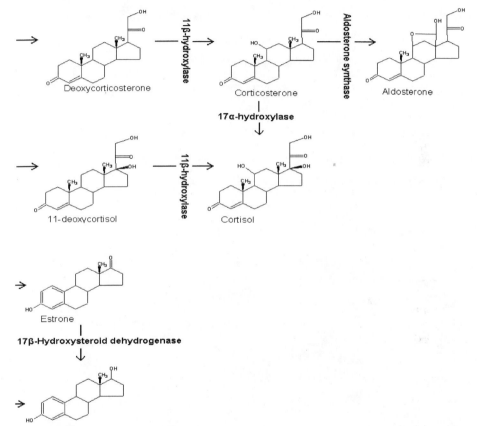

The Hammer Drills

Let's get busy improving your creativity, functional strength, hand-eye coordination, and muscle density and take you through your step-by-step learning of the hammer drills. I encourage new practitioners to be patient with the first few days of awkwardness as you build your skill. It is the kind of training that once you acquire the basic hand-eye coordination, you will begin to set new personal best records almost every day from then on.

Your training should begin with rubber mallets. It is recommended that you buy two rubber mallets, as well as a tennis ball and a golf ball to get started. I recommend the 16-ounce models shown below. These mallets happen to be *Pro Man Tools* purchased at ACE HARDWARE, which are nice because the ball bounces well off the surface of these mallets and they come with a fiberglass and rubber grip handle. However, any 16-ounce mallet you find at Home Depot, Loews, or other hardware store should be fine for your initial training.

Select either the golf ball or tennis ball as your practice ball.

Start by bouncing the ball one time and then catch it. Repeat this simple one-bounce run again and again. Your first goal is to do the one bounce and catch it without a mistake at least five times in a row.

The hand without the hammer must be ready to react to any miss that you might make by catching the ball and not allowing it to hit the ground. (Some of our practitioners started their hammer drill training by standing next to their bed so if they didn't catch the ball with their off hand, the ball landed right in front of them and didn't bounce down the hall every time they miss it.) If you can catch a missed ball with you off hand it only heightens the training of quick reflexes and hand-eye co-ordination.

After you have mastered the one bounce and catch routine, try to bounce it two times and catch it. Do this again, and then again, until you can bounce it twice, five times in a row and not make a mistake. Then go to three times in a row and catch it and then move to four times in a row and catch it. As you *climb the ladder* of the routine always do runs of five times without a mistake. Finally, on this Day One practice, move on to five times in a row and then catch it.

Now we're getting to the fun part. Put the mallet in your non-dominant hand and repeat the same routine just described, starting with one bounce, then catch it. You may find working the hammer drill from your non-dominant side much more difficult at first, so be patient with the awkwardness by allowing more practice at each step in the ladder. That is, do the one-bounce and catch routine ten times in a row before moving on to the two-bounces and catch level.

I have seen some people do these drills the first day with no problem, others have difficulty. Each person learns at his or her own speed, but the good news is everyone can develop a certain degree of proficiency with the hammers with patience and practice. For some people the golf ball is easier than the tennis ball. Some times I suggest if the tennis ball or the golf ball is too difficult, then try it with a balloon for a day or two. The reason the balloon works as a starting point is that it helps adjust the brain to targeting an object floating in space, but since it floats longer than a tennis ball or golf ball it gives the practitioner more time to adjust to the object's flight path. No matter what you use to start, build your confidence gradually with each success on the ladder.

The goal is to be able to bounce a tennis or golf ball off the hammer five times with both your dominant hand and non-dominant hand without a miss. Once you attain this level of proficiency, you can move on to *set your own new records each day*. There's no need to rush your progress, because time and practice will train the brain to eventually do runs of 100 hits without a miss from either your right or left hand.

Dual-Hammer Drill

Once you have the ability to easily do runs of 150 to 300 hits with the golf ball on a single rubber mallet with either hand without a miss, it will be time to add a new challenge to your hammer drills.

This is where the two rubber mallets are needed.

Take both mallets, one in either hand, and start your run by bouncing the ball with your dominant hand until you have full control. Then when you're ready, bring the other mallet into play and bounce the ball from your dominant hand to your non-dominant hand and then back to your dominant hand. This will be a difficult routine at first and it may feel like you've gone back to square one with the awkwardness of bouncing a ball back and forth between two mallets.

Again, try and do runs of three to five times without a miss, then rest, and start again. Your brain wants to learn this new skill and you'll be amazed that within a week or two you'll be doing dual hammer runs of 25-50 times without a miss.

Now you're not only firing both sides of the brain, but also lighting up your corpus callosum as the brain rapidly sends signals between both hemispheres to adjust for ball flight, hitting motion and hitting strength. This is a great exercise for your brain and body and will take you to a new level of hand-eye coordination, forearm and hand strength, and bone density.

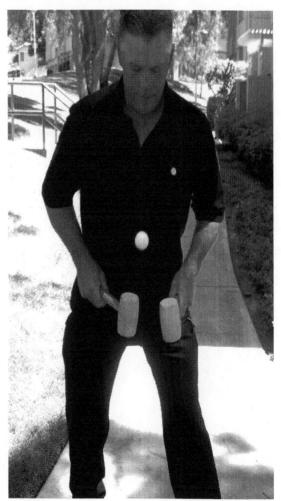

Advanced Hammer Drills

Once you have mastered the single mallet and dual mallet drills, and by master I mean doing runs of 300-500 hits without a miss, it may be time to consider moving on to either heavier hammers, or smaller diameter hammers. For the heavier hammers we recommend either a two-pound sledgehammer to start, and then a four-pound sledgehammer for those for whom the two-pounder is too light.

Heavy Hammer Drill

As you move on to the heavier hammers, moderation is the key as over-exertion can lead to injury. As with the rubber mallet training, there is no need to rush your progress with bouncing a golf ball off of the two or four-pound sledgehammer. The brain and the body will steadily improve your ability with the Heavy Hammer Drills so that in sixty to ninety days you'll be at the same level of skill you attained with the rubber mallets.

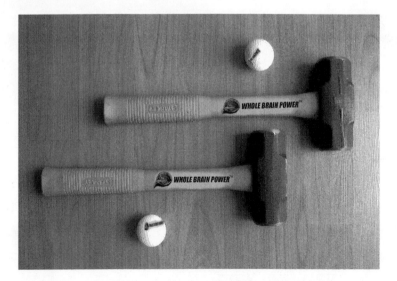

The four-pound sledgehammers shown are Stanley Tools hammers with fiberglass handles purchased at Home Depot. They are a nice quality and recommended. Unfortunately, Stanley Tool doesn't make six or eight pound sledgehammers in the short handle style, so we recommend STRIKER Tools[3] found at:

www.hammersource.com

for the heavier sledgehammers when you're ready to move on.

Begin with the one bounce and catch, one bounce and catch routine. You will find the heavier hammers much more taxing on your forearms and hands as you progress to runs of 25-100. In the process you are forcing the peripheral nervous system to super myelinate the axons throughout your upper body, arms, wrists and hands in order to accomplish this challenging new task. Some people start to see changes in their upper body strength and muscle density within a few weeks, but certainly within 90 days, whether you are female or male, you will notice significant changes in your body, not to mention the obvious increase in your hand-eye coordination.

3 http://www.hammersource.com/Sledge_Hammers.html?gclid=CIuFkc-TnZUCFQ0xawodJx2LOg

Smaller Hammer Drill

The other direction you can go after you have mastered the rubber mallets is to purchase hammers with smaller heads, such as the 28 ounce *Estwing* hammer shown below or any of the classic claw hammers on the market.

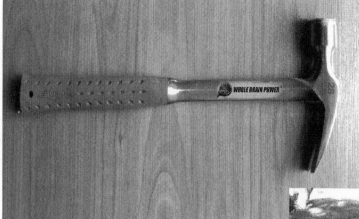

You want to begin your routines with the smaller hammer just as you did with the mallet, that is, one bounce then catch, one bounce then catch. Work your way up to five bounces then catch with both hands until that level is easy for you to do without a miss. It will be more difficult to get to five bounces without a miss compared to the mallets. While the smaller hammers don't have the same rapid muscle density improvement as the heavier sledgehammers, they permit a superior brain training for reflexes and hand-eye coordination, and they also have a significant myelination impact throughout the upper body.

164

I highly recommend that as you progress in your hammer drills from rubber mallets to either heavier sledgehammers, or smaller hammers, that you track your results either in a Whole Brain Power daily journal you've purchased for your penmanship drills, or here in the pages of this book.

Your Hammer Drills Progress Journal

Day One
Number of Consecutive Right Hand Rubber Mallet Hits:_____
Number of Consecutive Left Hand Rubber Mallet Hits:_____

Day 30
Number of Consecutive Right Hand Rubber Mallet Hits:_____
Number of Consecutive Left Hand Rubber Mallet Hits:_____

Day 60
Number of Consecutive Right Hand Rubber Mallet Hits:_____
Number of Consecutive Left Hand Rubber Mallet Hits:_____

Day 90
Number of Consecutive Right Hand Rubber Mallet Hits:_____
Number of Consecutive Left Hand Rubber Mallet Hits:_____

Day 120

Number of Consecutive Right Hand Rubber Mallet Hits:_____

Number of Consecutive Left Hand Rubber Mallet Hits:_____

Number of Consecutive Right Hand Sledgehammer Hits:_____

Number of Consecutive Left Hand Sledgehammer Hits:_____

Number of Consecutive Right Hand Claw Hammer Hits:_____

Number of Consecutive Left Hand Claw Hammer Hits:_____

Day 150

Number of Consecutive Right Hand Rubber Mallet Hits:_____

Number of Consecutive Left Hand Rubber Mallet Hits:_____

Number of Consecutive Right Hand Sledgehammer Hits:_____

Number of Consecutive Left Hand Sledgehammer Hits:_____

Number of Consecutive Right Hand Claw Hammer Hits:_____

Number of Consecutive Left Hand Claw Hammer Hits:_____

Day 180

Number of Consecutive Right Hand Rubber Mallet Hits:_____

Number of Consecutive Left Hand Rubber Mallet Hits:_____

Number of Consecutive Right Hand Sledgehammer Hits:_____

Number of Consecutive Left Hand Sledgehammer Hits:_____

Number of Consecutive Right Hand Claw Hammer Hits:_____

Number of Consecutive Left Hand Claw Hammer Hits:_____

The Hammer Man at work bouncing a golf ball between a 28 oz. claw hammer and the round end of a ball peen hammer.

Some day you will have the full arsenal of hammers on your workout bench. Gone will be the days of pumping iron for hours; now as a **WBP** practitioner, you will pick up a hammer or set of hammers and six minutes later you will feel the burn!

Chapter 6
System Killers – Violent Video Games and Television

If your goal is to develop Whole Brain Power™,

you must
increase active stress
on your brain through practicing our brain training methodologies,

and you must
reduce passive stress
on your brain by making healthy choices regarding your consumption of video games, television or movies.

V iolent video games, television shows and movies, as well as visuals that are hyper-edited with frenetic camera work and intense sound tracks, can have serious consequences for your brain and body health. For sake of simplicity, let's call these media concerns **virtual stress** as differentiated from the stress of *real life,* which we'll call **reality stress.** Please note, *I am not condemning* all television, film or computer-based entertainment. Quality story telling that doesn't pander to scenes of gratuitous violence and that incorporates slower-paced editing and camera work, and *thought-provoking content,* can have either a positive impact on your brain, or at the very least *neutral to less damaging impact.* It boils down to common sense and discernment in choosing your virtual stress. It is no different than walking into a supermarket and deciding whether to load up your cart with pastries in the bakery department or fill your cart with fresh fruits and vegetables in the produce department. One leads to hypoglycemia, the other to proper PH balance. What I want you to understand from this chapter is the impact on your brain, and by extension your body, of choosing one kind of virtual entertainment stress over another.

The analogy I like to make is that the impact on the brain of prolonged viewing of violent and/or hyper-edited video games, television and films is strongly correlated to a soldier returning from war with Post Traumatic Stress Disorder (PTSD). The soldier's hippocampi will have shrunk from the uncontrollable passive stress he or she has experienced on the battle field. I propose that the consumer of violent, hyper-edited audio/visual entertainment may also have a shrunk hippocampi and, in essence, a mild case of PTSD, not unlike that of the soldier.

Source: Dreamstime Images

The problem for society is that the entertainment industry which makes billions by attracting viewers and *(video)*gamers, has found that the more intense the visuals, either in graphic violent content or hyper-editing/camera work, the more viewers attracted to the product. Attracted may not be quite right; *addicted* may be more accurate. The **beta endorphins** pumped into the brain as the brain attempts to deal with the **passive virtual stress** of today's intense audio/visual entertainment are 18% to 48% more powerful a narcotic than morphine. Five minutes a day of this endogenously-produced "high" is probably harmless. But gamers are glued to their screens two to six hours a day, movies last two hours, and *Nielsen* research indicates that Americans average 4.5 hours of television per day. The brain can't be in this "blissed-out" state for this long without serious ramifications, especially on a daily basis.

169

People have fought to reduce violence in entertainment from a moralistic viewpoint; that is, Johnny absorbs the violence he sees on the screen with his *mirror neurons* and then, with his *moral compass broken*, Johnny runs out into the street and wreaks violence on his neighbors or his school mates (e.g. Columbine, Virginia Tech killings). Or, he is desensitized to violence he witnesses in real life (e.g. the hit-and-run incident in Hartford, Connecticut in June 2008 in which a 78-year-old man was run down in broad daylight by a couple of kids street racing and no one on the sidewalk went to his aid, much less the youth that ran him down).

The *mirror neuron theory* and the resulting broken moral compass should suffice as an argument against screen violence. A more persuasive argument might be: Johnny sees violence on the screen and Johnny suffers from sleep disorders, weight problems (too high or too low a Body Mass Index BMI), type 2 diabetes, impotence and eventually Alzheimer's. Consider this: Alzheimer's, which currently costs taxpayers $150 billion a year, is predicted to cost American taxpayers $1 trillion a year by the year 2050[1]. That's trillion with a "T".

It reminds me of when the Washington Public Power Supply System (WPPSS) tried to simultaneously build five nuclear power plants in the state of Washington in the 1970s. The environmentalists were protesting the plants from the environmental hazard point of view and lobbied in vain to get the huge project shut down. What eventually shut the project down was not the environmental hazard, which was great, but the cost, $24 billion. When the price tag was finally released by WPPSS and published on the front page of the state's largest newspapers for the Washington tax payers to see, the project was soon terminated.

Sometimes you just need to find the right hammer to pound the final nail into the coffin of bad ideas. Entertainment that glorifies violence and hyper-edited audio/visuals, were a bad idea for healthy brains from the start.

---

[1] According to an industry estimate for Medicare expenses associated with treating Alzheimer's patients in an article titled: National Institute on Aging / Rush University Medical Center By Terry McDermott, Los Angeles Times Staff Writer December 27, 2007.

The disappointing thing for me about the medical/scientific community's approach to chronic illnesses such as sleep disorders, obesity, type 2 diabetes, erectile disfunction, ADD, ADHD, Alzheimer's, dementia and osteoporosis, is that they seek a pharmaceutical solution to *symptoms* first and a natural solution to *prevention* second, if at all.

Grandma had it right: an ounce of prevention is worth a pound of cure.

It appears to me from twenty years of researching the brain that the goal of most scientific research is not to *prevent* or necessarily cure these diseases, but to *alleviate* the symptoms. After all, if people didn't get any of these diseases, how is the pharmaceutical industry going to meet its profit plan? Clearly, it is in the *best interest* of the scientific research community that is paid to produce drugs by Big Pharma, and the shareholders who make big profits off of their Big Pharma stocks, for drug manufacturers to perpetuate a sick society. God forbid the average citizen should pursue preventive measures to ensure they don't get sick in the first place.

If you think I'm out in left field with that observation, consider this lead in to Nathan Newman's July 25th, 2002 article in **The Nation**[2]:

"In June [2002], the New England Journal of Medicine, one of the most respected medical journals, made a startling announcement. The editors declared that they were dropping their policy stipulating that authors of review articles of medical studies could not have financial ties to drug companies whose medicines were being analyzed.

The reason? The journal could no longer find enough independent experts. Drug company gifts and "consulting fees" are so pervasive that in any given field, you cannot find an expert who has not been paid off in some way by the industry. So the journal settled for a new standard: Their reviewers can have received no more than $10,000 from companies whose work they judge."

---

[2] Link to the complete article: http://www.thenation.com/doc/20020805/newman20020725

Los Angeles Times Staff Writer Terry McDermott nailed the issue with Big Pharma in his article on Alzheimer's dated December 27, 2007.[3]

"There are currently five medications approved for treatment of Alzheimer's in the United States, one of which causes severe problems and is rarely prescribed. The other four take in an estimated $4 billion a year. They do nothing to stop the disease and have only marginal, often transitory effects on its symptoms. They're on sale because there is little else to offer people afflicted with the mind-crippling disease.

There are 56 more drugs in some stage of the clinical trials regulated by the Food and Drug Administration; few people other than their creators have great hopes they will work. Sometimes, not even the creators are optimistic."

It's apparent to me that Big Pharma's objective is to convince us that we're better off popping pills than practicing preventative medicine. My theory is all about the cause and natural prevention of diseases precipitated by violent, hyper-edited audio/visual entertainment.

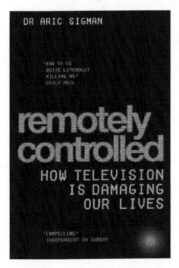

According to the compilation of research studies documented by Dr. Aric Sigman in his book, *REMOTELY CONTROLLED: How Television is Damaging our Lives*, television is a major factor in the decline of our brain health and strongly correlated to a decline in the health of our bodies.

Dr. Sigman researched scientific studies from government agencies across the world, including the Chinese Centre for Disease Control and Prevention, The Royal College of Psychiatrists, The American Medical Association, the National Academy of Sciences, Harvard and Stanford medical schools. He

[3] *Link to article:*
http://www.latimes.com/news/nationworld/wire/la-na-alzheimers27dec27,0,4521161.story?page=1

also researched countless articles in journals ranging from The Lancet and New England Journal of Medicine, Nature and Journal of Neuroscience.

Dr. Sigman arrived at disturbing conclusions about what both he and I believe to be the greatest health scandal of our time. We've learned that viewing even moderate amounts of television can produce a broad spectrum of diseases that are prevalent in our society and on the increase since the advent of television. Dr. Sigman's research supports my theories that television:

• *may damage brain cell development and function in the dentate gyrus, hippocampus, temporal and frontal lobes and cerebral cortex;*
• *is positively linked to Alzheimer's disease in people ages 20 to 60;*
• *is directly linked with obesity, more so than eating junk food or getting too little exercise; (Although, the combination of sitting on the couch watching television while eating junk food is America's favorite pastime. So most Americans, young and old are getting triple-whammied by this behavior and have the waistlines to prove it.)*
• *is linked to the significant increase in the risk of Type 2 diabetes*
• *may biologically trigger premature puberty;*
• *is linked to ADHD in pre-adolescent and adolescent children;*
• *leads to a significant elevated risk of sleep problems in children and adults, causing hormonal changes which in turn increase body fat production and appetite, damages the immune system and may lead to a greater vulnerability to cancer;*
• *is a major independent cause of clinical depression.*

Dr. Sigman's conclusions are based on clinical evidence that has been buried in academic journals, and has not been splashed on the front pages of USA TODAY or The New York Times.

One example was a study done at the University of Washington of 2,500 children which found "a strong link between early television exposure and attention problems by age seven which was consistent with a diagnosis of ADHD." For every hour of television a child watches a day, they noted "a nine per cent increase in attentional damage[4]." Another report in the medical journal *Pediatrics* studied the metabolic rates of 31 children while undertaking a variety of activities. The study found that when they watched TV, the children burned the equivalent of 211 fewer calories per day than if they did absolutely nothing. The authors of that study concluded that "television viewing has a fairly profound lowering effect of metabolic rate," with all of the health risks that entails.

Source: Dreamstime Images

Children now spend more time watching a television or computer screen than they spend in school. By age six the average child will have watched television for nearly one full year of their lives. Teenagers now spend on average 53 hours a week watching TV and computer screens — an increase of 40 per cent in the past decade.

[4] Link to article: http://www.sciencedaily.com/releases/2004/04/040406090140.htm

Research has found that television viewing among children under three appears to damage their future learning abilities. Sigman reports that scientists concluded television had "deleterious effects" on mathematical ability, reading recognition and comprehension in later childhood. The conclusion of the researchers was that the audiovisual output from TV is actually damaging the child's rapidly developing brain.

Dr. Sigman's research revealed that "by the age of 75, most of us will have spent more than twelve-and-a-half years of 24-hour days watching television. It has become the industrialized world's main leisure time activity, taking up more of our time than anything else except work and sleep."

My theory correlates an alarming rise in incidence of a number of diseases in American society (and other industrialized nations as well) with the introduction of television in the 1950s. That list of diseases includes sleep disorders, obesity, type 2 diabetes, decrease in male and female hormones, ADD, ADHD, osteoporosis, high cholesterol, erectile dysfunction, depression, Alzheimer's and dementia.

If that sounds like a litany of 21st century ailments that's not a coincidence. The argument I make is that the cascade of diseases and degeneration of the brain and body started with the introduction of *passive stress* ushered in by the "television age" and subsequently the "video game era." While I do not discount the potential for other environmental factors to play a role in the diseases listed above, such as pesticides and hormones in our food chain, less oxygen in the atmosphere, and increased carbon monoxide and other contaminants in our air and water supply. I contend that the main damage to our bodies is occurring through our brains, and more specifically than that, through our audio and visual senses.

175

Here is my organizational scheme for the rest of this chapter.

• The "Reader's Digest" Condensed Version

The simplified cause-and-effect of violent/hyper edited audio/visual entertainment on your brain and body. This is more of an overview that bullets the key issues we'll discuss in greater depth as the chapter unfolds.

• The "Reader's Digest" Enhanced Version

This segment of the System Killers chapter is an expanded description of the neuroscience and human biology behind the damage done to your system from violent/hyper edited audio/visual entertainment.

• The First-Year Neurobiology Student's Version

The segment of the chapter is the *"full monte,"* delving into the dense neuroscience and revealing the cascade of chemical and neurological system changes that are set in motion when one is exposed to the violent/hyper edited audio/visual entertainment in today's video games, television and movies.

So let's get to it.

The "Reader's Digest" Condensed Version

Catalyst

---> Violent or hyper visual edited/camera audio/visual entertainment is presented to the brain.

Result

---> *Brain waves in the temporal and frontal lobes transition from beta (high energy) to alpha (low energy) waves leading to sleep disorders.*

Beta wave: Alert/Working

Alpha wave: Relaxed/Reflecting

Theta wave: Drowsy/Day Dreaming

Delta wave I: Sleep/Dreaming

Delta wave II: Deep, Dreamless Sleep

---> *Sleep disorders precipitate hormonal changes that lead to obesity.*
---> *Beta endorphins flood the brain, anesthetizing brain cells and restricting blood flow to the memory and processing regions.*

---> *The "fight or flight" mechanism in the Limbic System initiates hyperactivity in the hypothalamic-pituitary-adrenal (HPA) axis referred to as the* **Axis of Stress.** *The HPA triggers release of cortisol (glucocortocoids) by the adrenal glands. Cortisol floods the blood stream docking with cells throughout the body and* **preventing the uptake of glucose** *by those cells. Without glucose cells begin to die.*

---> *Excess* **glucose in the body** *(which has been blocked from entering cells by the glucocortocoids) is deposited in the liver where it is converted to* **triglycerides** *(fats) which precipitates the onset of type 2 diabetes.*

---> *Excess* **glucose in the brain** *(which has been blocked from entering neurons by the glucocortocoids) over a long period of time causes a chronic inflammatory condition resulting in the release of* **excessive glutamate** *by the neurons as they begin to die.*

---> *Excessive* **calcium** *invades the neurons in this process and begins to damage cells leading to the cell's death.*

---> *When the degeneration of the brain's neurons caused by the inflammation reaches a critical point (essentially the point at which the microglial cells can no longer keep up with their job of cleaning up the excessive glutamate and dying neurons) then major neurofibrillary tangles are produced, massive neuron death accelerates, and lesions form in the hippocampus, temporal and frontal lobes and the cerebral cortex. This progression culminates in Alzheimer's or dementia and eventually death as the brain "rots" inside the skull.*

That sums up the basic cascade of biological changes that are put in motion by the virtual stress you experience from violent or hyper-edited entertainment.

The "Readers' Digest" Enhanced Version

The most important element of our thesis throughout this chapter is that passive stress from violent/hyper-edited audio/visuals leads to the production of glucocortocoids (cortisol) in the adrenal glands that flood the body and brain and block the uptake of glucose (sugar) by cells.

Excess glucose *in the body* triggers the release of *insulin* (a hormone produced by the pancreas that assists in the uptake of glucose by cells) as the body attempts to deliver more glucose to the cells. In a healthy body the insulin does its job properly and the glucose docks with cells normally. When a person develops a pre-diabetic condition his or her cells resist the action of the insulin and the excess glucose is not absorbed by the cells (all cells in the body use glucose for energy). The excess glucose in the blood stream, which has been blocked from entering cells by the glucocortocoids, is transported to the liver where it is converted into triglycerides (fat), initiating the *Type 2 Diabetes* condition and precipitating the downward spiral spawned by the *Axis of Stress*.

Number (in millions) of Persons with
Diagnosed Diabetes, United States, 1980-2005

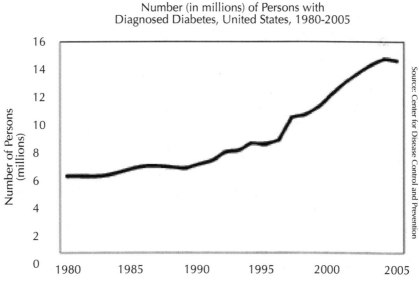

Excess glucose *in the brain* leads to the microglia expressing the ***Cytokine (protein) Interleukin 1***, which enhances the inflammatory response in the brain and leads to degeneration of the brain.

Common sense tells us that when we are exposed to violent, hyper-edited audio/visuals, we're tweaking the pharmacy of the brain and taking our brain out of homeostasis. Look at your own sleep patterns after watching violent or hyper-edited movies or television shows at night. If you're lying awake at 2:00 a.m. you might ask yourself, how is your brain is suppose to slip into a delta wave, deep sleep when your brain has been pumping beta endorphins and cortisol into your system for hours before going to bed? When combined with your temporal and frontal lobes languishing in an alpha state while awake, you've completely thrown your brain out of balance and into the H-P-A Axis of Stress.

The ***hypothalamic-pituitary-adrenal*** axis (***HPA-Axis***) is a complex set of direct influences and feedback interactions among:

• *the hypothalamus,* links the nervous system to the endocrine system via the pituitary gland and is responsible for managing homeostasis in the brain and body;

• *the pituitary gland*, a pea-shaped structure located below the hypothalamus, secretes hormones regulating homeostasis, including trophic hormones that stimulate other endocrine glands

• *the adrenal glands*, small organs located at the top of each kidney are chiefly responsible for regulating the stress response through the synthesis of glucocortocoids (cortisol) and adrenaline.

The homeostatic (balancing) interactions between these three organs constitute the ***HPA-Axis***, a major part of the *neuroendocrine* system that controls *reactions to stress* and regulates various body processes including digestion, the immune system, mood and sexuality, and *energy usage*.

Reality Stress versus Virtual Stress

Think of the *Axis of Stress* as your response mechanism to avoid hitting a child that has run out into the road in front of you at night. A stressful, potentially very violent situation to say the least. As you see the child appear before your speeding car you can imagine the broken bones, blood splattered across the hood of the car, the child's face against the windshield.

Source: Dreamstime Images

Our amygdala reacts in shock and fear, emotions in overdrive. It notifies the hypothalamus that instant response is required. The hypothalamus responds abruptly signaling the pituitary gland to *alert the system.*

The pituitary gland signals to the adrenal glands to pump adrenaline and adrenocorticotropic hormone (ACTH or corticotropin), into the system. Nerve impulses trigger release of glutamate (excitory neurotransmitter) from the *pre-synaptic cell.* In the opposing *post-synaptic cell,* glutamate receptors, such as the *NMDA receptor*, bind glutamate and are activated.

181

With our brain and body now slammed into high alert we simultaneously honk the horn to *alert the child* of the impending danger and we slam on the car's brakes. The car screeches to a halt inches from the little girl as the brakes lock the tires and rubber grabs the asphalt.

To bring our body to a halt after the trauma of seeing the child standing there wide-eyed in our headlights, *beta endorphins, glucocortocoids (cortisol)* and *GABA* (as well as *acetylcholine* and *dopamine*) are activated to help "brake" our brain and body, slow it down, help it adjust and release the stress the system just experienced.

Note that the brain and body's system needed to act quickly in response to the *reality stress*, expressing first *glutamate* to help fire our rapid response, followed by *GABA* to help shut the system down so that the stress can be relieved. It's all part of the brain's amazing ability to balance itself, to create homeostasis from the chaos of hyper stress on the system.

Here's the deal: you weren't in your car when the child ran out into the street in front of it. You were in a movie theatre and what was described above was not real but the "realistically" filmed opening scene in a horror movie, replete with screeching tires and screams from your favorite actress behind the wheel. Your brain is so engaged in the scene on the screen that it doesn't distinguish between the virtual reality of the movie and real life. Between "reality stress" and "virtual stress". So the HPA-Axis that is activated is the same as though it really happened to you as described. In real life the scene would end with you breathing a deep sigh of relief, signaling the little girl to get out of the street and then off you go. The brain recovers its homeostasis, its balance, and life goes on.

But you're in a movie theatre, and the director and editor of the film you're watching don't want your HPA-Axis to rest - not even for a minute. Suddenly, the little girl jumps up on the hood of the car and with one quick move punches her fist through the windshield and grabs your favorite actress by the throat. And the Axis of Stress fires right back up responding to the action on the screen. So now, what might have been over in a matter of seconds, continues for two hours until the climax of the film. Two hours of your body pumping beta endorphins, glucocortocoids, glutamate, GABA, acetylcholine and dopamine into your system. Is it any wonder you leave the theatre with the flush of anxiety still coursing through your veins?

What compounds this bombardment of chemicals is the fact your frontal and temporal lobes, the information processing centers of your brain, have been in an alpha state, or low energy state, the entire time. Your hippocampus, or short term memory center, the region that researchers indicate is the initiating region of Alzheimer's, has been anesthetized by beta endorphins, and lack of glucose and oxygen uptake. So while memory and information processing centers have been shut down, your Limbic System, or primal brain, has been in hyper stress attempting to help your central and peripheral nervous system deal with the perceived threats projected on the screen and blasting through the sound system.

Now multiply that experience times the number of hours you watch movies, television and/or play video games, remember, "by the age of 75, most of us will have spent more than twelve-and-a-half years of 24-hour days watching television." That's 105,120 hours in a lifetime.

Do you think if you spent 100,000 hours in your lifetime pumping iron you'd have pretty big biceps? Do you think if you spent 100,000 hours in your lifetime reading books you'd be pretty well read? So what do you suppose is the impact of spending 100,000+ hours pumping a drugstore full of chemicals into your system, far beyond what is natural for the system to handle? Might you expect the system to become out of balance? Could sleep disorders, obesity, Type 2 diabetes, hormone imbalances, osteoporosis, Alzheimer's, dementia, and heart disease be the result?

That's why I conclude: *this chronic imbalance is a system killer.*

The First-Year Neurology Student's Version

Now it's time to take you even deeper into your understanding of the brain dynamics of experiencing violent and hyper-edited audio/visuals.

---> With the brain in a "fight or flight" mode, **beta** (high energy) brain wave activity decreases in the temporal and frontal lobes, shifting these processing regions into an **alpha** (low energy) wave state (see chart on page 177). Being in an *alpha state* while one is awake is very abnormal and leads to **sleep disorders**, particularly an inability to experience normal periods of deep sleep known as **delta** wave with dream sleep (denoted by Rapid Eye Movement or REM state) or **delta** wave with deep, dreamless sleep.

---> **Sleep disorders** (chronic loss of delta wave or deep sleep) are **correlated to obesity** through hormonal changes that turn appetite on or off. Research showed that levels of *leptin*, a hormone produced by fat tissue when energy stores are low, were more than *15% lower* in those sleeping five hours compared with those clocking up to 8 hours of sleep per night. Similarly, *ghrelin*, a hormone released by the stomach to signal hunger, was almost *15% higher* in those with a five hour sleep quota versus those with 8 hours. Sleep loss also disturbs other hormones, including insulin, cortisol (stress hormone), and growth hormone, all of which are hormonal changes that could *boost the desire for calorie rich foods*. Finally, poor sleep sets up a vicious cycle where lack of sleep leads to fatigue, which leads to reduced levels of physical activity, which leads to lower energy expenditure which leads to obesity, which itself leads to poor sleep.

---> The reduction of *beta wave* activity in the temporal and frontal lobes, as well as the release of morphine-like *beta-endorphins* by the pituitary in response to the passive virtual stress, **reduces the amount of blood flow** to these regions. The dentate gyrus and hippocampi are also affected by the beta endorphins flooding

184

and anesthetizing the brain. Chronic lack of blood flow to the memory and pro-cessing centers leads to cellular degeneration of these regions and the resultant *loss of memory and mental functioning*.

---> *GABA*, an amino acid protein and a major workhorse is an *inhibitor of syn-aptic transmission between cells*. In a healthy functioning brain, *glutamate* and *GABA* work together to balance the system. But when the brain is experiencing "virtual passive stress," then excessive GABA is expressed because of the flood-ing of the *beta endorphins* into the brain. The GABA hyper-polarizes cells in the hippocampus, temporal lobes and frontal lobes, keeping these neurons from firing at all.

---> *Glutamate*, an amino acid protein molecule and major workhorse, is an *ex-citatory neurotransmitter* and normally associated with *exciting synaptic trans-missions between cells* as they communicate with one another. Glutamate recep-tor sites are found throughout the brain and are necessary for the formation of new memories. They are part of the *N-methyl-D-Aspartate* (NMDA) receptor activity. Most of the glutamate in the brain is within the intracellar matrix of the neurons and the glial cell population under normal conditions.

However, under a "virtual stress" condition in the brain, *glutamate is released excessively* by the cell. The excessive glutamate is not removed from the syn-aptic cleft and the cleft stays open allowing calcium to flood into the neuron. Lack of blood to the brain results in a lack of oxygen which leads to cell death, a condition known as *ischemia*.

---> Excessive calcium in the mitochondria swells this energy-producing struc-ture which leads to the death of the cell. It is known that neurons and glial cells will release glutamate into the system as they are dying. Excess glutamate in the system wreaks havoc, killing other neurons and glial cells in the brain.

---> As your brain is exposed to prolonged passive, virtual stress, the *hypothalamus* sends **corticotropin-releasing hormone (CRH)** to the pituitary which produces a 1-to-1 beta endorphin to **adrenocorticotropic hormone (ACTH)** molecule. The beta endorphins flood the information and memory processing regions, but the ACTH enters the blood stream where it initiates a response by the adrenal cortex to produce either epinephrin (adrenaline) or cortisol (glucocortocoids). The result is an over-production by the adrenal glands of *glucocortocoids* (cortisol), which slows the body down to conserve energy in anticipation of needing stored energy to handle the perceived threats produced by this "virtual stress." Your brain and body react with the *same cascade of chemical responses* to real life stress as they do to the "virtual stress" of violent scenes on television, in movies or on the video game screen.

According to an article on Medscape.com[5], researchers at the University of Iowa "monitored single neurons in the right pre-frontal cortex and found that these cells responded remarkably rapidly to unpleasant images, which included pictures of mutilations and scenes of war. Happy or neutral pictures did not cause the same rapid response from the neurons." According to principal investigator Ralph Adolphs, Ph.D., assistant professor of neurology, "The changes in firing pattern of neurons responding to the averse visual stimuli happened within about 0.12 seconds, which is very fast and probably prior to the patient consciously 'seeing' the image." The findings are consistent with the idea that the brain evolved systems that can respond extremely rapidly to potentially dangerous or threatening kinds of stimuli.

As the **glucocortocoids** get dispersed throughout the body, the *cerebral cortex,* now in alpha state, can't override the *amygdala* that's under massive stress from the violent or hyper-edited audio/visual information it is experiencing.

---

[5] Medscape article: http://www.medscape.com/viewarticle/412267

The following **bold-italicized** paragraph is perhaps the most important element you need to try and understand in this whole cascade of chemical reactions and interactions by your body's system when exposed to violent or hyper-edited audio/visual stimuli:

----> *The glucocortocoids (cortisol) that flood the system in response to "virtual stress" dock on cells throughout the body and brain. Once the glucocortocoids dock on a cell they block the uptake of glucose (blood sugar) by that cell. This leads to an excess of glucose in the blood stream and from there the downward spiral of biological consequences leads to the degeneration of the brain and body resulting in inflammation of the brain, collapse of the immune system, myriad diseases and eventually death from one or more of those diseases.*

---> In a healthy brain the *microglial cells* clean up neurotransmitter debris, help remove dying neurons, and respond to the system that is temporarily out of homeostasis. But in a brain that is experiencing chronic improper glucose metabolism the microglia express the **cytokine, Interleukin 1**, which enhances a pro-inflammatory response in the brain. This is because late clearance of glucose is damaging to brain tissue.

---> Excessive interleukin 1 creates a pro-inflammatory condition that leads to excessive **amyloid** precursor proteins (APP) production. These long-chain soluble proteins get clipped (cleaved) by the beta and gamma secreteses. Beta 42 is a form of a cleaved APP and in excess becomes toxic to neurons, microglial and oligodendrocytes.

---> When excessive glutamate enters the system it triggers the macrophages or microglial cells to clean up this invasion of glutamate and also clean up the neurons dying from excess calcium. If it fails to clean up all the dying cells and

187

glutamate then the microglial and astrocytes themselves begin to die and start releasing even more glutamate into the system. The downward spiral initiated by the production of excess glucocortocoids is now in full swing.

---> *Beta secretese* and *gamma secretese* are produced by the brain in response to the presence of APP. In a healthy brain under *active stress,* APP, beta and gamma secreteses are necessary for *synaptogenesis.* But in an unhealthy brain under *passive stress (tv, video games)* the inflammatory response leads to the clipped portion of the amyloid protein, becoming beta amyloid 42 which has the potential to become toxic to the glial cell population, the neurons themselves, and without proper removal leads to formation of the plaques that some scientists believe culminates in Alzheimer's.

Some of those researchers include scientists at the *Suncoast Alzheimer's Disease Laboratories at the University of Tampa, Florida,* who concluded that beta amyloid, *A beta42(43),* is involved in the formation of the plaque that causes the disruption of thinking, the hallmark of Alzheimer's Disease. *"This increase in A beta42(43) is believed to be the critical change that initiates Alzheimer's disease pathogenesis because A beta42(43) is deposited early and selectively in the senile plaques that are observed in the brains of patients with all forms of the disease."*

The problem is that the scientific community researching AD have not been able to conclusively determine the link between Alzheimer's and beta42. Controversy envelops the research on this degenerative disease with competing theories, including one called the *tau hypothesis.* Where beta amyloid generally aggregates outside brain cells, the protein tau aggregates into fibrous structures, called tangles, inside the cells. How either amyloid or tau cause brain cells to malfunction, and in some cases die, is still unclear.

---> No matter what science can or cannot prove at this point in time, eventually the degeneration in the brain reaches a point of no return in which the plaques, tau neurofibrillary tangles, massive neuron death and lesions, first afflicts the areas where new memories are laided down. Initial symptoms include the brief episodes of forgetfulness, jokingly referred to as "senior moments." This condition is referred to as *mild memory impairment*. The symptoms progress to more frequent memory lapses, then to broader cognitive problems -- confusion, disorganization, disorientation.

An estimated 5.5 million Americans have Alzheimer's today and by 2050 that number is expected to triple. But estimates are growing exponentially and so 15 million cases predicted now could be grossly under actual cases in forty years. Of course, there is a competing vision of the future. One in which there are fewer cases of Alzheimer's and dementia in 2050 then there are today. I believe we have within our power to make changes in our lives based on information readily available to anyone with an internet connection or a library nearby. I have tried to compile the most important, and to me, the most compelling theory against subjecting your brain to the constant virtual stress of violent video games, television programs and motion pictures.

There are only so many ways to explain the alarming increases in sleep disorders, obesity, Type 2 Diabetes, osteoporosis, erectile dysfunction, Alzheimer's and dementia since the advent of television in 1950. I believe all of these diseases are correlated to nutrition and violent/hyper-edited audio/visual entertainment, as well as a lack of proper physical and mental exercise. And maintaining a positive attitude on life does have a place in the equation, too. But more to the point, the brain is controlled by our five senses, by what we hear, smell, taste, see and feel. Certainly, environmental pollution, and our diet has changed for the worse since the 1950s, addressing what we breathe and eat in the equation leading to today's onslaught of degenerative diseases.

Beyond those factors though, Whole Brain Power™ is all about the *positive changes* we can stimulate through our sense of touch, ie. penmanship, ambidexterity, musicianship, art, etc. I have the conviction that it is our senses of sight and hearing, ones directly impacted by the proliferation of violent and hyper-edited audio/visual entertainment, that have the most negative bearing on the health of our brain. It is our brain's response to today's powerful passive virtual stress from the movie screens, the television screens and the computer screens, that has put our lives, and our society, at great risk of *system failure*.

The question for the reader is; how do you adjust to this knowledge? How would you quit a habit that is considered more addicting than morphin? Like morphine, the beta endorphins released into your brain by television and violent video games are psychologically, and to a lessor extent, physically addicting to the brain. Ultimately, what's the difference?

If you decided after reading this System Killers chapter that you are willing to reduce your consumption of television, movies and video games, what will you do with the hours each evening or weekend that you now devote to sitting in a chair or lying on a couch, your mind "blissed out" by the screen in front of you? As with the challenge facing smokers of what to do with their hands, or on their coffee breaks, or after dinner, when they normally light up, you will have to begin to redesign your lifestyle to adapt to a reduction or elimination of audio/visual entertainment. For starters, it may help to simply modify your viewing habits to eliminate violent and/or hyper edited television programming or movies from your choices. For video gamers, perhaps you could select more cerebral games like Myst, Guitar Hero, and Civilization III or IV, instead of Grand Theft Auto 4 or Doom.

To begin breaking away from any addiction, the most important thing is for the addicted person to acknowledge that they have the addiction in the first place. If you wonder if you're addicted to television, movies or video games, try and go five days without watching a show, movie or playing a video game. How strong will be the urge to get back to your media of choice? Even if you continue to watch television, how easy will it be for you to choose non-violent or non-hyper-edited programs or movies? People today are easily bored by programming that doesn't provide the beta endorphin "kick", or the "eye candy" stimulus of MTV-type filming and editing. I'm reminded of that scene in the film, *"Gladiator"* in which Russell Crowe slaughters six men in the ring, and then taunts the crowd, "Are you not entertained? ARE YOU NOT ENTERTAINED?" It took him ending the lives of six men to give the crowd its "kick", its beta endorphin high. It is sad for me to watch the rise of the "Ultimate Fighter" programming on *SPIKE TV*. The parallels to the Roman Empire, and the scenes of gladiators dying for the sheer entertainment of the masses, are a troubling evolution in our society's desensitization to brutal violence. How long will it be before *Ultimate Fighter* experiences its first death in the ring? What will be the network's, or the viewer's response?

If you *can't go* five days without watching violent television or playing violent video games, then it is a sure sign your brain is not getting the stimulus it needs to "balance" the reduction in beta endorphins it is used to getting. It's a sure sign that, "you are not entertained!" I suggest that you use your evening and weekend hours, now devoted to television, movies or video games, to begin transitioning to more Whole Brain Power™ practice routines. Explore beyond the hammer drills, penmanship and memory skill development, into other activities that develop your brain and body, such as playing sports ambidextrously, playing musical instruments, learning a new foreign language, learning to juggle, painting a picture, drawing your wife's face in pencil and charcoal, etc. Life is meant to be lived imaginatively, and your brain is perfectly designed to help you create your own amazing reality without the aid of a tv set or game box. Bring *your system* to life.

191

CHAPTER 7

CASE STUDIES
Whole Brain Power™ in Practice

I t's been an inspiration for me to work with some truly wonderful people who have pursued the health of their minds and bodies through practicing Whole Brain Power™. The case studies in this chapter include people of all ages:

- 15-year-old ambidextrous tennis players James Lavery and 17-year-old Chris Lavery
- 23-year old ambidextrous baseball pitcher Pat Venditte Jr.
- 27-year-old Whole Brain Power™ practitioner Dante Salazar
- 38-year-old ambidextrous baseball pitcher/switch hitter Chuck Mellick
- 43-year-old ambidextrous tennis player Suzanna McGee
- 52-year-old ambidextrous golfer Les Taylor
- 60-year-old ambidextrous all-around athlete Rolly White
- 77-year-old Whole Brain Power™ practitioner Patricia Ford
- 91-year-old Whole Brain Power™ practitioner Harry White

Please visit the site and check out our Whole Brain Power™ All Stars in action.

www.wholebrainpower.net

The Pat Venditte Jr. Story:
a Father and Son Journey into the Revolution of Ambidexterity

photos by Danny Wild

Pat Venditte Jr.'s success as the first ambidextrous collegiate All-American pitcher has fascinated the sports world this past year and inspired tens of thousands of fans across America. Of the millions of men that have ever set foot to the rubber of a baseball mound, including 19th century "ambidexters" like Tony Mullane or Elton "Icebox" Chamberlain, and 20th century player Greg Harris, no one has equaled Pat Venditte's dual-fisted accomplishments. Since Pat Jr. first pitched left and right-handed at the age of six in organized baseball he has already logged more innings as an ambidextrous pitcher than anyone in history. Pat was the first pitcher in NCAA history to record strikeouts with either arm in the same inning and led his team in strike outs his senior year at Creighton despite being a relief pitcher.

photo by Danny Wild

In June of 2008 Pat entered Major League Baseball as a reliever for the Staten Island Yankees Class A club for the New York Yankees' organization. After his recent professional debut (June 20th, 2008) his fame grew considerably. His face-off with a switch hitter at the bottom of the ninth inning delayed the game for almost ten minutes as both sides argued as to who must commit first, a switch pitcher or a switch hitter. The following week Minor League Baseball was forced to institute a new ruling regarding the situation of a switch hitter at the plate and a switch pitcher on the mound. This represents a paradigm shift in baseball when a minor league pitcher in Single A ball causes a change in the rules of the game. This episode made all of the major sport shows and the video of the turmoil has more than 80,000 hits on YouTube. You can watch a video clip of this historic event at:

http://www.youtube.com/watch?v=dPVCbXDiaTE

Controversy of the rules for switch pitchers aside, the best is yet to come for the young Staten Island Yankee pitcher.

I originally contacted the Venditte family in the fall of 2007. I had been following Pat's collegiate career for about a year on the Internet. Then in September of Pat's senior year at Creighton University, I left a message on the family's answering machine. Soon I got a return call from Pat Venditte Sr. and a long conversation ensued between two fathers who have raised their sons to be ambidextrous. We talked about Pat Sr.'s philosophy and early attempts to teach Pat Jr. to pitch ambidextrously. Pat Sr. believed his son had a predisposition to right-handedness in childhood, however, Pat Sr. was convinced that nurture and dedication to training overrode the dominant-hand gene factor.

Photo courtesy the Venditte family.

Pat Sr. and Pat Jr. (at 3-years-old) taking batting practice.

I explained to Pat Sr. my own history in the study and practice of ambidexterity, and my interest in the accomplishments of his son, including my desire to share information about how to best train an ambidextrous athlete. Pat Sr. was delighted to talk to someone who shared his intensity about this fascinating concept of ambidexterity and was very open to working with me to help take his son's pitching skills to the next level.

I began consulting with Pat Jr. in October of '07 while the young ambidextrous phenom was still busy with his studies at Creighton. I learned that his mom Jan had encouraged many of the things we discussed, such as writing with the left hand, when she home-schooled Pat Jr. as a boy.

I shared some of my other training methodologies with him such as the hammer drills and the memorization drills. We discussed nutrition as well as that is an important component of brain health. He started to work the four-pound sledgehammer drills and within a short period of time started to see improved wrist and forearm strength. His dad often catches him in the off season, and this past winter prior to his final year at Creighton (2007-2008), he said that his son's curve ball was breaking better than ever and from both sides.

When Pat Jr. told me about his musical talents and the fact that he had not practiced the violin for a while, I encouraged him to take it up again. I pointed

out that a number of professional athletes have tremendous musical aptitude and that seemed to strike a chord with him. We talked about the discipline that musical training evokes, and the tempo that music brings forth. With pitching, a lot depends on rhythm and tempo. Research has shown that musicians have a larger corpus callosum and right brain hemisphere than non-musicians, and this bit of brain trivia intrigued Pat. I directed him to our www.wholebrainpower. net web site so that he could have a place to go to learn more about my Whole Brain Power™ theories and training methodologies. GW soon built a page on our site devoted to Pat and his ambidextrous journey into baseball history.

He resumed playing the violin much to the joy

Photo courtesy the Venditte family.

of his parents who had missed the sound of their son's music. Of course, musical instruments are excellent tools for developing ambidexterity, beyond their power to train the brain.

196

Now that Pat Jr. is off and running in his professional baseball career, Pat Sr., with whom I consult regularly by phone, tells me that his son has been staying with the penmanship exercises both right-handed and left-hand mirror image. Nothing could be better for his fine motor control over his pitches than the power of the pen.

Ben Hill, a writer for the MLB.com and MiLB.com, recently captured Pat's amazing story and his family history in this article for MiLB.com.

Venditte: Pitcher or Pioneer?

by Ben Hill (provided courtesy of Ben Hill and MiLB.com, Major League Baseball trademarks and copyrights are used with permission of MLB Advanced Media, L.P. All rights reserved.)

Pat Venditte is not a biological oddity. The Omaha native is a natural right-hander, and his ambidextrous abilities were developed over two decades of backyard exercise with his father. "I had always wondered, "Why can't a person pitch with both arms? Or kick with both legs?'"

recalled the elder Venditte. "My thought when I started doing this with Pat was that if we devoted the time to it, or, in this case, devoted double the amount of time, that he could be ambidextrous." So that's exactly what they did.

"We worked on punting, placekicking and throwing. It was awkward at first and just seemed impossible. But the more you do it, the more you see that road getting smoother," added Pat Sr. "I attribute a lot of this to the fact that we had the facilities, including lights at night and Astroturf. And home schooling also had a lot to do

Photo courtesy the Venditte family.

with it. To have that level of control of a youth's time makes a big difference. Whether it was 10 o'clock in the morning or two in the afternoon, it didn't matter. We both had the desire to continue to work and strive toward this goal. It sounds like a lot of work, but it was a lot of fun too."

"When you start doing something at such a young age, you don't realize it's different," Venditte said. "It's all I have ever known. And growing up in Omaha, I played baseball with the same kids from the time I was 7 or 8 years old. Being ambidextrous was no big deal." Nonetheless, Venditte's unique abilities have been confounding to the opposition ever since he first started playing organized baseball.

"When Pat played in his first game at the age of 6 or 7 years old, he took two gloves out to the mound and the umpire wouldn't let him do it," recalled Pat Sr. "And after that game, the opposing coach told our coach, 'Those twins you've got on your team both did a hell of a job today', and our coach said, 'Those aren't twins, that was just one guy.'" While Venditte is now intent on working his way up the Minor League ladder, he harbored very few dreams of baseball stardom growing up.

"Honestly, my initial baseball goal was just to be able to pitch in college," he said.

At times, even that modest goal seemed out of reach. Upon graduating high school, Venditte drew very little interest from college programs. He ended up attending nearby Creighton, where he made the team as a walk-on.

Photo courtesy the Venditte family.

"I first saw Pat when he was a high school senior, because my son and his son were the same age," said Creighton head coach Ed Servais. "When I saw him throw for the first time I thought he was interesting and unique, but to be honest I thought he came up a little short on both sides. I never thought much about him afterwards, thinking that'll be the end of that. But that summer, I received a call from his Dad asking for a tryout. I said, 'Why not?'"

Venditte was just impressive enough to make the team, but his first season as a collegiate player left much to be desired.

"In the spring of his freshman year, Pat made the travel team. But he pitched just a little over an inning the entire season and got hit hard," said Servais. "At the end of that year, we told him he needed to get in better shape, pitch through-out the summer and come back having shown some real improvement." Venditte did just that.

"When he returned, Pat had dramatically changed in terms of his body type, velocity and confidence," said Servais. "It was clear that he was now ready to become one of the team's main players." Venditte was low-key and modest in explaining what sparked his dramatic turnaround.

"I just became a lot more focused and it really helped that I was a lot more comfortable in my surroundings, now that I had a year of college under my belt," he said. "My goal was basically to outwork everyone around me."

Once Venditte had proven that he was ready to take his game to the next level, the coaching staff needed to find a role for him that suited his unique skills.

"We figured that he would give us the biggest advantage if he was pitching from the bullpen, and he quickly went from pitching in out-of-hand games to pitching in critical situations," said Servais. "Over the last two years, he was pitching in pretty much every game, as early as the third inning and as late as the ninth." Of course, one of the greatest attributes of having an ambidextrous pitcher is the wealth of favorable matchups it creates.

"With switch-hitters, we would predetermine which side of the plate we would want them to hit from," said Servais. "Then, when they came to bat, we would just yell to Pat from the dugout, 'Throw right-handed!' or 'Throw left-handed!'" The more Venditte's role on the team increased, the better he pitched.

"Never in my wildest dreams did I think he'd achieve what he achieved with us," Servais admitted. "He pitched 41 1/3 consecutive scoreless innings as a junior, in college ball, against players using aluminum bats! That is just phenomenal and really says what you need to know."

Gradually, Venditte realized that Division I college ball wasn't necessarily going to be the pinnacle of his baseball career.

"In May of my junior year was when I really started to change my goals," he said. "I initially didn't think I would ever be drafted, but I was really fortunate that year. We had a very good team top to bottom, which allowed me to be seen by a wide variety of people."

After a senior year in which he went 9-3 with a 3.34 ERA over a team-leading 86 1/3 innings, Venditte was drafted in the 20th round by the New York Yankees. He was then sent to the Staten Island to begin the long and arduous road to the Majors.

photo by Danny Wild

"Every hitter you face here is good. You can't take any pitches off," said Venditte, who had yet to allow a run after his first six professional appearances. "I'm just working hard, trying to control the things I can control. I need to keep getting ahead in the count, locate my breaking stuff better and add velocity. I'm never going to have a plus-plus fastball, I just need to keep the ball down."

Venditte sounds like just about any other aspiring hurler trying to make it to the Majors. The difference being, of course, that he needs to work twice as hard in order to achieve his goals.

"I throw as much as I can, but the Yankees have really cut me back a lot when it comes to that," he said. "I got so used to throwing every single day, so that's been a change. The most important thing for me is keeping muscle memory."

Venditte also has to deal with a far greater level of attention than the average New York-Penn League ballplayer. So far, he has proved adept at taking it all in stride.

"I have a unique talent, so it's understandable that people have an interest in what I do," he said. "But as I continue to get better, I hope to just be known as a pitcher. I just want to get out there on the mound and close the game down."

Pat Venditte is currently professional baseball's only ambidextrous pitcher, but in the long history of the sport there have been several others who have also possessed this unique talent. Nineteenth century star Tony Mullane, Little League World Series hero Angel Macias and, more recently, reliever Greg Harris were all ambidextrous, but were generally treated as oddities as opposed to pioneers. That may now be changing. Ambidexterity is a learned skill, as Venditte has so ably proven, and it is a talent that provides a player with many physical and strategic advantages. Is it possible that we may soon see a wave of self-taught "ambidexterians," not only in baseball, but throughout the sporting world?

-- Ben Hill

Pat Sr. in his Peru State uniform.

Pat Sr. and I also share a lot of baseball talk. We discuss the difference between being a thrower and being a pitcher. The elder Venditte knows baseball and the value of changing speeds. Pat Jr. realizes that in order to be an effective pitcher in the Major Leagues, he cannot overpower Major League hitters and he needs to rely on location and set up his pitches. He also has an unusual ability to pitch effectively with either arm, and no organization in the last century has ever had this type of pitching phenomenon on its roster.

Pat Sr. has long held the belief that *long toss training* has been very beneficial to the training of Pat Jr. In fact, Pat's ability to throw the baseball with either arm 335 feet (the distance from home plate out over the fence in most MLB stadiums) means that both arms are at about equal strength. This relates to the potential to throw the baseball over ninety miles an hour from either side of the mound. However, at present Pat Jr's clocked speed is about 88-92 mph righty and 78-85 mph lefty.

Pat has two different personalities when he switches his pitches from the right to the left side. Right-handed he comes from a ¾ position fastball and he has a great breaking curve ball. From the left side he throws more from a side-arm position and relies heavily on the slider as his strike-out pitch.

The Yankees' closer had a stellar rookie year for the Staten Island Yankees. As the season ended he had 23 saves in 30 games. His ERA was a phenomenal 0.83. Interestingly, Venditte did slightly better from the left side with a .71 ERA on the season, even though he's considered to be a natural right-hander at birth.

Photo courtesy the Venditte family.

Hitters batted a scant .117 against him. He broke the All-Time Staten Island Single Season record for saves, surpassing Matt Brumit, who held the previous team record of 22 saves for the Baby Bombers. His strike out to walk ratio was 4.2 to one, a tremendous statistic for a relief pitcher.

From my Whole Brain Power™ perspective, I theorize that Venditti is still expanding his brain power through his ambidextrous training and pursuit of perfection on the mound from both the right and left sides. Undoubtedly, he is inspiring a whole generation of young pitchers who aspire to attain his unique dual-arm pitching skills.

To answer Ben Hill's question in the title of his article on MiLB.com, I say Pat Venditte Jr. is a pitcher, a legend in the making; and that he, ***and his dad***, are both *pioneers in this ambidextrous revolution.*

Pat Jr. on the mound for Staten Island Yankees.
(photo by Danny Wild)

Below, Pat Venditti's rookie season final stats.
Source: milb.com

2008 Season

Team	League	W	L	ERA	G	GS	CG	SHO	SV	IP	H	R	ER	HR	BB	SO	GO/AO	AVG
STA	NYP	1	0	0.83	30	0	0	0	23*	32.2	13	5	3	2	10	42	0.62	.117
Minors		1	0	0.83	30	0	0	0	23*	32.2	13	5	3	2	10	42	0.62	.117

* 23 saves = New Staten Island Yankees team record for single season saves.

203

The Lavery Boys - The Y Generation of the Ambidextrous Revolution

Two of the people that have been practicing Whole Brain Power™ the longest besides myself are my sons James (15) and Christopher Lavery (17). They have had the most exposure to these concepts and at this writing each has developed an incredible potential to play ambidextrous tennis at a very proficient level. Both of my boys claim that their intentions are to excel in high school tennis, then play in college and possibly further. These are ambitious goals and I support their efforts wholeheartedly.

Chris, me and James, summer 2008.

When my boys were infants I would physically move both their hands and feet. Even though they were unaware of what I was doing they seemed to enjoy the stimulation. I would hold their small hands and move them as though they were throwing an object or hitting a forehand or a serve. I believe this manual manipulation of their limbs stimulated their brains and helped to accelerate their ambidextrous ability. I also feel strongly that there were no negative ramifications from overriding their natural predisposition to favoring one limb over another.

Arguments against such thinking in some scientific journals suggests that one should not tamper with what is "natural." I believe the "ambidextrous" training of young pianist and violinists and other musicians completely debunks these arguments.

Chris lets rip a flying right-handed forehand.

My son Chris showed a natural propensity to left-handedness from a very early age, even though his mom and dad were both right-handers. Did my development of ambidexterity in the years before Chris was conceived influence the genome and awaken silent gene expressions? Is it possible that I influenced my DNA to manifest this ambidexterity in my children? It is interesting that my sons all have a mixed-handedness and mixed-footedness ability. For example, Chris punts a football better with his right leg and kicks it off the ground better with his left leg. In tennis he has a tremendous slice backhand from the right hand even though he is a natural left-hander. My son James is very much mixed-handed. He writes better with his right hand but he throws a baseball extremely fast with his left hand. He serves a tennis ball very well with his right hand and now is moving toward ambidexterity in all of his athletic pursuits.

Chris sets up his left-handed 115 mph serve.

205

As discussed in Chapter One, I told bed time stories to help my boys be open to ambidexterity. I would make up a twist at the end of each story as to how the hero always had the "ambidextrous edge." I made up a word that was the opposite of ambidexterity. I would tell my sons that I was going to play tennis against a person that was "ambiflugerous." This meant that this person could not play the ambidextrous way. I would use this word often with my boys and they assumed it was a real word used in the real world. Sometimes when my sons would see me play against a certain player and they saw that indeed I was getting the upper hand on the opponent, they would come over to the court and ask the person, "Why are you ambiflugerous?" Hearing this unusual word my opponent would ask me, "What did your kid say?"

In teaching my sons to become ambidextrous, I demonstrated my own aptitude for these motor skills across the board. It would not matter if I was playing ping pong, throwing a football, hitting a wiffle ball, throwing a frisbee, etc., I would try it from either side. When playing catch with my sons I would always throw to them with the opposite arm that they were using. This automatically exposed their brains to the Mirror Imaging Methodology™ that we use in our training of athletes in Whole Brain Power™.

From my perspective, the fastest way for a child or an adult to learn the ambidextrous motor skills of throwing a ball or serving a ball is to utilize this Mirror Imag-

Chris and me on the court.

ing Methodology™. I always tell my boys to check out their left-handed motion in the mirror. "When you watch your technique in the mirror you are seeing the mirror image of your mechanics. So as a result you look as though you are a right-handed person and your technique looks pretty good. Now make the attempt to do the motion with your right arm and see

Chris slams a left-handed forehand.

if you can detect any flaws with your pitching or tennis serving style."

One of the comments that Chris would often make to me is, "Dad, you did not start to do this ambidextrous training until you were 29-years-old. So I will be much better than you because I started when I was just a baby." He gets it now at the age of 17. When I observe him practicing his service motions during summer tennis camp I can see his mind working out the mechanics. There is healthy competition that each side of his brain and body brings to the equation. He is now claiming that he believes that his right-handed serve will outdo his natural left-handed side. Chris is realizing that he is his own coach and protégé simultaneously.

Through this whole experience I have reminded him that what he is doing is at present very uncommon. You will always come up against those who say that this is an anomaly, that "It will never work at the college or professional level." I tell him, "Chris, results will always silence your critics." He is very much aware that any serious success higher up the ladder in the tennis world will naturally bring attention to his unusual game. His potential at tennis could possibly

James sets up his
left-handed serve.

parallel what Pat Venditte Jr. is doing in professional baseball. It is very interesting to consider that Pat Venditte Sr. and I were on to this ambidextrous concept pretty much at the same time twenty years ago. Is this the universe in synchronicity?

Many people have tried in the past to persuade me to get Chris to play the conventional way. At this point in his development neither he nor I am willing to end the ambidextrous experiment. Even his coaches are now completely in acceptance of his ambidextrous abilities. Clean forehand winners from his nondominant right hand side are becoming more frequent all the time.

My third son James is also well-trained in his ambidextrous tennis skills. He has experienced being on the other side of the net when Chris is ripping those ambidextrous forehand winners, and he wants no part of being the lackey for his older brother. Boys, let the games begin!

The goal of teaching ambidextrous tennis is not to abandon the backhand but to expand on the possibilities of potential weapons in one's arsenal. I teach my sons to mix it up. The slice backhand is a very effective weapon, just as a change up can be in a pitcher's repertoire. The Lavery boys are manifesting this expanded

James slams a right
hand forehand shot.

way of playing the game. The fun of all of this is that the numbers of ambidextrous tennis players are growing. My youngest son Steven also has this skill. When there are four ambidextrous players on the court at the same time (myself and three of my sons) it is very difficult to deny that this paradigm shift is occurring.

Chris (right) and James (top and below) practice their Whole Brain Power™ training routines.

The Chuck Mellick Story - A "Roy Hobbs" of baseball?

Chuck Mellick, age 38, from Tracy, California, posted some videos on You-Tube in the fall of 2007 of himself throwing baseballs against the wall in a rac-quet ball court. What interested me when I found these clips in early 2008 was that he was pitching right and left-handed. In his description on his YouTube site he told of his quest to be the first baseball pitcher in history to be documented throwing 90 mph with either arm. I looked at his pitching mechanics and saw the potential in him. This lead to sending him an e-mail through his contact page and he responded to my comments almost immediately.

Our first conversation on Jan, 20th, 2008, lasted an hour and he elected to have me consult with him to harness this switch pitching ability. He told me the story about the 17-year layoff from baseball and his comeback attempt a year earlier at age 37. He impressed me with his serious passion for playing competitive baseball again, striking an emotional chord when he said, "Michael, I feel most at home when I am on the mound." I was once a pitcher myself and I could relate. Chuck said, "People think I am a little bit crazy, but I believe that this is what God wants me to do with my life; this is my destiny."

I had a strong sense of art imitating life at this moment, not just with the movie *The Natural*, but a story of my own making. Years ago I had written a screenplay called *The Art of Baseball.* It was a saga about a guy who learns to pitch ambidextrously late in life and makes it back to professional baseball. So talking to Mellick was a déjà vu moment, for on the other end of the line was a man who was telling me

Lavery and Mellick in Tracy, CA. 2008.

of his dream to do just that. I was more than excited about teaching him all that I could, helping him tap into Whole brain Power™.

Since Chuck lives in Northern California and I am located in Orange County, the training was conducted over telephone conversations and emails in which we covered training methodologies. He went after all of the tenets of Whole Brain Power™ with the dedication of a warrior.

Chuck is mixed-handed, he writes with his left hand and does his pitching with his right hand. I encouraged him to embrace the uniqueness of his uncommon brain wiring and to bring it to a new level.

211

I stressed with him the need to do some role reversals in his ambidextrous training. I convinced him to do mostly right-handed penmanship drills and a lot of throwing left-handed. "When you have the urge to write left handed, make an effort to do it the mirror image way and expand the brain's plasticity in your visual fields. After all when you are making your hand and eyes go to the left, this is activating the right hemisphere of the brain in a very intense way." He went after every detail of the training like no other practitioner. He mastered the three different alphabet sequences, the coding of the alphabet, too. He memorized the A=1, B=2 ... Z=26 version, as well as the Z=1, Y=2 ... A=26 code. I challenged him by writing emails in the different codes. He would then respond back to me in the same manner.

I asked him to send me penmanship samples in all of the required directions, left, right, and mirror image. From his handwriting it was obvious that he was indeed re-wiring his brain through the fine motor controls that the pen can evoke. "Michael, I am definitely seeing and feeling results and the crazy part of it is that I have to eat like a horse just to maintain my weight." He would go to the racquet ball courts and throw off the wall and videotape each session. Then he would post his pitching mechanics on Youtube. GW would then work the MIM magic (editing the video with the right hand pitches flipped over) and this would allow for Mellick to see the flaws of his left-handed pitching as opposed to the better mechanics of his right-handed side.

For the first two months Mellick and I worked well together and he was constantly telling me of the strength increases that he was seeing in the gym. Chuck has always enjoyed the intensity of doing heavy squat lifting, and now he was putting 450 pounds on the rack and doing ten repetitions. He eventually pushed it to 475 pounds. He was excited about the progress, yet I was having reservations about his flexibility. Upon my request, strength and flexibility expert Dean Brittenham reviewed the footage of Mellick pitching and he told me bluntly,

"Chuck is very tight in the gluteus muscles, the hamstrings and the hip flexors. This is definitely robbing him of his velocity on the fastball." I used Brittenham's observations to reinforce with Mellick that it was time to move away from the standard absolute-strength weight training he had been doing all his life and into the functional-strength training methods of Whole Brain Power™. My phone conversation with him didn't convince him that this was the best way to go.

A few weeks later on March 30, 2008, GW and I flew into Sacramento, California to film Chuck in his first game of the season. When Chuck shook my hand for the first time he realized where I was coming from with this functional strength conditioning. I certainly surprised him with some of the leverage lifting that I performed with the 10, 12 and 16 pound sledge hammers. He admitted that he was a bit perplexed at my muscle density.

"Michael, how is it that I am doing heavy workouts with curls and bench presses in the gym and you never pump iron and yet your overall muscle density far exceeds my own?"

"Here's the deal, when you are doing slow deliberate movements with the heavy weights, you are not stimulating the *Central Nervous System* and the *Peripheral Nervous System* in the same manner that I achieve with my methods. For example, when I have two, four-pound sledgehammers in my hands and I am bouncing a golf ball from one hammer to the other 500 consecutive times without a miss, the overall brain and body work out is incredible. Plus the improvement to my overall hand-eye coordination and athleticism is off the charts. Not only do I get the pump from this intense hammer drill, but I theorize that this particular exercise forces my Central and Peripheral Nervous systems to *myelinate the axon sheaths* like crazy in order to accommodate the increased demand on my body to perform this extreme skill. My research indicates that this myelination results in a cascade of chemical interactions leading to the synthesis of steroids, otherwise known as *steroidogenesis*. I believe this is where

213

the superior functional strength increases occur. It takes me only about 2 1/2 minutes to do a run of 500 hits on the hammers, not the two hours in the gym that you spend pumping heavy weights. While I bounce the golf balls, I also recite the Powers of 2 up to the 30th power. This is turbo-charging my work out with the hammers, as doing the numbers drill combined with the dual hammer drill forces my brain to light up like the Fourth of July. If I ever get hauled into a lab at some neurological research facility and they wire up my brain I think it will be a thrill for them when they see how much energy my brain is outputting, how much neurotransmitter activity, glucose absorption, and action potentials are being achieved." At this moment I had his attention, and high hopes of getting Mellick out of the gym and onto the hammer drills in earnest.

At dinner that evening with Chuck, his wife and two boys, and his mom and dad, I pursued the issue of weight training further. I asked his dad, Gus Mellick, "Did Chuck throw harder before he started the intense weight training in high school?" Gus did not hesitate a bit and he shared with me in Chuck's presence, "Michael, in Chuck's junior year, he was throwing in the high eighties. After he started to pump iron, he lost 5 mph from his fast ball by the time he was a senior." That was all the confirmation I needed from his dad, and I was glad Chuck heard it as well. After dinner we stood in the parking lot and I proposed an agreement with Chuck. "Please commit to 30 days with no weight lifting, and instead do the hammer drills, as well as all the tenets of Whole Brain Power. I guarantee you that you will be amazed at the results." I handed Chuck the weighted two and four-pound metal juggling balls from my training kit and suggested that he add the juggling routine to the program. We shook hands on the agreement and the metamorphosis of Chuck Mellick began.

Since then Chuck has begun to experience a growth spurt that is difficult to fathom for a man in his late 30s who is not on anabolic steroids. He has had to get a larger hat size, shoe size and ring size since starting on Whole Brain Power™ training. He, as much as anyone, has been totally surprised at the changes in his body. At the same time I made suggestions that Chuck change some of his nutritional habits. We communicated on an almost daily basis, mostly through emails. As his curiosity about his growth spurt increased, I sent him internet links to the sites that explained the latest discoveries that confirmed that the mammalian brain has all of the machinery in place to achieve the whole cascade of endogenous steroid production. "Chuck, if you keep up with the training you will keep growing the neural connections in your brain, and as the wires thicken then the chemistry will change and you will get dense muscles that can move fast."

A sports writer from The Oakland Tribune [The Bay Area News Group] got interested in Mellick's story. He learned of some of Chuck's achievements on our web site and others from the Orange County article by Tom Berg. The

writer, Carl Steward, has covered all of the greats that have come through the Bay area. He watched the *"Bruise Brothers"* Jose Canseco and Mark McGuire grow into supermen, and has seen and written about the effects of the Steroid Era in Baseball. When he met Chuck in person he called me after the interview and said, "This guy has arms like a lumber jack. I cannot believe how good this guy looks for an athlete nearing the age of 40." He was quite impressed with the results of Mellick's training and he wrote a story that hit the front sports page of three major Bay Area newspapers.

215

Throwing Baseball a Curve

by Carl Steward

(Courtesy Carl Steward and The Oakland Tribune.)

Imagine a pitcher who could throw blazing fastballs right-handed to Manny Ramirez, then turn around and throw sharp-breaking sliders left-handed to David Ortiz.

The New York Yankees can imagine it. They drafted an ambidextrous pitcher, Creighton Universtiy reliever Pat Venditte, in the 20th round of the 2008 amateur draft. You can watch the turmoil he created in his debut performance with the New York Staten Island Yankees at:*http://www.youtube.com/watch?v=-2oD8KzxS14*

Chuck Mellick of Tracy — and also of the semipro Tracy Yankees — believes he is going to be even better than Venditte very soon, and so does the ambidexterity mentor who has counseled both pitchers. In fact, within the next six months, Mellick hopes to be the first man timed by a radar gun to throw 90 mph with both arms. He's already been clocked at 93 mph right-handed and estimates he's at around 82-83 mph left-handed, a quantum leap from where he was six months ago.

Mellick believes if he continues rapidly escalating his performance levels, it will earn him a professional baseball contract — he'd love it to be with the A's — before next year.

"If you put me on the Oakland Coliseum mound and had Billy Beane standing right next to me with a radar gun, I would hit 95 easy right-handed, I'd be so jacked," Mellick said. "Then they would just have to say,

'You know what, Chuck? That is awesome. We want you to throw 95 right, 90 left, and become a pitcher for us.' And I could do it, but they have to give me that shot."

Crazy? You haven't heard the half of it yet.

Start with the fact that Mellick is 38 years old. He has a wife and two kids and a day job in Manteca as an auto parts account manager that he's held for

15 years. Once a hard-throwing high school and junior college pitcher with pro aspirations, he'd been out of baseball for 17 years until he joined a 35-and-over league last summer.

"I always felt like I missed my calling because I had dominant stuff for a high schooler," said Mellick, who produced a newspaper clip reporting a no-hitter he once threw for Oak Ridge High School in El Dorado County.

"In college, my coach never really taught me anything so I didn't get much better. But with the right teacher, I could have done well, got drafted, and I think made the pros.

"So, 17 years later, I thought, `What could I do to make people notice me?'"

Nope, we're not even to the really crazy parts yet.

Mellick, who writes and bats left-handed but throws right-handed, decided to test his ambidextrous abilities only last year. He made enough progress that he downloaded videos of himself on the Internet, after which he was contacted by Michael Lavery, a Laguna Beach man who runs a company called Whole Brain Planet and searches out ambidextrous athletes to teach his radical but highly scientific brain-training methods.

Lavery, aka "The Hammer Man," has appeared on TV demonstrating his own amazing feats of ambidexterity. He can plays tennis with both hands.

When he was 43, he was a 40-handicap golfer who never broke 100. In four years, using his ambidextrous training methods, he learned to hit crisp, straight drives of more than 300 yards from either side of the ball. He is now a scratch golfer contemplating the PGA's Champions Tour when he turns 50.

Lavery says it's all about training the brain to work its less dominant hemisphere through physical and mental regimens, which also improves the dominant side. Citing Venditte, Mellick and other athletes he has counseled, he believes ambidexterity will soon lead to new horizons in athletics with quarterbacks who can throw on the run with either arm, tennis players who hit only forehands and pitchers who routinely pitch from either side.

217

"I think it eventually will turn into a revolution," Lavery said.

Lavery has his subjects juggle two- and four-pound steel balls while counting by powers of 2 to the 50th power (1,125,899,906,842,624). He has them bounce a golf ball off the end of a sledge hammer, left- and right-handed while reciting the alphabet backward. He has them write with a pen left- and right-handed, forward, backward, upside down and in mirror image. The rationale?

"Every normal brain has a savant capacity to it," Lavery said. "So my theory is that by teaching somebody to write with either hand, that mentally and spatially taps the brain, you get outside of your comfort zone, and you have a more spatially advanced brain to throw a ball or do any form of athletics."

That's just one of dozens of notions Lavery spouts, but back to Mellick. After practicing Lavery's unusual techniques, he can now throw a ball over 300 feet right-handed and more 250 left-handed. Unable to touch the rim a year ago, he can now dunk a baseball. He's running faster than he did when he was 20, he said.

He can hit a fungo 350 feet from either side or the velocity on his throws has been steadily raising. He believes if he could work regularly off a mound in training, he could accelerate his velocity and his progress that much more.

More Twilight Zone material: At 38, Mellick said his body is actually growing. He had to resize his wedding ring from a 9 to a 10. His hat size

Mellick's WBP routine includes launching a tire 25 feet in the air.

went from 73 8 inches to 75 8. He wears a half-size larger shoe, and he believes he has grown more than a half-inch as well. Lavery's explanation is that Mellick's brain work is generating additional amounts of a natural steroid called Pregnenolone.

Mellick is hoping Venditte's example opens a door for him, even though he understands the age factor and his belated development as a righty-lefty. Venditte started when he was 3. "It's a shame that I'm 38 years old because no one's going to give me a shot unless I can throw 90 miles an hour left-handed and 97 miles an hour right-handed," he said. "Hopefully, at that point, they wouldn't care how old I was. But I will be the first guy to throw 90-90."

Greg Harris is the only man who has thrown from both sides of the plate in the modern-era majors, and he did it as a one-inning lark with the Montreal Expos. Mickey Lolich and Billy Wagner were right-handed pitchers as kids who succeeded as left-handers after being forced to change because of injuries.

But you have to go back to the 1800s and Tony Mullane, who won 284 games and struck out over 1,800 batters, to find the major leagues' one true ambidextrous pitcher. Mullane played without a glove, started his windup with both hands on the ball, and hitters didn't know until his leg kick with which arm he was going to throw. Today's rules state that a pitcher must complete an entire at-bat from the same side, as must the batter. But an ambidextrous pitcher would represent a new baseball weapon.

Lavery thinks Mellick has at least as good a chance as Venditte.

"Chuck definitely throws harder (Venditte clocks high 80s right-handed, low 80s left-handed)," Lavery said. "I think he'll eventually throw 97-90, because training his left side is making his right side better. He will make the breakthrough. And think about it. The guy's 38, and he's got a daytime job? What if he was younger and really funded to do this full-time?"

*Mellick, who has 45 strikeouts in 30 innings in his summer semipro league -
he's "moved up" to a tougher 28-and-over circuit - was reminded that by throwing 82-84 mph lefthanded, he's already in a velocity league with the beleaguered
Barry Zito.*

*"I've had a couple of friends tell me that," he said. "But I'm getting better
results."*

*Yes, it's crazy. Totally crazy. But it may not be so hare-brained for somebody
besides a curious reporter to give Mellick a look.   --- Carl Steward*

Soon after the Steward article ran, a radio interview followed on station KKIQ
in the Bay Area where Wayne Coy, the Morning Show DJ, opened the segment:
"We are embarking upon one of the best human interest stories I've heard this
year and its about a baseball player named Chuck Mellick."

This was soon followed by CBS television affiliate in San Francisco going to
Tracy, Mellick's hometown, with a correspondent and a film crew to investigate
this phenomenal story. Mellick took the news crew to the local park where he
impressed them with his baseball long toss and hitting exhibition in which he
launched a huge tire with a 16-pound sledgehammer.

Greg Wilson, a pitching coach who runs a baseball school, was present to
answer questions. Wilson stated that the thing that impressed him about Chuck
was what great shape he is in. He also said that he believes that with the proper
training Mellick has the potential to become a major league hurler. They prom-
ised that the segment would air that weekend. Well, it would air as soon as the
correspondent made a few phone calls to local doctors in the Bay Area. Apparently, she needed to discuss with the local medical community Mellick's story
and the claims of this *steroidogenesis* factor leading to his superior strength, athletic skill and larger hat, foot and hand sizes. When three weeks went by without
the story airing we knew there must be a problem.

It turns out that the CBS affiliate pulled the plug on Mellick's story because the doctors they called "the experts" said that it was impossible for a man aged 38 to be having these physiological changes in his body, unless, of course, he was taking anabolic steroids.

I got an email from Carl Steward who knows the CBS-affiliate correspondent, and he said that he made an attempt to persuade her to at least discuss the theories on steroidogenesis that are turning Mellick into a beast at 38; but neither she, nor her boss, would have any part of it. Was the steroid issue in baseball too much of a taboo or was Chuck looking too big and too strong? One thing we know for sure, Mellick is *not* juicing on artificial steroids of any kind. Nonetheless, it would appear the story was too unbelievable for "the experts" to investigate one of the most inspirational stories of the year.

But the story is on the street now, thanks to writers like Carl Steward and Tom Berg with the Orange County Register, and Ben Hill with the MiLB.com, Bob Brownne with the Tracy Press, and Wayne Coy with KKIQ FM in San Francisco. We anticipate more reporters will investigate this man Mellick, a man on a mission to be the first pitcher in history to throw more than 90 mph from both the left and right side.

Suzanna McGee

Suzanna with 80 lb. kettle ball.

Suzanna McGee, age 43, is a trained athlete and personal trainer from Venice Beach, California, and Whole Brain Power™ practitioner for 6 months. Originally from Czechoslovakia (now Czech Republic), in her twenties she moved to Sweden for ten years, and then immigrated to the United States and settled in Venice Beach in the 1996. She has had extensive training as an athlete, including cross country and telemark downhill skiing, and for years has been a competitive member of the National cross country ski racing team. She has always trained with elite athletes since she was a young girl, enjoying competition against the boys in her age group in soccer and basketball. She's been training in the gym since she was a young girl with the intent to become a stronger, faster and better athlete. It has always been her natural functional strength that has impressed her coaches in the different sports in which she has trained. Suzanna's YouTube website (http://www.youtube.com/watch?v=eHihk0EfTLY), shows her working out with an 80 lb. kettleball with an ease that makes most people stand back in awe. When I witnessed first hand her athleticism I was very much inspired to help train her in the method's of Whole Brain Power™.

Suzanna has had success in women's natural (drug free) body building. In 1999, she won the International title for the "Miss Natural Olympia" women's body building championship. She previously had won the 1999 Redbull

National Roller Dancing competition. Five years ago, after 7 successful years in bodybuilding, she set her eyes on the game of tennis and it has become one of her passions.

Like others that have been shared videos of their ambidextrous athletic skills with the world on YouTube, I noticed Suzanna's dual-handed forehand posts on her YouTube site. I then visited her personal web site (http://www.sixftlion.com) and sent her an email inquiring whether she might be interested in learning more about how to enhance her ambidextrous tennis game. She responded soon after and said she had already seen our *www.wholebrainpower.net* site.

We soon realized that we have common contacts in the tennis world. When she saw the link on our site to the page of the Battistone brothers, she told me how she met them at an ambidextrous tennis camp run by Lionel Burt. I mentioned that I knew of Lionel Burt, the inventor of the two-handled tennis racquet. The Battistone brothers liked the unique racquet so much that they acquired the patent for the racquet which is named "The Natural."

For a few years, Lionel observed Suzanna practice her conventional tennis game of forehand and backhand style of play. He noticed her strong work ethic and persis-

Suzanna with the "Natural Tennis" two-handled tennis racquet.

223

tence in pursuit of her goals. He thought she would be a perfect spokes model for his racket, so he approached her and introduced the two-handled racket to her, explaining the benefits.

Suzanna was already well aware of the importance of balance in sports and in life. She's been teaching her balanced health philosophy to her clients for many years. She thought that playing tennis ambidextrously was an excellent idea: healthy for the body and the mind. She feels it is very important for the longevity of an athlete. As with Dr. McQueen, she believes many injuries result from the overuse of the dominant limb, and these slowly creep in from all the imbalances in the body.

She tried to hit with the two-handled racket and to her surprise the left side was not good, in fact, she felt clumsy on the left side, and her hand-eye coordination suffered. As an athlete, and an ex-champion bodybuilder, she couldn't accept that her body wouldn't function the same way on both sides. Thus, from this point forward she started to play ambidextrously. It's been an amazing journey, full of frustrations, realizations and great accomplishments. After pursuing her ambidextrous tennis goal for about a year she was ready to step into tournament quality play.

Within a week of our first few communications by phone and through e-mail, we arranged an in-person training session with my son Chris Lavery and me. She was already hitting the ball with great authority from both sides and she enjoyed the whole range of shot selection that Chris and I had in our arsenals. What impressed her most was that Chris and I each had the ability to serve with our opposite arms and to really put some "pop" into our serves. To this point, Suzanna has been mostly focusing on her ambidextrous ground stroke game, and did not put much effort into practicing her left-handed serving. The training session with Chris and me made her realize how important the left-handed serve is, and that more practice is all that was needed.

224

I explained the Mirror Imaging Methodology™ (MIM) theory and the connection to harnessing the subconscious strata of the brain through the use of the pen. I demonstrated my ambidextrous writing skills and showed her my working journals. When she saw page after page of the cursive penmanship, my drawings and the pertinent scientific articles, she understood how committed I was to my training methodologies.

Suzanna and me at our first training session.

Chris commented that only lately has his right-handed service motion finally felt natural. "For a while I never thought too much about my father's ideas about this handwriting training, but it really does work." I was proud of him for confirming that one of the most important aspects of the program can have immediate results. Without prompting Chris grabbed the *28 ounce Estwing claw hammer* and ripped off 100 hits in a row with the golf ball with each hand.

She soon invested in the hammers and a journal and began practicing the tenets of Whole Brain Power™ with great enthusiasm. Suzanna is a very intelligent woman who speaks six languages, is very mathematically inclined and has taught computer science at the University level. I felt honored to be working with such a sharp mind.

Penmanship is the gateway to accelerating motor control enhancement. Suzanna wasted no time at all writing in the left-handed style and in all of the prescribed directions. She called one day to proclaim, "Michael, the more I write left-handed the easier it is to write right-handed." She explained that at first it

225

was mentally exhausting and that she would even get a cramp in her hand. She sent me scans of her writing and told me how much fun it was to get back to the feeling of when she was a little girl in her home country where they disciplined the students to write properly. Her penmanship is quite "girly" looking, she asserted.

Suzanna's left-handed (non-dominant) forward writing.

I told her, "Find a style that is pleasing to you and develop the uniqueness that feels good to you. Bear in mind that if you intend to communicate to others through cursive writing, make a concerted effort to allow them the ease of reading your penmanship. The goal with writing should always be first and foremost the ability to communicate your thoughts to yourself and then to others."

Suzanna was receptive to my ideas and wrote on a daily basis. Within ten days she started to do long runs with the hammer drills. She was giving me constant progress reports on her tennis game and the breakthroughs that she was making with her left-handed serving motion. This woman truly is a testament to the plasticity that can occur in the human brain. She has not been content to just accept the principles that I promote, but seeks out and consumes the latest brain-training literature.

She called me one evening and said, "Michael, I am reading a wonderful book by Dr. Norman Doidge, it's called *The Brain That Changes Itself*. This book parallels so many of the things that you are teaching me. These stories of people who have miraculously come back from debilitating brain injuries and problems make me more motivated than ever. If people would just realize that it takes only 20 minutes a day to practice this stuff they would see what a difference it makes."

Suzanna gets ready to deliver a powerful forehand shot.

Suzanna is on the forefront of the ambidextrous revolution. She has come to realize that the old dominant/non-dominant model is one that does not offer nearly as much balance in the body or brain development. Even though Suzanna has re-wired her brain in each hemisphere over the last few years since starting to play tennis ambidextrously, she is now seeing an amazing acceleration of her skills and functional strength. She is committed to being a champion and has every intention of playing in National Championship Tennis tournaments.

The Les Taylor Story - a Man on a Mission

Soon after the Orange County Register article entitled *Mind and Muscle* by Tom Berg hit on May 12th, 2008, I got a call from Les Taylor, age 52. We spoke briefly about my program and what I could do to improve his golf game. Without hesitation, he signed up for *Whole Brain Power™* training. At the time, he did not realize that we had already met, but I recognized his name from a few years ago. I had entered a Long Drive contest in August 2005 at a golf course in Bakersfield, California. Les convincingly won the senior division (45-55 age group) even though the conditions that day were blustery and we were hitting into a strong head wind. He hit his first ball 335 yards and sat down. No one could beat that stroke and victory was his.

Michael at the driving range with Les Taylor

I had come to know of his teaching reputation as a long-ball coach, and was very interested in working with Les because of his own legendary long ball skills. He has coached two of the most recent World Champion Long Drivers.

He has also had success playing in tournaments, but beyond his golfing skills, it was his natural athleticism and "take no prisoners" attitude that inspired me to work with him.

The amazing journey that Les has undertaken in the last 90 days prior to the publishing of this first edition of *Whole Brain Power* is nothing short of miraculous. A natural right-hander, Les had never hit golf balls from the left-hand side. Now, three months later, he is hitting his left-hand driver 275 yards, and accurately. His left-handed golf swing is almost a perfect mirror image of his right-handed swing. How could this happen when the man is 52 years of age?

With Whole Brain Power™ age is only relative in relationship to your commitment to your training.

Les started to write left-handed mirror image immediately. Within days it was looking extremely fluent. He felt as though the mirror image writing was a dormant skill that always existed in his brain. I confirmed that sense by sharing that my co-author GW had experienced the same sensation the first time he wrote left-handed mirror image. For both of them it was easy and from that first sentence ever attempted in the mirror image (backwards left-handed penmanship) it

looked almost like their right-handed forward penmanship. Talk about proof that the brain controls the hands!

Les went out and bought the several types of hammers I recommended for his hammer drill training. He immediately started to practice the fine motor control skill of stopping the golf ball on his golf wedge, and on the face of his putter. To show his commitment to ambidexterity, he went out and purchased a complete set of left-handed golf clubs!

Les practicing his left-handed shots at Oak Creek driving range.

People are watching Les at the driving range and he tells me that the golfing crowd is getting quite curious. "What's up with this left-handed stuff?" they wonder aloud. I've been there and have heard that in my early days of ambidextrous golf. I warn him about the ramifications of stepping outside the box. He takes it all in stride because he's been around the block a few times and he's fully aware of the rich history of sports legends that have bucked the system.

"Michael, people must realize that different is not deficient. You have to accept the fact that some people think that your ideas are a little bit out there." He knows of Mac O'Grady, the ambidextrous golf guru who teaches out of Palm Springs, California. Mac has had his share of run-ins with the PGA. He has lobbied the PGA for years to allow him to enter tournaments as a right-handed pro and a left-handed amateur, all to no avail.

At the driving range, the new look by Les Taylor is to have two golf bags. People see him working on his swing from the opposite side (left) and it really "trips" them out. They have known this man for years and suddenly there is a change in him that they cannot explain. Their incredulity is heightened by the knowledge that he is a better than a scratch golfer at this point in the journey. "So why would you start to practice something that is so difficult to do?" they ask. He does not really want to talk about it; he prefers to post rounds of 67 instead!

Les is a different cat, that is for sure. When he visited our website, he saw the video clips of the different athletes and their skills, and he decided he wanted to join the baseball pitching competition. As with Mellick, he likes the idea of being the first man in history to pitch 90 mph from both sides. This twist in the training completely confused me. I believed at first that Les wanted to concentrate only on his golf, but sure enough, the story would get more complicated. When he told me that he had a special surprise to help his baseball pitching, and that it was coming in from Hawaii, I was intrigued.

"I just ordered the Speed Chain from a company that is on the cutting edge of helping athletes to improve their performances in a host of sports." Each time we talked about his golf he kept bringing up the 90/90 mph baseball pitching quest. To my amazement, he has been making phenomenal strides and now his pitching mechanics are getting smooth from

Les practices his baseball pitch with the Speed Chain.

both the left and the right hand sides. They are very much mirror imaged. This transfer of skills is paralleling what is occurring with his golf swings from both sides.

231

The athleticism that Les is developing at age 52 is Whole Brain Power™ at work. As I have at age 49, he is also seeing tremendous change in his muscle density in his forearms and back muscles. Again, we believe this is *steroidogenesis* at work. He is driving a golf ball on the course over 350 yards and hitting his fairway shot on a par 5 with his five iron, 230 yards. This is the stuff of the top PGA pros, and only a handful of players at that. The brain of this man is still expanding and making new connections. I believe it has to be related to the increase of the insulation on the white matter tracks; how else can one explain the tremendous skill that he has developed in a three-month period? It is his whole golf game that is improving, too, including his chipping and putting. Any golfer knows the saying, "You drive for show and you putt for dough." Don't bet against Les, with either his putting, chipping or his driving.

The important message in the Les Taylor story is that this can work for anyone. It worked for VJ Singh after he started to practice opposite side golf. As a matter of fact, some of VJ's best golf came after his sessions with ambidextrous golf guru Mac O'Grady. VJ can smash a drive from the left side 260 yards and put it straight down the fairway. He even turns his right-handed iron upside down in tournament play if the situation calls for it and strikes the ball left-handed.

I recently spoke to Les about how well his right side golf game is doing and he said, "I have never hit a ball this well from the right side. I just played the Black Gold course up here in Yorba Linda, and shot a 67. The round included eight birdies and three bogies. I feel that I have more capacity to dial it in at any time these days. There definitely is a heightened sense of focus and my ball-striking ability is the purest it has ever been." From my perspective, Les Taylor is to the golf world what Satchel Page was to the baseball world. For perspective, Page pitched his last major league game at age 59 and worked three innings and struck out six guys. The inspiring aspect of Les's story is that he is still getting stronger and more coordinated in many areas of his athletic pursuits *at age 52.*

Les is also a father and his children are beginning to understand how this all works. He has a boy named Sean (coincidentally, both GW and I have sons named Sean as well), age eleven, and now father and son are practicing ambidextrous pitching. Dad is showing that you can teach an "old dog" new tricks, and Sean doesn't want to be left behind! Now his boy will push through the awkwardness of his ambidextrous training until he gains the muscle memory to throw strikes left-handed.

Exciting things seem to be in store for Les. It has always been his intention to secure sponsorship for his bid to play on a professional tour. He certainly does not lack for power, and his short game is better than ever. So it just might be in the cards for him. *The Best Damn Sports Show* has expressed interest in *The Taylor Story,* and if this happens he will most probably get an opportunity to show a national audience his metamorphosis as an ambidextrous athlete.

Les writing both left mirror image and right hand simultaneously.

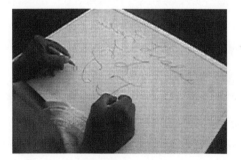

Dante Salazar Story - Mind and Muscle

Lavery and Salazar with sledgehammers.

Dante Salazar, 27, a college student and an aspiring attorney, happened to read Tom Berg's Orange County Register article in May 2008. Soon after scrutinizing the basic tenets that Tom described on page two of his article, Dante began the alphabet drills and the numbers training. He saw results and this led him to email me. He described his goals to attend Law School next year and a willingness to commit to the disciplines of Whole Brain Power™. We met at the local athletic field soon afterwards and I started him on the program.

Dante is another person, like Les, who is "going off the charts." One of his immediate goals is to take the LSAT and get a super high score, so his is more of an academic goal with his Whole Brain Power™ training than an athletic one. Nontheless, after only two months his athletic prowess is now bending the minds of the boxers at the gym where he works out. He has always felt frustration at not having balance in the size and definition of his arm muscles, especially the biceps and triceps muscle groups. He added the hammer drills to his penmanship training and began on the memorization of the powers of two to 2^{30}. Within weeks he was seeing phenomenal results. By his own account he is

234

leaner and his muscle tissue is denser then ever before, accounting for an increase in five pounds of additional muscle weight.

Like Les at the golfing range, people in the gym where Dante boxes are starting to gossip about his rapid strength improvement. He is doing six, one-legged squats in a row, and from each side. For perspective, he never was able to do a single one-legged squat prior to participating in WBP training. This feat, among other dramatic improvements in Dante's speed and quickness, has his buds wondering, "Dante looks as though he is juicing." I shared with him my theory of how Whole Brain Power™ taps in to the well of steroidogenesis. I asked him to research pregnenolone and the endogenous steroid cascade informa-

Dante in the middle of a one-legged squat.

tion easily available on the web. He began to experiment with an increase in egg consumption as he learned of the importance of cholesterol synthesis into pregnenolone and other endogenously produced anabolic steroids.

I caution readers about increasing cholesterol consumption without first reviewing this dietary change with their doctor. If you have a predisposition to elevated LDL's (low density lipoproteins) then increasing blood plasma levels of cholesterol is not advised at all. However, if one's cholesterol levels are normal and the blood pressure is normal and ph levels are optimum, then cholesterol *can act* as the precursor to maintaining proper cellular function if you are outputting enough mental and physical energy.

235

Dante tells me that he looks healthier than ever. In theory, because Dante *is* outputting so much more mental activity, he is raising his neural activity and consequently the levels of beta wave activity. This then leads to increased ATP production from a greater efficiency of the astrocyte cells and more glucose absorption. One side benefit that Dante is getting from the program is that he is learning about organic chemistry and actively stressing his short-term memory.

I teach him about the gesture preparation theory as it is applicable to being a great communicator. When we meet in person we play the five-syllable word game and he enjoys it immensely. I stress the less-is-more concept. "Dante, when you become articulate with your communication skills, you will be that much more effective at defending an argument in court. Eliminating the fill words takes more energy than you would imagine."

He responded. "You're right."

"No Dante, I am correct." It takes great energy to output flawless language, verbally or in writing. I continue my lessons with Dante by impressing upon him that if you want to be a great speaker, you must become a great writer, and the best way to achieve that goal is for you to put pen to paper. The great thinkers in the past all had excellent penmanship skills. As of his latest e-mail to me, he is pouring through the dictionary gathering up a bounty of four, five and six syllable words. He is entering them into his journal in the most exquisite left-handed penmanship possible. Each time he writes them down he is growing his hippocampi and improving neural plasticity. He is now approaching the memorization of 2 to the 50th power. This expanded use of his energy during the day is tasking his brain so much that Dante is experiencing more restful sleep. He said to me that in the past people have always considered him to be a workaholic and that as a result he was looking run down and haggard. "Back then, they were telling me to slow down. Now the opposite is happening; people say I look great and they want to know the secret of my restful sleep."

I explained to him about nutritional changes that are important for maintaining good health, such as proper pH balance, glucose and insulin levels, and the dangers of hydrogenated fats.

After just two months, his cursive writing looks 1000% better than it did on day one of his training. He takes notes in class with his left hand and his retention of new information is steadily improving. He is bouncing golf balls off the hammers in his home and his roommates that are sitting around watching television are wondering what's up, saying "Dante is really acting weird these days." One of them even jokingly asked him, "Hey dude, are you in a cult or something?"

He chuckles to himself and rips off another run of 100 bounces on the sledgehammer without a miss. He states that he is more energetic, alert and alive than at any other time in his life. He is working with the whole arsenal of hammers recommended in the program. He invested in the heavier sledge hammers and he is starting to impress at least one professional boxer down at the gym who has noticed the dramatic changes in Dante and is curious how he has achieved those results without steroids. What this professional boxer sees is Dante's transformation in functional strength and hyper hand-eye coordination, not the absolute strength gained from pumping heavy weights in the gym. Outside the gym, Dante is seeing increased traffic to his political blog, which he believes is directly correlated to his improved written communications skills from his Whole Brain Power™ memorization and penmanship training. Dante is a man on a path to make his case to the world around him.

Patricia Ford - Reunited with her piano playing

Pat Ford and GW, August 6th, 2008

After a long career as a manager in the computer operations at a *Children's Hospital* in Seattle, Pat Ford "retired" to become a full-time owner and chief post-production manager of her own video production facility cleverly titled, *Ford Video*. That was more than twenty years ago. Co-author GW, a long-time filmmaker in search of an edit facility found Ford Video back in 1996 and it quickly became his home away from home for seven years, editing more than 100 videos at Pat's place during that time.

GW came to know the now 77-year-old mother of seven and grandmother of 14 as one of the smartest people he's ever known. Thus, it was only natural for him to think of Pat as a potential practitioner of Whole Brain Power™.

He began teaching her and her son Matt the training methodologies on June 6th, 2008. At the conclusion of the two hour session, GW gave Pat his two rubber mallets so that she could get started right away.

On Day One Pat recorded in her journal, in both right hand cursive and left hand mirror image her results, "Today I started my Whole Brain Power training by bouncing the golf ball off a rubber mallet three times with my right hand. I was not as successful with my left handed hammer drill, barely getting two hits before missing."

As we wrote this case study, Pat was on Day 60 of her training. She likes to practice her hammer drills next to her bed "to avoid chasing the ball down the hallway!" she exclaimed. She recently surpassed 80-hit runs without a miss on three occasions with her right hand, and regularly has runs in the mid-20s with her left hand.

Pat practices her left-handed mirror image writing.

Pat in her backyard on a left-hand run.

Pat credits her mirror image left hand penmanship drills with much of her overall skill improvement. She is determined to bring her left hand hammer skill up to compete with her right.

"I love the fact that there is a sense of achievement every time I surpass my personal best. It keeps me striving for higher and higher records." As her family will attest, Pat is a tenacious learner and will achieve whatever goal she sets her sights on.

For her memory drills, she and her son Matt have developed a long list of difficult memory exercises to help improve their hippocampi. That list includes the 50 United States by geographical region, the 13 original states, the 12 Apostles, the 9 Planets, the 7 Deadly Sins, the 7 Holy Virtues and, of course, they are working on the Powers of 2 to the 30th power.

Pat is most proud of her application of her amazing new memory ability. Sixty-two years ago was the last time she memorized sheet music for the piano. It's been forty years since she's played the piano. Inspired by her Whole Brain Power™ training, Pat borrowed an electronic piano keyboard from one of her five daughters, and picked out *Josef Hayden's "Gypsy Rondo,"* a six-page piece of sheet music for piano.

Pat playing Hayden's "Gypsy Rondo" by memory.

To her great surprise she has memorized the entire piece and now enjoys playing it from start to finish. Now Pat laments, "I guess I'll probably have get myself a real piano now, this is too much fun.

Pat's right hand signature.

Pat's left-handed mirror image signature.

Pat's left-handed mirror image signature flipped over to match her right-hand.

Whole Brain Power™ All Star Pat Ford

241

Rolly White

My good buddy Rolly, a conservative businessman from Orange County, has a knack for carefully analyzing anything new that appears on his plate. I'd say he has a healthy skepticism about newfangled ideas and he found my *ambidextrous revolution* pretty far-fetched. My first golf teacher pondered my Whole Brain Power™ training methodologies for four years before he committed to become a practitioner.

It was the summer of 2007 when Rolly finally began working the program seriously. So what was the catalyst that finally got him off the sidelines and into the game? It was witnessing the major transformation of my golf game. Apparently, the master (Rolly) was tired of watching *"Grasshopper"* (me) pluck the pebble from his hand.

We used to go out golfing three to four times per week in the early mornings. I was still being given the complimentary golf by the Club and Rolly was in Aliso Viejo's Player Development Program, which included early morning rounds for only $20. During this period of the spring and early summer of 2007, *Aliso Viejo* was in the process of building a new Club House and redesigning the course layout, so they had only 11 holes open.

During this stretch of my golfing journey I was posting very good scores on this shortened course, one I had come to know like an old glove. My score card would usually say one to two under par after the eleven holes. It was enough to capture Rolly's attention. He is a very competitive athlete and we would talk "smack" as many golfers do. Whoever would control the tee box had the bragging rights for the day. For non-golfers, this implies that the person who wins the last hole is allowed to tee off first on the next hole. One day I was "on fire," ending at four under par while Rolly scored a miserable eight over par for the eleven holes. He joked about forgetting to put his "clown suit" on for the morning round. That was the straw.

On our next round at Aliso Viejo, as I was approaching the tee box on the 7th hole he asked, "So, where should I begin?"

"Begin with what?" I kidded with him.

"With this Whole Brain Power stuff, because I'm tired of watching you, my golf student, kick my ass."

At last, my old friend was willing to have some fun with this ambidextrous revolution. "It has much to do with balance and memory. There are times when you hit the ball perfectly and you have a run of great golf for three to four holes. Then, bam, all the wheels fall off your cart. I believe that you could become a much better golfer if you would let your whole brain in on the equation." That is I when asked him about his ability to juggle and his level of ambidexterity. He said that he had never juggled, and that he had no skill with his left hand.

Our conversation continued to the parking lot after our round. I went over to my truck and pulled out my bag of hammers and the handwritten working notes for this book.

"So Rolly, how much do you task your brain during the day with cursive penmanship? Do you ever train both of your hemispheres by writing cursive with your right hand *and* mirror image with your left hand?

243

"Of course, not," he shrugged.

I pointed to a page of my handwriting where the first line was mirror imaged and the second line was the normal direction left to right across the page. Rolly noticed there were no pencil lines. "Writing on blank paper is all about spatial intelligence and firing neurons in the deep strata of your brain," I explained.

"Do me a favor, hold up your hands like this." He held his hands up in the air. "Look at these gifts and admit to me that you use them in a lop-sided manner that may, or *may not be*, what nature intended. The same could be said of the way that you are using both hemispheres of your brain. My theory is that *your hands grow your brain*, but if you do all your large and fine motor skills with just your right hand, then the muscle development, the reflexes, all the signals are out of balance. You hold the golf club with two hands; but the left hand and the right hemisphere are neglected, not only in your golf swing, but in most of the waking hours of your life."

"I would argue, Rolly, that the reason your golf game has not improved in the last decade is not a symptom of your aging, but the result of your brain not providing your body with the balance it needs to take your game to a new level." I had his attention now and drove hard to make my point. "Why is it that your nephew Harrison is making such great strides in his baseball and golf skills and you're not?"

Rolly offered, "Is it because he is young (age thirteen) and his brain is able to learn quickly, while my brain is getting too set in its ways ?"

"Absolutely correct. Now let's make your brain act young again." His eyes lit up at this suggestion. At this point in his life Rolly was on a supervised hormone replacement program. He had been doing extensive research on life extension and this concept of de-aging his brain was highly intoxicating. "Okay, do you believe that your right hemisphere is still expanding its neural connections? Do you believe that your grip on your left hand is as strong as your right hand?"

At this point I stuck out my *left hand* to shake his hand and he extended his left hand. "This is what I am talking about," as I applied some pressure with my grip. He knew that it was not my intention to hurt his hand but to make a point.

"I get where you are going with this, Michael," he said.

I opened my sports bag with its collection of hammers and took out a four-pound sledge. I gave it to him to hold and then I got out a tennis ball and had him do a few bounces on it. "Okay bud, your first assignment as a full-fledged practitioner of Whole Brain Power™ is to go to Home Depot and get two, four-pound sledge hammers. They'll cost about twenty bucks each. It will be the best investment you could ever make for your golf game."

I gave him some tips on how to climb the ladder (steadily improve the number of hits with the ball on the hammer without a miss), and I discussed the importance of memorizing the powers of two up to 2^{30}. That night I emailed him the full training program, including the alphabet drills, coding drills, and penmanship drills.

A few days later I called to schedule our golf game and he excitedly stated he had the alphabet drills honed solidly as well as the memorization of the Powers of two to the 30th power. Amazingly, he had been spending time on YouTube watching some juggling training videos and he was starting to get the juggling skill down.

Juggling coordination was the breakthrough that he needed. He also started training with a rubber mallet and a four-pound sledge hammer using a tennis ball. I taught him *the Buzz game* and he got the gist of it very quickly. We soon started challenging each other to rounds of *Buzz* and would complicate the game by adding a 4th rule in which one would also have to *Buzz* on Prime #'s in the teens and the thirties. The #'s would be 13, 19, 31, and this brain game entertained us as we practiced the "art of being in focus."

He nailed the alphabet sequences and the coding aspects of the program without hesitation. I also introduced him to other Whole Brain Power ™ practitioners here in Orange County and they bonded quickly. He gave the alphabet and the powers of two assignments to his two nieces, Natalie age seven and Alexandria age nine, and they had them memorized in a matter of days. He would then report back to me and exclaim, "You would not believe how fast my young relatives are getting this stuff."

About thirty days after being on the intensified program Rolly started to hit the ball better than ever. He began to clear the fairway traps with his drives and then stick his second shot for a chance at birdie. His improving power on the golf

course began to carry over to other areas of his life, from his more erect posture to more confidence in his business dealings. He was a man being transformed by his brain training program.

Two months later Rolly called. "Hey, Hammer, something very unusual is happening to me. I am feeling a surge of power in my tennis game and my softball game that I have never felt before in my life. I am seeing the ball better than ever in my tennis playing and easily beating guys that I was on a par with just four months ago. And I'm hitting the ball out of the park in softball. It's insane."

I explained my theory to him that what he was experiencing may have to do with something that neuroscientists called *steroidogenesis*. "Without going into it in too much depth, the gist of steroidogenesis is that if you have all of the elements working properly, you can naturally lift the performance of your endocrine system and thus raise your hormone levels back to youthful levels."

"That's very interesting," said Rolly, " because I just got back my latest report from the lab concerning my hormone levels. My latest readings on testosterone were completely off the charts for a man my age. Hell, they were good for a man half my age! Get this, Michael, my doctor has to reduce my hormone replacement dosage now. She's going to test again in two months to see where I'm at."

Two months passed and again the levels were higher than expected even though he had reduced his artificial hormone therapy. Now the decision was made by his endocrinologist to completely take Rolly off the testosterone replacement.

By this time he was so motivated by what was happening to him that I started to call him one of the *Whole Brain Power™ All Stars*. Eight months into the program and Rolly had mastered the memorization of two to the 60th power and was writing daily in his journal in all of the penmanship sequences. He also invested in six-pound and eight-pound short-handled sledgehammers.

The more he experienced his potential using Whole Brain Power™ in the training of his brain and body, the more he encouraged me to stay the course and finish this book. He saw the greatest value of my theories on training the brain to be in transferring my skills to other people.

Clearly, Rolly has improved his motor functions (ambidextrously) and his memory processing which support my theories that he has created new growth in his brain. Scientific evidence indicates that his rapid improvements in strength and hand-eye coordination and improved reflexes were the result of an elevation in his endogenously produced pregnenolone levels. The data suggests that this increase in the master steroid has a direct correlation on mood and can directly affect one's personality. Sometimes that mood-altering feeling manifests itself in improved motivation to achieve. In Rolly's own words, his motivation levels are off the charts as is the athletic performance of this man who turned 60 this year. He is now moving on to higher levels of Whole Brain Power™ training, hitting golf balls from the *left side* and learning *left-handed* tennis strokes as well as the *left-handed* serve. He is certainly inspiring those who live in his community in Mission Viejo, California. He has his dad Harry White, age 91, on the program and he tells me that his father is enjoying it very much. When Tom Berg, the writer for the *Orange County Register,* became interested in the

Mind and Muscle story, he pulled me aside and said, "Michael, of all of the practitioners of your program, Rolly White's story is the one that my readers will relate to most. Not that the other people who are doing the ambidextrous feats are not impressive, but the baby boomers will be very intrigued by him." This was after Rolly did a hammer drill demonstration using the eight-pound sledgehammer and golf ball. Now that's a Whole Brain Power™ All Star training routine! Since the Berg article hit on May 12th, 2008, Rolly has taken the Powers of two into the stratosphere having wired his memory with 2^{70}, eclipsing even my ability to recite up to 2^{64}. Now it is me in the role of "Master" and Rolly as *"Grasshopper"* snatching the pebble from my hand! Seeing Rolly achieve so much through his Whole Brain Power™ training is the best thing that could ever have happened to me.

Soon afterwards he gave me an article in *Fortune* concerning business tycoon, T. Boone Pickens, and the brain scans that they had performed upon the multi-billionaire. Even though Mr. Pickens happens to be 80 years of age, his brain has the functional ability of a 55-year-old man. This article had Rolly really turned on because it hit home as to what I had been telling him only months prior. "Michael, I am so much sharper in my recall of technical data, and I believe it gives me an edge in my business meetings. I do not have to refer to my notes nearly as much as I used to."

"Now I know what this gesture preparation and impulse control can really do for a person. I recently had an experience in a board meeting where I could have easily lost my composure. But I maintained my cool. In the past, I might have acted in a way that was detrimental to my objective."

"I can honestly say that at this point of my life I have never felt better. I am playing the best golf, tennis and softball of my life. The fact that I have recently posted four rounds of golf in the 70s should be testament enough to the affects of Whole Brain Power™ working miracles in my life."

Harry White (Rolly's dad), me and Rolly.

Harry White

Rolly's dad, Harry White, 91-years-young, is a devoted practitioner of Whole Brain Power™. Rolly inspired him to join the program more through actions than words. Harry had been hearing his son talk about the benefits of the training, but it was not until he saw Rolly post a round of 73 on a difficult golf course at Palm Valley Country Club that he asked how he could get involved in this new training program that had Rolly playing the best golf of his life. Rolly was

thrilled that his dad wanted to learn "the secret" of his consistently playing at or near par golf.

Rolly began with the basics, teaching his dad to write left-handed mirror image, memorize two to the powers of 30, and to do the hammer drills. Recently, Rolly showed me a letter that his father had written to him that was done completely left-handed. It looked very good. Rolly was beaming because he has his dad all fired up about the program.

His transformation is fascinating to watch as he is only 60 days into the program. He's hot on the track to memorize Mark Anthony's well-known and oft-quoted speech from

Harry bouncing a tennis ball on a rubber mallet. Shakespeare.

"Friends, Romans and countrymen, lend me your ears. I come to bury Caesar not to praise him. The evil that men do lives after them, the good is oft interred with their bones. So let it be with Caesar..." Thus far, Harry has memorized 35 lines of this famous speech.

Harry claims he's playing the best tennis of his life.

Harry is now writing left-handed penmanship as well as practicing his right-handed cursive. One can imagine how much greater long-term potentiation Harry is experiencing in areas of his motor strip, pre-motor strip, the cerebellum, basal ganglia, pre-frontal and frontal lobes. And as a result of higher levels of ATP production, his brain appears to be functioning at a higher level than he's experienced in decades. The outcome? Better control of his tennis stroke, (or as Harry describes it) "...better than ever."

As Harry's family and friends see his improved energy levels and obvious coordination increases, they scratch their heads in disbelief. After all, Harry is in his 9th decade of life. Yes, he is more motivated than ever to improve his quality of life. Rolly chimes in, "My dad has people buzzing. He says he's hitting the tennis ball better than at any point in his life."

253

(Check out Harry's page on our web site to see this nonagenarian in action on the courts and his recitation of Shakespeare.)

The amazing thing is not simply this 91-year-old Whole Brain Power phenom's accomplishments, but the impact he is having on his family, friends and community. Harry is so pleased by the transformation that he has experienced that he wants to share his story and training regimen with the people in his retirement community. As of the publication of this book, he has set up what amounts to a weekly "Whole Brain Power™ training club". After an initial presentation to 65 members in mid-September, we anticipate at least 50 of Harry's neighbors will attend these weekly sessions, perhaps more. We'll report updates on how this is going on our website. If this takes off at Harry's community, we anticipate the template created can be replicated at retirement communities elsewhere. Tom Berg with the Orange County Register is writing a feature story on Harry and his community of Whole Brain Power practitioners.

But Harry's biggest thrill is competing against his grandchildren Harrison (13), Alexandria (9) and Natalie (7), in Whole Brain Power™ drills such as the hammer drills, alphabet game and the Buzz game. Harry's enthusiasm for his new brain training and his sense of accomplishment is infectious, as everyone

Harry and his grandkids, Harrison, Alexandria and Natalie.

around him is seeing the obvious changes in his mental acuity and improved athleticism. As Harry says, "The best is yet to come."

Harry's grandchildren practice their hand-eye coordination drills.

Natalie uses the ping pong paddle and ping pong ball in her practice.

Alexandria bounces the golf ball off of a mallet.

Harrison rips off a run of 200 hits with the dual hammer drill.

Chapter 8

NUTRITION

"The doctor of the future will give no medicine, but will invest patients in the care of the human frame, in diet and the prevention of disease."

-- *Thomas Edison*

In this chapter we will discuss some of the basics about how what we eat and drink interacts with our brain and body. Proper education of what to eat and just as importantly -- why -- has never been an important part of the educational system or mass market information. Supermarkets are stocked to the ceiling with highly processed foods that the food industry would rather you eat and not question the bio-chemical results of its products on your body and brain. There is an old saying, "You are what you eat." which is accurate in terms of your body's chemistry. Other factors influence what we consume and how we digest foods, such as our genetic predisposition, cultural mores or availability of food seasonally or geographically. Setting aside those factors, I want to review some of the latest research and revelations about nutrition and how best to incorporate healthy choices into our diet.

There are seven areas of nutritional guidance I want you to learn about and hopefully adapt into your decisions as you grocery shop, prepare a meal at home or dine out.

The Glycemic Index - *The glycemic index is a measure of how quickly the carbohydrates in food are absorbed into our bodies and converted to glucose.*

Insulin - *Insulin produced and released into the blood by the pancreas is a master hormone of metabolism. It assists with the assimilation of glucose by cells in our body.*

pH Levels - *The health of the body is very much governed by the measure of the balance of acidity versus alkalinity in our blood and bodily fluids referred to as the pH level. Optimally, our blood will have a pH of 7.4, or slightly alkaline.*

Protein/Calcium Connection - *Consuming high levels of protein actually result in our body using stores of calcium in our bones to help balance our pH levels which ultimately leads to osteoporosis -- the degeneration of our bone density.*

Hydrogenated Fats - *Partially hydrogenated oils make you gain weight the same way that saturated fats do -- by making you consume even more fat to get the essential fatty acids you need.*

Somatids - *When your immune system is weakened, somatids, the smallest living organism known to science, expand from their three basic forms to as many as sixteen higher pathogenic states. It is the mutation or evolution of the three basic somatids that interfere with cell activity and the immune system making your body prone to disease and infection.*

Trophology - Food Combining - *Correctly combining foods is important to proper digestion, cholesterol and metabolism. Without complete digestion, nutrients cannot be fully extracted and assimilated by the body.*

The Glycemic Index

The *Glycemic Index* is a measure of how quickly the carbohydrates in food are absorbed into our bodies and converted to glucose. As mentioned in Chapter Two, that three-pound organic computer called your brain can consume up to as much as 30% of the available glucose in your blood stream. When it comes to sustained brain power, I recommend foods with a low glycemic index, that is, foods that will make glucose available over an extended period of time. Foods with low glycemic levels are complex carbohydrates found in the cellulose or fiber of the starches of grains, beans, potatoes, fruits, vegetables or lentils. They are also found as everyday food in the form of oats, apples, oranges, bananas, rye, brown rice, whole wheat.

Foods with high glycemic levels include simple sugars or refined carbohydrates that cause major swings in blood sugar levels. White breads, sweetened cereals, pastries, croissants, baguettes, white rice, cakes, sweets, chocolates, alcoholic drinks, sweetened cold drinks and other foods highly processed with sugar sweeteners are foods with high glycemic levels.

Refined carbohydrates and excess sugar deplete your body's vitamins (especially the *B* vitamins) and minerals, and supply almost nothing in exchange. Furthermore, they are implicated in fatigue, eating disorders, diabetes, learning and memory problems, hyperactivity and attention deficit problems, Alzheimer's and heart disease as well as emotional responses such as aggression, anxiety, phobias and suicidal thoughts. All these negative effects of excess sugar are often referred to as *"the sugar blues"*. Even though a bowl of sugary cereal and a bowl of old-fashioned oatmeal may have the same number of carbohydrates, they have very different glycemic loads, that is, how fast or slow they are converted to glucose. Sugary cereals and other types of pastry foods get into your body quickly and cause a spike in blood-sugar levels, but soon after, your energy levels fall dramatically. Oatmeal, on the other hand, is absorbed slowly, which promotes a slow rise in blood sugar and enough energy to last for hours after consumption.

Results of a study in which children were given either a sweetened cereal or a bowl of oatmeal with a natural sweetener (honey) showed that when given academic tasks, such as memorizing the names of countries on a map, the oatmeal eaters did up to twenty percent better than the sweetened cereal consumers. It should be noted that the calorie count was the same, except that the oatmeal had a higher amount of protein and fiber than the highly processed sweetened cereal. Processed sugars not only affects our glucose, blood sugar and energy levels, but it also affects our cognitive functions giving us those proverbial "blood sugar blues".

Disglycemia and toxic glucose

When your blood sugar levels can't be kept stable glucose becomes toxic, creating a condition called *disglycemia*. This is a diabetic condition in which glucose becomes toxic to the brain, resulting in eye, nerve and brain damage that some diabetics experience. Keeping your blood sugar levels stable is of vital importance to allow proper delivery of glucose to the cells and for early clearance of glucose from the bloodstream. As with so much of what I have discussed in this book, achieving homeostasis within your brain and body should be your goal. The two most important things to keep in balance are your glucose levels and your pH levels because when these two are chronically out of balance disease and ill health are sure to follow. Ways that your glucose can get out of balance most easily are through *passive virtual stress* (as discussed in depth in Chapter 6: System Killers) or through the *consumption of too much food containing simple sugars or refined carbohydrates, or the lack of physical or mental*

259

exercise. The combination of experiencing passive virtual stress (watching tv) while consuming refined sugary food is asking for trouble.

Refined sugar, adrenalin and glucocortocoids (cortisol)

Excess simple sugars and unrefined carbohydrates also spike adrenalin and cortisol levels and makes for an undesirable chemistry for the brain and the body. If your blood sugar level dips, you have one of two ways to raise and stabilize it again. First, is to consume more glucose in the form of food or drink. Second, if glucose levels are not raised by more food and drink, your body will correct the problem by increasing the level of the stress hormones, adrenalin and glucocortocoids (cortisol). When the body detects the presence of low blood sugar, glucocorticoids are secreted by the adrenals to minimize glucose absorption by the brain and the body. This is why it is better to have six smaller meals per day than to skip meals and then eat excessively. As discussed in Chapter 6, glucocortocoids prevent glucose from docking with cells throughout the body and brain and result in excess glucose being transported to the liver, where it is converted into triglycerides (fats) and leads to inflammation in the brain and the body. When our bodies boost the production of glucocortocoids to deal with virtual stress or nutritional stress, the result is a downward spiral likely to lead to to obesity, Type 2 diabetes and inflammation of the brain.

Insulin

Insulin produced and released into the blood by the pancreas is a master hormone of metabolism. It affects virtually every cell in the body and regulates blood sugar, controls the storage of fat, helps direct the functions of amino acids, fatty acids, and carbohydrates, and it regulates the liver's synthesis of cholesterol. It also functions as a growth hormone, affecting appetite control, kidney function and much more. But insulin can be a double edged sword.

When the body senses a rush of sugar, (from eating too much of the wrong kind of food, such as refined sugars and starches) your pancreas panics and over-compensates, producing an overabundance of insulin in an effort to normalize (lower) blood sugar levels. This rush of insulin causes blood sugar to plummet. Some people experience nervousness, shaking, mental fogginess, and profuse sweating if their blood sugar levels drop too precipitously. This condition is called *hypoglycemia*. Too much insulin on a consistent basis creates a set of serious problems including:

• *raising blood pressure and cholesterol levels*

• *storing food as fat instead of using it for fuel*

• *causing the kidney's to retain excess fluid,*

• *damaging arteries*

• *elevating triglycerides*

• *and changing needed protein and sugar into fat*

Insulin Resistance

Learn to recognize the signs of *insulin resistance*:
• *fatigue*
• *low blood sugar, and sleepiness*
• *mental fogginess*
• *intestinal bloating*
• *increased fat storage*
• *increased triglycerides*
• *increased blood pressure*
• *depression*

One of the toxic effects of high insulin is that cells become insulin resistant as they try to protect themselves. The pancreas pumps out more and more insulin because the receptors on the cells are no longer reacting properly to it. This causes the insulin sensors to be less responsive as they become more and more overloaded. Inevitably, your body demands more and more insulin as it attempts to affect cells. The result for some people is the onset of Type 2 diabetes as they become so resistant to insulin that their pancreas can no longer manufacture enough insulin to effectively lower blood sugar. But scientists are now beginning to correlate even more serious health problems related to insulin resistance including cardiovascular disease, high blood pressure, high cholesterol levels, and osteoporosis. They are addressing the insulin resistance issue itself as the trigger to these other problems.

Excess Insulin: Magnesium, Calcium, Vitamin C, Body Fat

Excess insulin interferes with *magnesium* storage in cells, leading to high blood pressure. Thus if your cells become insulin resistant you can't store magnesium and it is excreted in the urine. Magnesium plays an important role in muscle relaxation. Since the smooth muscle cells called the *endothelial cells* need magnesium to relax and then contract, without proper amounts of magnesium in your blood stream, your blood vessels constrict. The result: higher blood pressure.

Excessive insulin also depletes *calcium* from the system. Both calcium and magnesium are instrumental in the bone building matrix, therefore an ongoing deficiency of calcium and magnesium sets the stage for osteoporosis. When insulin levels are too high it affects the body's ability to absorb *vitamin C*. Since vitamin C is essential to the manufacture of collagen, the main structural protein that makes bone, muscle fiber, tendons, ligaments, skin, hair, and strong arterial structures, the body is compromised on all fronts. Since Vitamin C and glucose (sugar) have similar chemical structures, they compete when entering cells. If there is more glucose and higher insulin then there is going to be less vitamin C allowed into the cell.

Eating foods that cause a spike in blood sugar create excess food "energy" in your system. It is not as simple as caloric input and caloric expenditure. This might be true when the body is in a state of homeostasis, however, when the wrong foods are eaten and you're in a state of passive stress, then there can be systemic weight gain. In order to have someplace to put this excess energy the body makes *new fat cells*, with insulin being the facilitator for the creation of these new cells. Since cholesterol is the framework for cells, when new fat cells are created, so is cholesterol.

To recap this section on the Glycemic Index.
---> *Excess glucose* results from eating too much refined sugars and carbohydrates

---> *Excess insulin* results from excess glucose

---> *Excess fat* storage results from excess insulin

---> *Excess cholesterol* results from excess fat storage

---> Decreased magnesium, calcium and vitamin C result from excess insulin

So if you don't eat foods that cause an excess production of glucose and insulin in the first place, you won't trigger the fat storage cycle. Foods that enter the bloodstream slowly do not cause excess insulin to be produced and therefore don't contribute significantly toward fat storage, provided that cortisol levels (and passive virtual stress levels) are under control. It is the combination of high processed sugar foods and carbohydrates, and high levels of passive stress, that trigger the greatest likelihood of fat storage.

Ironically, people believe that they need to be on a low fat diet to lose weight and so they are taking the good fats out of their diet and eating more refined sugars instead. Eating healthy, natural dietary fat does not create body fat unless it's eaten with glucose raising carbohydrates. The body will use dietary fat, and stored body fat, for energy. The key to maintaining normal body weight is to have the food you eat be used as energy to fuel your body. Both fat and fiber in natural foods help to slow the rate of entry of carbohydrates. Plus, healthy fat contains the hormone *cholecystokinin (CKK)* that tells the brain you're full and to stop eating. This is why non-fat foods are disastrous for people trying to lose weight, and to make matters worse, many non-fat foods replace the fat with extra sugar. Take a look at the labels and you'll notice fat has been replaced by various forms of sugar, like corn syrup, fructose, etc. – insulin raisers.

Processed foods such as bran muffins, rice cakes or breakfast cereals that are perceived to be high in fiber, and therefore "healthy", are deceiving because they contain the wrong kind of fiber, called *insoluble fiber.* Natural foods contain *soluble fiber.* The more a carbohydrate is "processed" (using man-made processing methods), the more you break down its cell structure, and the more it negatively affects insulin levels. This also applies to foods that are specifically processed to make them "instant", like instant potatoes, instant rice, and instant oatmeal. Processing negatively affects the beneficial soluble fiber.

Natural, unprocessed foods also provide many vitamins, minerals, enzymes, and other nutrients that have been removed or destroyed in the refining process. These nutrients contribute toward keeping the whole body in good repair. When cells are not insulin resistant the entire process of sugar regulation is kept in balance. Then, if the body goes for a long period without food, fuel reserves stored in the liver are called upon giving a steady supply of glucose, or fuel.

The food refining process creates "sugar concentrates" that spike blood sugar because they have been stripped of their naturally occurring fiber. In addition, refining strips food of vital nutrients necessary for the body's energy requirements, repair, and digestion. Artificially adding synthetic nutrients back into refined foods so they can be labeled "fortified and enriched" creates harmful nutrient imbalances. Fortification adds only a handful of virtually useless synthetic vitamins and minerals instead of the full contingent of inter-reacting, co-factors that existed naturally before the refining process. Most nutritionists offer the following guidelines which I ascribe to: refrain from eating processed foods packaged in a box, a bag, a can or some kind of package. The more you rely on foods processed for convenient preparation, the greater you put your health at risk.

Understanding pH Balance

The health of the body and mind are very much governed by the measure of acid versus alkaline in our blood and bodily fluids referred to as pH levels. The pH scale ranges from 1-14. The highest acid level possible is 1 pH and the most alkaline level possible is a 14 pH. What is measured is the proportion of hydrogen ions (H+) relative to hydroxyls (OH-) within arterial blood. It is expressed as a negative logarithm. This means that a drop in pH indicates an increase in hydrogen ions and a decrease in hydrogen ions is demonstrated by a rise in pH.

It reflects a balance between acids and bases (alkaline) rather than a measure of total acids in solution. Body chemistry (fluids) can range between 6.8-7.4 pH for proper maintenance of health. Optimally, the pH of the blood is exactly 7.4 just like optimum body temperature is 98.6 degrees. These numbers are critical for homeostasis, otherwise the human system gets out of balance and disease can overtake the body.

Our body is comprised of approximately 10 gallons of water. The pH of this fluid, which is contained in every cell throughout the body, is either acid or alkaline. The ideal situation is for all of these cells to be in a slightly alkaline solution. Our bones, lungs, kidneys, liver and other processes all keep our pH at or near 7.4. However when testing the pH of urine or saliva indicates a number below 7.4, it means that all the water in the body is too acidic, not simply the urine or saliva. This affects the chemistry of the entire body and if the body is chronically acidic it can precipitate a long list of health problems including: arthritis, immune problems, oxygen levels dropping in the blood stream, bad parasites multiplying and good bacteria decreasing in the small intestines, and allergies intensifying. Additional affects include poor circulation, kidney and liver problems, as well as chronic constipation, skin problems, high cholesterol and weight problems.

According to research, total healing of chronic illness only takes place when and if the blood, intra-cellular and extra-cellular fluids are restored to a normal, slightly alkaline pH level of 7.4. There are two organs of the body where acid is supposed to be in abundance. They are the stomach and the mantle of the skin. All other areas of the body are meant to be in an alkaline state. However, due to the poor diet and frenetic lifestyle of our modern culture, the intestinal tract is generally more acidic than nature intended it to be. This creates a climate where parasites and bacterial infestation can manifest.

Most people do not know or understand how their diets create a toxic, acidic, anaerobic (oxygen deprived), parasite-laden, and systemically diseased body. The first step to maintaining proper pH balance is to monitor your pH levels. It is very easy to do and the cost is minimal. Most health food stores or pharmacies carry pH testing kits (paper strips for testing urine or saliva). It can be done in the privacy of the home and takes only seconds. The urine and/or saliva strip can indicate the state of the pH of the blood, whether your body fluid is acidic or alkaline. From this reading one can take the necessary steps to keep it at the right levels or bring it within a healthy range. Urine runs slightly acid pH and it is normal for readings to range from 6.0 to the 7.4. Throughout the day, the readings will vary. Usually in the morning the level will be lower because no food has been eaten for eight to ten hours. With the consumption of food, pH will rise during the day, depending upon each individual's circumstances. If the proper ratio of alkaline to acid foods is eaten, the pH of the urine or saliva will be the indicator. For example, the pH of milk is alkaline; however it is metabolized as an acid. Likewise, the pH of lemon juice is extremely acidic, but it is metabolized as an alkaline. It is the amount of these waste products in your blood stream, in the intracellular and extracellular fluid, that determines the state of the pH of the blood.

When *hydroxyls* outnumber *hydrogen* ions in your body fluids, the pH is a slightly alkaline. If the reverse is true, then the body activates the buffer system, by adding alkaline minerals into the bloodstream. This in turn brings the blood pH within the proper range. By eating foods containing too much acid, the body is put in a state of stress as it attempts to return to homeostasis. If the pH of the body is constantly in the high acid range of 6.0 or below, this is called *acidosis*. Additional factors beyond food consumption, such as toxins, stress, lack of exercise, inadequate water intake and failure to control weight all push the body to a more acid state. They used to say that the body's first line of defense is the immune system. However, there is a growing consensus among scientists that pH is a more important factor.

Check pH Balance

One of the first tests that a doctor should look at when helping you fight a disease should be the pH balance results. Since more than 90% of Americans become overly acidic during their lifetimes, there is almost always some basis for the system to be out of balance as the result of the pH level being out of balance, normally too acidic.

pH and Oxygen

One way we use up more of the blood's oxygen reserves than usual is eating junk food. In order to metabolize the preservatives and what few nutrients may actually be in the food the body taps its stores of oxygen. The percentage of oxygen in fats is less than 15 percent. The percentage of oxygen in protein is between 20 and 40 percent, depending on the proteins amino acid profile.

Dense food compounds, such as fats and proteins, are not only low in oxygen content, but also require extra oxygen from our bodies to convert them into energy which further depletes our oxygen reserves. Other oxygen-robbing foods include processed sugar, white flour, alcohol and caffeine drinks. To balance these food's acidity, our bodies have to divert needed oxygen from primary metabolic functions, such as heartbeat, blood flow, brain function and immune response, just to oxidize and metabolize them.

Any excessive stress, heavy workload, traumatic or intense events in your life, prolonged depression and anxiety, can also rob our bodies of huge amounts of its much-needed oxygen. Emotional stress produces adrenaline and adrenaline-related hormones, requiring our bodies to draw on its oxygen reserves for their production and eventual oxidation.

The constant lack of oxygen in the blood creates a breeding ground for many of the diseases that confront modern society. When the body is in a chronic state of acidosis, the body is spending all its oxygen reserves trying to neutralize the acid. Consequently, it neglects the function of metabolism and toxic waste removal.

On the other hand, complex carbohydrates and raw fruits and vegetables, are high in oxygen with as much as 50 percent of the weight of these foods made up of oxygen.

Also, aerobic exercise increases oxygen intake and helps us perform two very important functions. First, the additional oxygen permits the creation and release of more energy for the exercise. Second, the increased supply of oxygen is utilized to remove by-product wastes that are the result of higher metabolic rates. Conversely, a sedentary lifestyle can inhibit the removal of toxic wastes from our bodies perpetuating a system prone to disease.

In 1931, Otto Warburg of Germany won his first Nobel Prize for his discovery of oxygen deficiency in the cancer growth process. He proved that unlike healthy cells, cancer cells do not require oxygen. Their growth instead involves a process of fermentation. Thus when the pH is off, our bodies are running more acid, and our cells are getting less oxygen. The conclusion is that cancer thrives in an acidic pH/oxygen deficient environment.

Just how important is oxygen? Stop breathing for a minute and you can easily get the picture. All cells in the body need to breathe and the amount of oxygen they get is related to the pH of the body. Now can you see why it is important to monitor the pH and how this can directly improve the quality of life?

As stated before, healing of chronic ailments can only happen in a slightly alkaline state. When the pH is too acidic certain enzymatic reactions fail to occur and cellular metabolism becomes difficult to regulate. Connective tissue repair is especially dependent upon proper pH levels. When extra-cellular fluid (ECF) is acidic then these cells bathe in, and eventually die in, their own wastes. When connective tissue cells die, they close the critical bridges between the cardiovascular system and the rest of the cells and organs of the body. When these passages are closed, nutrients can no longer be supplied nor can wastes be removed. This situation, if left untreated, is harmful to our health. The storage capacity for wastes is exhausted and the body begins to corrode in its own acidic wastes. Over time, these accumulated wastes begin to damage the veins and arteries, destroying cell walls and eventually entire organs.

Cleansing diets are often recommended to help restore the proper climate of the digestive tract and allow for the colon and the small intestines to return to their proper pH balance. Once cleansed, the body's pH climate is prepared to assimilate the proper nutrition for balancing pH, healing and health. Many people attempt to correct their pH without going on a cleansing program and they do not see a major change in their pH levels. This is because the mucus buildup, toxins and dried fecal matter have not been removed from the digestive tract and the "good" foods seem to have little benefit because they are not being assimilated by the intestinal walls.

Alkaline Forming Foods ------------------>>

Alfalfa sprouts

Almonds

Apples

Apricots

Avocados

Bananas

Beans, dried

Beet greens

Beets

Berries

Blackberries

Broccoli

Brussels sprouts

Cabbage

Cantaloupe

Carrots

Cauliflower

Celery

Chard leaves

Cherries, sour

Collard greens

Cucumbers

Dates, dried

Dulse

Figs, dried

Fresh corn

Goat whey

Grapefruit

Grapes

Green beans

Green peas

Green soybeans

Kale

Kelp

Lemons

Lettuce

Lima beans, dried

Lima beans, green

Limes

Mangoes

Maple syrup*

Melons

Milk, goat

Millet

Molasses

Mushrooms

Muskmelons

Mustard greens

Okra

Onions

Oranges

Parsley

Parsnips

Peaches

Pears

Peppers

Pineapple

Plums

Potatoes, sweet

Potatoes, white

Prunes

Quinoa

Radishes

Raisins

Raspberries

Rhubarb

Rutabagas

Soy beans, green

Spinach, raw

Strawberries

Tangerines

Tomatoes

Vinegar, cider

Watercress

Watermelon

Acid Forming Foods

Alcohol

Aspirin

Bacon

Barley grain

Beef

Blueberries

Bran, oat

Bran, wheat

Bread, white

Bread, whole wheat

Butter

Cake

Carob

Cereals

Cheese

Chicken

Chickpeas

Chocolate

Cod

Coffee

Corn

Corned beef

Crackers, soda

Cranberries

Currants

Eggs

Flour, white

Flour, whole wheat

Grains, except millet

Haddock

Honey

Lamb

Legumes

Lentils, dried

Lobster

Macaroni

Milk, cow's

Mustard

Nuts

Oatmeal

Oysters

Pasta

Peanut butter

Peanuts

Peas, dried

Pike

Pork

Rice, brown

Rice, white

Salmon

Sardines

Sausage

Scallops

Seeds, dried

Shrimp

Soda crackers

Soft drinks

Spaghetti

Squash, winter

Sugar

Sunflower seeds

Tea, black

Turkey

Veal

Vinegar, distilled

Vitamin C

Walnuts

Wheat germ

Yogurt

Canned, glazed &

sulfured fruit

All dairy products

All animal, foul and

sea animal products

<----------------------*Acid-forming foods*

The Protein, Calcium Myth

As calcium is lost, the bones and teeth become more porous until they become fragile and susceptible to breakage. Our medical profession has responded by telling everyone, especially women that they need to consume more dairy products to prevent the disease. Current figures show that this has done little to stem the rise in incidence of osteoporosis.

Is osteoporosis a disease of old age or a symptom of stress, improper diet and pH balance? As discussed previously, when the acid levels of the blood are too high the buffer system releases calcium and magnesium from the bones. Milk and cheese are rich in calcium; however they create acid ash when metabolized. Thus, their intake makes the body more acidic. They also are mucus forming foods and they line the walls of the digestive tract preventing assimilation of vitamins, minerals and other nutrients our body needs. I believe that osteoporosis is a disease that reflects our modern lifestyle.

I base that belief on the cumulative research of the last twenty years that pinpoints the causes of osteoporosis. We take in too much protein, especially the protein that is found in meat, dairy products, poultry and fish. All of these proteins are metabolized as acid wastes thus lowering the body pH and stressing the buffer system.

The human body has very low protein requirements and cannot store excess protein. Once the protein is digested and converted into amino acids, if not used, it is left circulating in the blood. When the amount of amino acids and their by-products accumulate in the blood, the pH level drops as Hydrogen ion (H+) concentration rises. In order to balance the blood pH the body must take its most

273

readily available alkaline minerals (calcium and magnesium) and draw them from the bones. The result is high levels of uric acid, calcium and magnesium in the urine. On the other hand, experiments show that when fed a meal dominated by plant-based foods, there is little or no calcium in the urine.

Why is this information not common knowledge?

The medical system is designed to treat and cure through diagnosis, prescription and/or surgery, rather than adherence to holistic lifestyle methods. And when you see your favorite sports star with a milk mustache, or eating a hamburger at a fast food chain, you feel comfortable about consuming dairy products and meat products. These athletes seem to be the epitome of health and we are induced to follow suit and be like them.

Before you stock up on cheeseburgers and grow a milk moustache keep this simple equation in mind.

Consumption of high quantities of animal proteins:

---> *raises acidity in your body causing your pH level to drop*

---> *the body responds by taking alkaline minerals, calcium and magnesium from your bones, to balance your pH levels*

---> *drains your bones of calcium and magnesium resulting in the development of osteoporosis if you don't bring your pH levels back into balance.*

Dietary Recommendation: *reduce animal protein consumption and increase raw, organic, unprocessed plant-based foods.*

What's Wrong with Hydrogenation?

The difference between a "fat" and an "oil" is temperature. A "fat" is a lipid that is solid at room temperature. An "oil" is one that is liquid at room temperature.

Unlike butter or virgin coconut oil, hydrogenated oils contain high levels of trans fats. A trans fat is an otherwise normal fatty acid that has been "transmogrified", by high-heat processing of free oil. The fatty acids can be double-linked, cross-linked, bond-shifted, twisted, or messed up in a variety of other ways. Basically trans fats are poison-like in that they interfere with metabolic processes in your body by taking the place of a natural substance that performs a critical function. That is one definition of a poison. Your body has no defense against trans fats, because they never even existed in our three million years of evolution -- so we've never had the need or the opportunity to evolve a defense against them.

But the worst part is that in the last stages of oil processing (or "refining"), the oil is literally steam distilled to remove its odor. But hydrogenated oil is much worse than rancid butter in odor. So if it did smell, it would smell worse than the most rancid butter. So the next time you see "partially hydrogenated oil" on a label, think "rancid butter".

Partially Hydrogenated Oils Make You Fat!

Essential fatty acids are vital to every metabolic function in your body. But *consumption of lots of saturated fats will lead to obesity* because saturated fats contain only small quantities of the *polyunsaturated fats that contain the essential fatty acids you need.* The key to being normal weight is to consume foods containing polyunsaturated oils such as fish, olives, nuts, and egg yolks. These foods also help diminish your sense of hunger.

275

Partially hydrogenated oils make you gain weight the same way that saturated fats do -- by making you consume even more fat to get the essential fatty acids you need. Partially hydrogenated fats are even worse, for not only do they produce disease over they long term, but they interfere with the body's ability to ingest and utilize the good fats!

Most partially hydrogenated oil is partially hydrogenated soybean oil. That's a problem, because soybean oil depresses the thyroid, which lowers your energy levels, makes you feel less like exercising, and contributes to fat accumulation in your body's fat zones, belly, hips and thighs. Despite the health concerns, Americans are consuming soybean oil and partially hydrogenated soybean oil, in many of our processed foods.

Avoiding Hydrogenation

When you start reading food labels, it is astonishing how many products you will find that contain partially hydrogenated oils. In the chips aisle, there are maybe two brands that don't: Lay's Classic Potato Chips (not their other brands), and Laura Scudder chips. Most every other package on the shelf does.

Even some items on the "health food" shelf, like Tigers Milk bars, contain partially hydrogenated oils. So beware of products marketed as a "health food" that could contain partially hydrogenated oils. Read the labels of everything you consume. Watch for key words, like hydrogenated oil, high fructose corn syrup, glucose, and soybean oil.

Instead, look for foods with *omega-3 oil, as this is a healthy fat for the brain and body.* Omega-3s will help make cell membranes become more fluid so nutrients and waste pass in and out of cells as intended. Omega 3 oil, or alpha linolenic acid, can be found in flaxseed oil, deepwater fish, fish oil, salmon, halibut, eggs, avocados and walnuts.

Deep-Fried Foods: The Ultimate Killer

If you're going to fry, use a fully saturated fat like lard, or coconut oil. 50% of coconut oil consists of lauric acid, a medium-chain fatty acid that's anti-bacterial, anti-viral, anti-fungus, and anti-yeast. Or use butter which consists mostly of short-chain saturated fats that are easily burned for fuel.

To learn more about coconut oil read Eric Armstrong's work on this topic on his web link:

http://www.treelight.com/health/nutrition/CoconutOil.html

At restaurants, deep frying with butter is prohibitively expensive. Things were better when restaurants fried in beef tallow and coconut oil, because they had a lot of flavor and the saturated fats aren't harmed by the heat. But all that saturated fat sounded bad, so restaurants switched to partially hydrogenated vegetable oils.

One "healthy" Mexican restaurant even advertised that they fried in vegetable oil. That would be somewhat better than partially hydrogenated oil, assuming that they weren't using partially hydrogenated vegetable oil. Subjecting the unsaturated fatty acids contained in a vegetable oil to the high heat of a deep frying vat is very bad for your body, especially when the oil is used and reused all day long. The result would be the same kind of trans fats that you get in the hydrogenation process!

But the absolute worst commercial frying is done by the fast-food chains, which almost uniformly do their deep frying in cheap, partially hydrogenated oil. Any fats that escaped being transmogrified in the hydrogenation process are now subjected to the deep frying process. It would be a miracle if any of the unsaturated fats escape being transmogrified.

Somatids - The Blood is Life

Through a technology called dark field microscopy, science discovered that the blood of every healthy mammal contains three basic forms called protits or somatids. They have mapped out the mutations that proper cell division occurs in the presence of the three basic somatids. When the body's biological terrain changes, then the somatids, the smallest living organism known to science, expand their three basic forms to higher pathogenic states. It is the mutation or evolution of the three basic somatids that interfere with cell activity and the immune system.

There are 16 stages or macro cycles that somatids go through when the biological terrain is out of homeostasis. Clinical experience demonstrated that in healthy people there is a strong gate control to keep the somatidian cycle from expanding out of the normal three cycles. A scientist named Gaston Naessens observed with his somatoscope that it takes 90 hours for the macrocycle to be completed. Naessens used time-lapse photography to capture the shape of the three normal somatids and the 13 other pathogenic forms.

In the book, "Politics in Healing" by Dan Haley, he outlines the findings of Naessans' work. *"Naessens described the somatids as the following, 1) basic somatids , 2) spores, 3) double spores, 4) bacteria, 5) double bacteria, 6) little rods, 7) double spore bacteria, 8) granulated double spore bacteria, 9,10) mycrobactia with bubbles, 11) a bursting phase, 12) yeast phase, 13) ascospores, 14) asci, 15) filamentous thalli, and finally, 16) bursting phase of new somatids. According to Naessens, each advancing form of life evolved from the previous one."*

Naessens has been able to culture the normal somatid cycle and by creating adverse conditions has seen the complete 16-stage cycle repeated. Naessans has theorized that when the immune system is weakened by exposure to chemical pollution, radiation, electrical fields, poor nutrition, depression, shock, broken bones, or accidents, the gate is opened for the advance stages of the somatids. Essentially, the sicker the patient the greater the macrocycle of somatids are visible in a live blood specimen. When patients become healthy again, somatids revert back to their first three stages.

This in itself is of tremendous importance for people that believe in the body's ability to heal itself of an array of diseases. Imagine the potential for screening diseases by live blood analysis through dark field microscopy. This is the preventive medicine that Thomas Edison envisioned would be the practice of the doctors of the future. Naessens has the capacity to pre-diagnose conditions in advance before they clinically appear. The ability to culture somatids and to associate the health of a patient with their somatid cycle is the paradigm shift to the new world of microbiology. Like Bechamp, Enderlein, Warburg, and others before, Naessens unequivocally states, "germs are not the cause but the result of disease".

Trophology - The science of food combining

Daniel Reid[1], a Tao Master, reminds us that *"Correctly combining foods makes all the difference in the world to proper digestion, cholesterol and metabolism. Without complete digestion, the nutrients in even the most wholesome food cannot be fully extracted and assimilated by the body.*

Moreover, incomplete digestion and inefficient metabolism are the prime causes of fat and cholesterol accumulation in the body."

A diet of processed and overcooked foods leads to impurities in the blood stream that can cause heart disease. While your heart normally pumps about three thousand gallons of blood every twenty-four hours, a circulation system

---

[1] http://www.danreid.org   http://www.hps-online.com/food/index.htm

clogged by sediments must pump twenty-five thousand gallons of blood in twenty-four hours. This enormous stress can lead to heart attacks and heart disease.

The stomach secretes *pepsin* in order to digest animal protein, which can only do its work in a highly acidic solution that is present for several hours. Starches such as potatoes and bread on the other hand require the secretion of *pytalin* and other alkalines into saliva as they are consumed. Once swallowed, the alkalized starches need the stomach to be in an alkaline state for complete digestion.

The problems for your body begin when you eat a starch and a protein at the same meal, resulting in the pepsin and the pytalin, the acid and alkalines, neutralizing each other. This leaves a weak solution in the stomach unable to properly digest either type of food. Thus, you end up with the starches fermenting and the proteins putrefying, causing discomfort ranging from gas, to heartburn, from cramps and bloating, to constipation, foul stools, bleeding piles, colitis, etc.

Allergies can also result from not eating food in proper combinations as toxins are picked up from the putrefied or fermented food in the intestines. Symptoms of these toxins include skin rashes, hives, headaches and nausea.

It's been pretty common knowledge for some time that the average American has five to ten pounds of undigested, putrefied red meat in their bowels. This creates a septic-like condition in the intestinal tract causing the colon to secrete mucus in order to entrap toxic particles before they damage the colon's sensitive lining. This is, of course, a serious problem for Americans who consistently combine proteins and starches at every meal for years on end. The mucus that forms, accumulates and gets impacted in the folds of the colon, which results in a pocket ballooning outward through the colon lining, a condition called diverticulosis. Colitis, irritated bowel syndrome, and colon cancer are the next stages of colon deterioration caused by these conditions. These problems are serious, pervasive and yet, easily preventable once you understand the dynamics of trophology or more commonly known as food combining.

Try and plan your meals around either a protein or a carbohydrate, but not both. When you eat a meal of meat or dairy protein, give your system a couple of hours to digest that meal before consuming a carbohydrate such as oatmeal, potatoes or fresh fruit. Our suggestion is to have a meal of fresh fruits or salad, then later in the day, or at the next meal, consume your protein. Remember, the body doesn't need that much protein and the excess protein (an acid) must be balanced by taking magnesium and calcium (alkalines) out of our bones.

Organic foods verses the petroleum based farming

Earthworms are a dying breed in today's world of mega-*agribusiness*, they have been driven out by petroleum-based fertilizers, and that is a shame. The lowly worm helps to "turn" the soil—bringing down organic matter from the top and mixing it with the soil below, thus making him nature's greatest natural fertilizer manufacturer. If there are 500,000 worms living in an acre of soil, they can make 50 tons of castings. That's like lining up 100,000 one pound coffee cans filled with castings. These same 500,000 worms burrowing into an acre of soil can create a drainage system equal to 2,000 feet of six-inch pipe.

Pretty amazing for just a little old worm, don't you think?

Having worms around in your garden is a good sign that you have a healthy soil. It's one main reason your home grown vegetables always taste rich in flavor, unlike the "plastic" looking pesticide and fertilized produce you buy at the store. If you can afford it, try and shop in the organic produce section of your supermarket. Organic produce should still be grown the old fashion way, with earthworms!

Nutrition in Review

This final chapter encourages you to make healthy nutritional choices in your diet with the goal of balancing your pH, glucose, and insulin in your system, and to be careful about hydrogenated fats and food combining. Everything has a balance, everything we eat is interconnected in our body's chemistry.

All throughout this book I've tried to convey enough scientific information for you to understand what is happening when you either practice my training methods or change your lifestyle habits. I acknowledge how difficult it is to make these changes, especially if you are fairly healthy right now. Perhaps you may be more motivated if you or a family member are suffering from some disease or illness described in this book. It could be that you may want to excel in some athletic endeavor and see the power in my recommendations for improvement.

Whatever your level of commitment to making changes in your life, I hope that you will take from this material a comprehensive understanding of not only what I recommend, but why I recommend it. I also believe that what I have presented here are methodologies and guidelines that are within your control, within your ability to bring these things into your life. Nothing I recommend is very expensive (hammers cost between $5 and $35), nothing is too time consuming (hammer drills take six minutes a day, penmanship another five to ten minutes, memorizing maybe five minutes), nothing is out of your reach (every grocery store has a produce section, every TV has other channels to watch).

Because we have such a wealth of options in our food choices in American supermarkets, it is exceedingly challenging to pick those foods that balance our system and strengthen our immunity against disease. But the rewards of understanding and choosing the right path to health can literally change our lives for the better in a short amount of time.

Photo courtesy: United States Department of Agriculture.

Conclusion
Perfecting Whole Brain Power™

Dear Reader,

I decided to write the conclusion in my cursive handwriting because the end of my book is the beginning of your journey into Whole Brain Power. As film-maker and co-author GW would say I want to make this transition seamless between your learning and your practice.

The important things that I want you to take away from this book are these:

1) Believe that you can change your your brain to make it faster, stronger, more creative, a more effective servant of your dreams and desires for your life. Your brain is not some inert processor inside of your skull, it is the most amazing organic three pounds in the Universe. It is capable of changing your life and the world.

2) Understand that one of the most important themes in this book and in your life is that your hands grow your brain--both hands growing both hemis-

pheres in your brain. Get back in touch with the power of using your dominant and non-dominant-hand in your every day life, whether through penmanship or athletics, brushing your teeth or painting a masterpiece, make your hands skillful in everything you do. Ambidexterity is more than just a skill with either side of the body, it's an empowerment of both sides of your brain, the flawless analytical left side and the creative genius right.

3) Practice penmanship, memory and hammer drills, not as an end unto themselves, but as just the beginning of your transformation. Develop these skills and then apply them to your lives as our case study participants have done in their lives. Use your enhanced memory as Patricia Ford did to improve her learning of sheet music after a 62 year hiatus. Or as Rolly White did to improve his golf game, or his dad Harry to improve his tennis game and memorize Shakespeare. Whole Brain Power is about reinvigorating your life with a sense of your power to change your life, to bring new meaning to what you do and how you do it. Chuck Mellick woke up one day at age 38 and decided that he wanted to become a Major League Baseball player. Whether or not he fulfills that dream, his days are now filled with purpose and energy around that journey.

4) Know that practicing Whole Brain Power training methodologies is only part of the journey, that reducing or eliminating passive virtual stress from violent or hyper-edited television shows, movies or video games is equally important to a healthy brain and body. This virtual stress is so damaging to your system that I titled Chapter Six: System Killers. Now that you know the cascade of chemical changes that take place as the result of daily exposure to this insidious stressor, you can take control of what you watch on the screen. If Americans stop watching violent or hyper-edited entertainment, Hollywood and the video game manufacturers will have to change their focus to brain healthy productions.

5) Pay attention to what you eat and drink. "We are what we eat" is not just a clever platitude. In today's world it has become a truth we live or die by. Use our Nutrition chapter as the starting point for changing your diet toward one that improves your brain power, your energy, your heart health, your bone and muscle density and your longevity.

6) Become at ease with the terminology about the brain. Chapter Two wasn't solely meant to be a refresher course in human biology, it was intended to acquaint

you with your brain and body's operating software. By now you should be comfortable talking about your hippocampus and dentate gyrus, about neurons and the glial cells that support them, the astrocytes and oligodendrocytes. And you want to focus on pumping up your action potentials so that your brain fires faster and you can be on top of your game. Don't be intimidated by your cerebral cortex or cerebellum, they are simply integral parts of your body that are here to serve your life dreams. Communicate with them through your hands, grow them, nurture them, and develop their Whole Brain Power.

I leave you with this one bit of inspiration: Geniuses are not born, they are made. You have within you the creative intelligence of an Einstein or a Da Vinci. You have only to realize that fact and to tap into the unlimited resources that have always been there at your disposal. If you believe you can re-wire your brain then you can. I have presented to you ways that I have found that make it easier and faster to achieve this re-wiring process. It's up to you to take this knowledge and transform yourself. What I believe is that if Americans were to tap into Whole Brain Power we would see an amazing transformation of our society, nothing less than a renaissance in the twenty-first century.

Michael J. Lavery

APPENDIX

Resources, References, Links and Suggested Reading.

Armstrong, Thomas. The Myth of the A.D.D Child:50 Ways to Improve Your Child's Behavior and Attention Span Without Drugs, Labels, or Coercion. Penguin Group. 1997

A Theory of Cortical Neuron-Astrocyte Interaction. http://www.antanitus.com/hypothesis

Batmanghelidj, Fereydoon. Your Body's Many Cries for Water. Global Health Solutions, Inc. 1997.

Baulieu, Etienne-Emile and Schumacher, Michael. Progesterone as a neuroactive neurosteroid, with special reference to the effect of progesterone on myelination. INSERM U 488, 80 rue du Général Leclerc, 94276 Le Kremlin-Bicêtre, France Collège de France, Paris, France. Available online 4 December 2000.

http://www.biomedx.com

Blenz, Richard M. Stop Inflammation Now. G. P. Puttnam's Sons. 2004.

Braverman, Eric. The Edge Effect. Sterling. 2005.

Brittenham, Dean, Brittenham, Greg. Stronger Abs and Back: 165 Exercises to Build Your Center of Power. (Paperback) Human Kinetics. 1997. http://www.humankinetics.com/

Brown, Rachel C., Cascio, Caterina, and Papadopoulos, Vassilios. Pathways of Neurosteroid Biosynthesis in Cell Lines from Human Brain: Regulation of Dehydroepiandrosterone Formation by Oxidative Stress and b-Amyloid Peptide. Interdisciplinary Program in Neuroscience, Division of Hormone Research, and Departments of Cell Biology and Pharmacology, Georgetown University Medical Center, Washington, D.C., U.S.A. Blackwell Publishing. Journal of Neurochemistry, Volume 74, Number 2, February 2000, pp. 847-859(13).

Burroughs, Stanley. Master Cleanser . Burroughs Books. April, 1976.

Chandler, Daniel. The Phenomenology of Writing by Hand. http://www.aber.ac.uk/media/Documents/short/phenom.html

Colpo, Anthony. The Great Cholesterol Con. Lulu.com. October 2006.

CONRAD , C. D., JACKSON J. L., and WISE, L. S. CHRONIC STRESS ENHANCES IBOTENIC ACID-INDUCED DAMAGE SELECTIVELY WITHIN THE HIPPOCAMPAL CA3 REGION OF MALE, BUT NOT FEMALE RATS. Department of Psychology, Arizona State University, Neuroscience. Published in final edited form as: Neuroscience. 2004; 125(3): 759–767.

Danzig, Allison, Schwed, Peter. Fireside Book of Tennis. Simon and Schuster Adult Publishing Group. July 1972.

Doidge, Dr. Norman. *The Brain That Changes Itself.* Penguin Books. 2007.

Edwards, Betty. Drawing On the Right Side of the Brain. Penguin Group. August 1999.

Food and Cholesterol - Beyond The Myths: 10 Reasons Why We Need Cholesterol In Our Food. http://www.wellness-monitor-online.com/food-and-cholesterol.html

Gelb, Michael. How to think like Leonardo Da Vinci. Dell Publishing. 1998.

Genazzani, AR, Facchinetti, F, Petraglia ,F, Pintor C and Corda R. Hyperendorphinemia in obese children and adolescents. Journal of Clinical Endocrinology & Metabolism, Vol 62, 36-40, Copyright © 1986 by Endocrine Society.

Graveline, Duane. Lipitor Thief of Memory Publisher: Duane Graveline; 1 edition (November 1, 2006)

Gray, Henry. Gray's Anatomy. Gramercy Press. 1988.

Haley, Daniel. Politics in Healing. Potomac Valley Press. 2000.

Hypothalamic-pituitary-adrenal axis. http://en.wikipedia.org/wiki/Hypothalamic-pituitary-adrenal_axis

Jaffe, Eric. Mirror Neurons: How We Reflect on Behavior, Association for Psychological Science, Volume 20 May 2007.

James, Bill, Neyer, Rob. The Neyer/James guide to pitchers: An Historical Compendium of Pitching, Pitchers, and Pitches. Published by Simon and Schuster, 2004

Journal of Neuroendocrinology, Volume 19, Number 11, November 2007 , pp. 860-869(10)

Karri, S.1; Dertien, J. S.2; Stocco, D. M.3; Syapin, P. J. Steroidogenic Acute Regulatory Protein Expression and Pregnenolone Synthesis in Rat Astrocyte Cultures. Blackwell Publishing.

Kendrick, Dr. Malcolm. The Great Cholesterol Con: The Truth About What Really Causes Heart Disease and How to Avoid It. Publisher: John Blake (October 1, 2008)

Klingberg,Torkel. Development of a superior frontal–intraparietal network for visuospatial working memory. Paediatric Neurology, Karolinska Institute, Astrid Lindgren's Children's Hospital Q2:07, 171 76 Stockholm, Sweden. Revised 24 October 2005.

Large Martin. Set Free Childhood: Parents' Survival Guide to Coping With Computers and TV (Early Years). Hawthorne Press. 2003.

Lavaque, E., Sierra, A., Azcoitia, I. and Garcia-Segura, L.M. Steroidogenic acute regulatory protein in the brain. Laboratory of Neuroendocrinology, The Rockefeller University, New York, NY 10021, USA Departamento de Biología Celular, Facultad de Biología, Universidad Complutense, E-28040 Madrid, Spain. Accepted 31 May 2005. Available online 7 December 2005.

Marchione, Marilynn. Study: 'Pre-dementia' is rising, especially in men. AP Medical Writer Mon Jul 28, 10:29 PM ET. http://news.yahoo.com/s/ap/20080729/ap_on_he_me/med_pre_alzheimer_s

McDermott, Terry, Scientists can't get their minds around Alzheimer's. Los Angeles Times. December 27, 2007. http://www.latimes.com/news/nationworld/wire/la-na-al-zheimers27dec27,0,4521161.story?page=1

Mota, Sean. For a switch, why doesn't baseball go ambidextrous? http://www.satelliteguys.us/sports-section/41926-switch-why-doesn-t-baseball-go-am-bidextrous.html

Palmer Method. http://www.zanerian.com/Palmer.html

Parker, Jim. Neuropeptides: Unlocking the Secrets of the Brain. Do It Now Foundation. July 1983.

Pennisi, Elizabeth. NEUROSCIENCE:Enzymes Point Way to Potential Alzheimer's Therapies. Science 22 October 1999:Vol. 286. no. 5440, pp. 650 - 651 http://www.sciencemag.org/cgi/content/summary/286/5440/650?ck=nck

The best natural ways to raise low testosterone levels. http://www.thefactsaboutfitness.com/research/lowtest.htm

Ratey, John. Spark the Revolution Between Exercise and the Brain. Little, Brown and Co. 2008.

Sapolsky, Robert. Why Zebras Don't Get Ulcers. Henry Holt & Co. 1994.

Sapolsky, Robert M., Uno, Hideo, Rebert, Charles S, and Finch, Caleb E. Hippocampal Damage Associated with Prolonged Glucocorticoid Exposure in Primates. Department of Biological Sciences, Stanford University, Stanford, California 94305, University of Southern California, Los Angeles, California. September 1990.

SEROTONIN AND OTHER MOLECULES INVOLVED IN DEPRESSION. The Brain From Top to Bottom. http://thebrain.mcgill.ca/flash/a/a_08/a_08_m/a_08_m_dep/a_08_m_dep.html

Sigman, Aric. Remotely Controlled: How Television Is Damaging Our Lives. Vermilion; New Ed edition (1 Feb 2007).

Sisodia, SS and Price, DL. Role of the beta-amyloid protein in Alzheimer's disease. Department of Pathology, Johns Hopkins University School of Medicine, Baltimore, Maryland.

Snowdon, David. Aging With Grace: What the Nun Study Teaches Us about Leading Longer, Healthier and More Meaningful Lives. Bantam Books. January 2001.

Society for Neuroscience. Testosterone's Influence on the Brain. Brain Briefings, April, 2002.

Stoffel-Wagner, Birgit. Neurosteroid Biosynthesis in the Human Brain and Its Clinical Implications, Steroids and the Nervous System, The New York Academy of Sciences, Volume 1007, December 2003.

Talbott, Shawn. The Cortisol Connection. Hunter House, Inc. 2002. 2007.

THE RITALIN CONSPIRACY. http://www.geocities.com/northstarzone/RITALIN.html

Wade, Nicholas. Brainpower May Lie in Complexity of Synapses. Nature Neuroscience. June 10, 2008.

Waters, Rob. Dementia-Dreading Baby Boomers Spur Race to Invent Brain Games. Bloomberg, April 4. http://www.bloomberg.com/apps/news?pid=20601124&sid=a.u9pPbC3qYM&refer=home

Zwain IH, Yen SS. Dehydroepiandrosterone: biosynthesis and metabolism in the brain. Department of Reproductive Medicine, University of California-San Diego School of Medicine, La Jolla. National Center for Biotechnology Information Endocrinology. 1999 Feb;140(2):880-7.

REVENUES, PROFITS

Ra nk	Company	Global 500 rank	REVENUES $ millions	REVENUES % change from 2006	PROFITS $ millions	PROFITS % change from 2006
1	Johnson & Johnson	107	61,095	15	10,576	-4
2	Pfizer	143	48,418	-8	8,144	-58
3	GlaxoSmithKline	151	45,447	6	10,432	5
4	Roche Group	175	40,315	16	8,135	29
5	Sanofi-Aventis	178	39,977	8	7,204	43
6	Novartis	181	39,800	8	11,946	67
7	AstraZeneca	265	29,559	12	5,595	-7
8	Abbott Laboratories	312	25,914	15	3,606	110
9	Merck	332	24,198	7	3,275	-26
10	Wyeth	381	22,400	10	4,616	10
11	Bristol-Myers Squibb	427	19,977	12	2,165	37
12	Eli Lilly	453	18,634	19	2,953	11

Source: Fortune Magazine. July 21, 2008 issue

INDEX

Michael J. Lavery

Co-Founder, Whole Brain Planet

Michael was born in Arlington, Massachusetts, in 1959 to Robert and Beatrice Lavery. One of five children (three brothers and a sister) he was blessed with parents who emphasized academics, the arts, as well as athletics. Michael attended Exeter Academy, and then in 1979 he went on to Amherst College. While at Amherst he excelled in sports, earning four varsity letters in football, hockey, baseball and squash.

Upon graduation with a degree in Fine Arts in 1982, he was drafted by the Toronto Blue Jays. After a short stint in their organization, Michael realized his true passion was in the arts. He moved to the art colony of Laguna Beach, California in 1984, where he established himself as one of Southern California's premier land and seascape painters. His other artistic endeavors include singing, song writing and guitar playing, with two original music CDs to his credit.

His world-class hand-eye coordination skills, demonstrated by his ability to bounce a golf ball on the round end of a ball peen hammer, earned him a spot on a pilot show for golf enthusiasts. It was on the set of that show that he met filmmaker Walsh. Since then he has collaborated with Walsh on the writing and publishing of *Whole Brain Power,* Michael's theories and training methodologies related to brain and body health and fitness.

Michael is the proud father of four sons, Sean, Christopher, James and Steven.

Gregory S. Walsh

Co-Founder, Whole Brain Planet

GW has spent most of his career as a screenwriter/director/editor in the film and video world, winning regional and national awards and producing more than 650 projects over the past twenty-two years. A native of the Great Northwest, he is now focused on helping Lavery communicate and teach Whole Brain Power™ theories and training methodologies through books, documentaries, training videos and films.

A graduate of the University of Washington with a B.A. in English, and minors in Editorial Journalism and Film, GW spent the first two decades of his career within the corporate structure of Seafirst Bank, the top performing regional bank in the country. At the bank he spent most of his career as manager of Corporate Television, and creative director for large corporate events, as well as executive presentation trainer. He left the bank in 1999 after Bank of America took control of Seafirst, and formed a small film and video production company.

In September, 2007, GW was in development on a reality television show being shot in Laguna Beach, California, and Lavery was one of the guests on the show. The exchange of business cards on the set culminated in the formation of Whole Brain Planet, a company co-founded by GW and Lavery with the mission of teaching the world Whole Brain Power™. This book is the foundation of that mission.

GW is the proud father of two sons, Ryan and Sean.

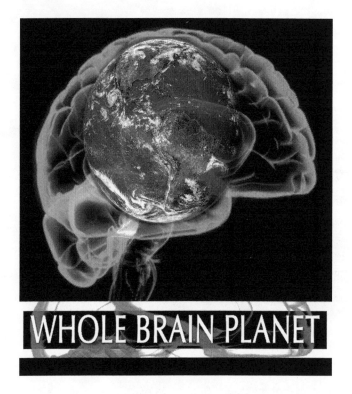

WHOLE BRAIN PLANET

www.wholebrainplanet.com

The Whole Brain Planet mission statement:

Changing the planet one brain at a time.

Made in the USA
Lexington, KY
08 January 2012